STEVIE
WONDER
A MUSICAL GUIDE TO
THE CLASSIC ALBUMS

Suim

STEVIE
WONDER
A MUSICAL GUIDE TO
THE CLASSIC ALBUMS

STEVE LODDER

STEVIE WONDER
A MUSICAL GUIDE TO THE CLASSIC ALBUMS

STEVE LODDER

A BACKBEAT BOOK
First edition 2005
Published by Backbeat Books
600 Harrison Street,
San Francisco, CA94107, US
www.backbeatbooks.com

An imprint of The Music Player Network United
Entertainment Media Inc.

Published for Backbeat Books by Outline Press Ltd,
2a Union Court, 20-22 Union Road, London, SW4 6JP, England.
www.backbeatuk.com

ISBN 0-87930-821-4

ART DIRECTOR: Nigel Osborne
EDITORIAL DIRECTOR: Tony Bacon
EDITOR: Paul Quinn
DESIGN: Paul Cooper Design

Origination and Print by Colorprint Offset (Hong Kong)

05 06 07 08 09 5 4 3 2 1

CONTENTS

INTRODUCTION

"Right about now, ladies and gentlemen, we'd like to continue with our show by introducing to you a young man that's only 12 years old – and he is considered as being the genius of our time. Ladies and gentlemen, let's you and I make him feel happy with a nice ovation as we meet and greet – Little Stevie Wonder… How about it, huh?"

I t's the Regal Theater, Chicago, early 1963. Stevie Wonder is 12 going on 13 years old. He's already recorded some singles and an album for Motown, but nothing has really broken through. Despite his tender age he's recognised as a potentially huge artist, but the process of realising that potential, and turning it into record sales, is proving harder than anyone thought.

The head of the Motown record label, Berry Gordy, has noticed that Stevie's live set always succeeds in lifting the crowd – he seems to be in his element on-stage. The other acts appearing in the *Motown Revue* tend to follow the disciplinarian clockwork timing developed to keep the show rolling forward, whereas Stevie is always clearly bathing in and soaking up the audience's reaction, often oblivious to the demands of the other musicians around him. So a risky strategy has been put in place, to record a live show and try to capture the two-way energy exchange that sparks back and forth between Stevie and the audience.

Stevie played bongos on the original studio version of the tune 'Fingertips', and he's also been trying out some piano and organ ideas, but tonight he wants to play a harmonica solo, and so asks permission of his producer and musical director, Clarence Paul. A reluctant Paul finally agrees, after a conversation with the MC: "Man, you might as well let him play … What's he gonna do?"[1]

What Stevie does is start by playing bongos to set the groove while he speaks to the audience, working them like a seasoned trouper:

"Yeah! … Yeah! … Ladies and gentlemen now I'm gonna do a song taken from my album, *The Jazz Soul Of Little Stevie*. The name of the song's called, uh, 'Fingertips' … Now I want you to clap your hands, come on… come on… Yeah! … Stomp your feet, jump up and down, do anything that you *wanna* do… Yeah! *Yeah!*"

Then, when the drums join in, down go Stevie's bongos and up comes the harmonica.

A few testing up-and-down phrases before he blows a bluesy line and then the band is in with a fairly stock but appropriate set of chord changes. They play the tune, while Stevie plays some unmistakably Stevie-style harmonica licks (even at 12 years old), as well as getting far too excited and carried away.

The music drops down to harmonica and lighter drums for eight bars before hitting the tune again with a blast... the trumpets are blowing too hard and losing their tuning, but Stevie hasn't had enough yet. "Everybody say *yeah!...*" He's basking in the sound of the audience as they clap along, confident enough to sing and play on his own with just their handclaps for accompaniment.

After a few more minutes you can almost feel the band thinking, "How do we get him off the stage?" Stevie's tongue-in-cheek 'Mary Had A Little Lamb' riff on harmonica (playing the cute kid card or what?) seems to provide the perfect opportunity for a big finish, as the MC's words ring around the auditorium: "How about it, let's hear it for him – Little Stevie Wonder..."

Cue ultra-slick 'curtain-down' music, meant to round off the number and introduce the next act... But hang on, Stevie's still not drunk his fill, even though Mary Wells' band is coming on to take over for her set. It's chaos on-stage, not to mention in the audience. As Clarence Paul would put it: "Man, I'd never heard noise so loud. It scared me. I picked him up and took him off the stage. But them kids were hollering and he wanted back on-stage. He jumped right back out there."[2]

Mary Well's bass player Joe Swift is plugging in, but with Stevie suddenly back on-stage the band has to strike up again, in the best showbiz tradition. You can hear Swift's panicked shouts of "What key? What key?" (to which, according to Clarence Paul, trumpeter Herbie Williams quips back, "What do you care, you play everything in the same key anyway…")

The track bursts back for a storming encore, before it finally winds up and Paul leads a still-reluctant Stevie off-stage. (The false-ending routine proves to be such a crowd-teaser/pleaser it's deliberately incorporated into Stevie's show finales for a while afterwards – a bit like James Brown throwing off his cape and coming back for more.)

After some consideration, Motown will decide to release the whole of the live 'Fingertips' recording as a single – 'Part 1' on the a-side, and the extended encore section as 'Fingertips Part 2' on the b-side. As it turns out it's the shambolic but infectiously anarchic and energised encore that becomes the big selling point, rather than the bulk of the song itself. But a Number One hit is a Number One hit. The track goes on to top the US pop charts for three weeks in August 1963, becoming Motown's second Number One single, after The Marvelettes' 'Please Mr Postman'.

And so a new musical phenomenon was launched on an unsuspecting world. With hindsight, early tracks like 'Fingertips' bear little relation to the crafted and era-defining compositions and productions Stevie would create in his 1970s heyday, but this was where his extraordinary career kicked off.

Marvin Gaye, originally one of Motown's in-house and uncredited drummers, made the point that, "You really had to start paying attention to Stevie after 'Fingertips'. No matter what else you might be doing, you'd always know that Stevie had a superior musical intelligence and was learning as fast as you."[3]

In the Motown 'family', that's quite a compliment from one sibling to another. Stevie really was learning fast: he'd spend hours picking up tips from musicians and generally hanging out at the studio, sponging up all that anyone would show him. For the next ten years or so he would continue to absorb sounds and musical styles, before gradually forming and honing his own mature and highly individual writing style, which emerged in the early 1970s.

It's that crucial period of Stevie's career, from 1970 to 1980, that will be the main focus of this book (from Chapter 3 onwards) – largely because it's the most musically adventurous, groundbreaking and influential (not to mention funkiest) in his history. But by way of setting the scene, we'll start by looking at Stevie's background and his formative years, from disadvantaged blind kid to musical 'boy wonder', as well as the complex relationship with Motown, Stevie's long-time musical home.

CHAPTER 1
FAMILY, DETROIT & MOTOWN

"I wanted a place where a kid off the street could walk in one door an unknown and come out the other a recording artist – a star."

BERRY GORDY, FOUNDER OF MOTOWN

Stevland Hardaway Judkins Morris, to give him his full complement of names, was born in Saginaw, Michigan, on 13th May 1950. He was the third son of Lula Hardaway – Lula's own remarkable life story is told in full in the book *Blind Faith*, but it's worth looking at least at the bare bones of her background here. Born in one of the poorest areas on the outskirts of Montgomery, Alabama, in Depression-ridden 1930s America, Stevie's mother didn't have an easy life. Known as 'Little Red' on account of the red tinge in her hair – a likely sign of Celtic genes in her family tree (just like Billie Holiday) – Lula was brought up mostly by her great-aunt and great-uncle, Virge and Henry Wright, on the Alabama cotton farm they managed. But both died when she was in her early teens, and Lula was then passed around various other relatives (including another great-uncle Robert Morris, a Methodist Episcopal deacon, and his wife), before eventually ending up with her uncle, Hone McGee, in Saginaw, about 60 miles north-west of Detroit.

It was the kind of south-to-north migration that was common at that time, though for different reasons: many southerners moved to the big northern cities in search of work, or to escape racist persecution. Motown boss Berry Gordy's parents, for instance, made some money in the 1920s and were anxious to avoid drawing attention to themselves for fear of alerting the Ku Klux Klan (who were still keen on lynchings, as chillingly related in the Billie Holiday song 'Strange Fruit').

Lula, who already had a son (Milton) from a previous relationship with a man called Paul Hardaway, became drawn to a local gambler, and unenthusiastic worker, Calvin Judkins. Before long they were married and had their own son together, also given the name Calvin. There was often no money around, and the teenage Lula was forced into prostitution by her husband.

When Stevie was born he was two months premature and weighed less than 4lbs (2kg). He was put in an incubator, where he remained for 52 days. Towards the end of his stay in hospital, doctors noticed Stevie wasn't responding normally to movement and light, and they declared him blind.

Their explanation was that he might have been given too much oxygen in the incubator – although without that extra oxygen for his under-developed lungs he would probably not have survived at all. It seems as if there was a period in the late 1940s to early 1950s where the mixture of oxygen given to premature babies was too high, causing a nasty side effect that damages the blood vessels in the retina. Known today as retinopathy of prematurity, it was previously termed retrolental fibroplasias – basically the blood vessels linking iris and retina grow abnormally and can pull away, causing a detached retina.

As he grew up, though, Stevie would never be in the habit of playing the blindness-as-weakness card – perhaps his most famous quote expresses his attitude best: "Just because a man lacks the use of his eyes doesn't mean he lacks vision."

One man who did seem to lack vision was Calvin Judkins. Stevie's father physically abused Lula till finally she snapped and, responding to his violence one day, ran a knife into his arm. That spelled another enforced move, the end of life in Saginaw and the beginning of life in Detroit. Accommodation was found at Brewster Projects, a block of flats funded by the city government, and Lula found herself working in a fish market from 4.30am till midday.

She later described her situation there as "ghetto life", although Stevie recalls a "lower middle class or upper lower class" existence. Whatever the socio-economic label, the fact is food was often in short supply, and in the depths of winter (and Detroit winters are cold) coal was appropriated under cover of darkness from a local yard using Stevie's baby carriage as a delivery truck.

It wasn't all hardship, though. Stevie's lack of sight may occasionally have been taken advantage of by his elder brothers, but it's clear he was as game for a spot of trouble as any other boy. There are incredible tales of leaping across shed rooftops, or his brothers trying to help Stevie see playing-cards better by lighting a newspaper fire in the middle of the sitting room floor. Stevie also acquainted himself with some of the physical attributes of the opposite sex by indulging in the odd game of doctors and nurses. All in all, the usual explorations of youth.

World of sound

Medical investigations into Stevie's blindness had yielded no positive hope of a reversal, but it became clear his lack of sight was at least partially offset by a highly developed sense of hearing. He had a musician's ear for mimicry, could tell the difference between the sound of a dime and a quarter coin dropping on a table, and was often glued to the radio in the evening.

"I listened to everything I could hear," Stevie once said. "Music was my communication to the world. Different languages, voices, singers – I heard everything."

He was innately musical. He loved beating out rhythms, using spoons to play on pots and pans, or anything he could lay his hands on. Eventually he got a home-made cardboard drum kit, a Christmas present that barely lasted the year before needing to be replaced. He was later given a set of drums by a charity at a party held for blind children. He found access to a piano at the age of three, and owned one of his own by age seven.

"A lady who lived down the hallway from us had an acoustic piano. She was going to move back to New Orleans, and she wanted to know if I wanted the piano because she knew I loved it very much. So they gave it to me."[4]

Hours would be whiled away picking out tunes he had heard on the radio. He also sang in the choir at the Whitestone Baptist Church, until one day when a whiter-than-whitestone lady churchgoer found Stevie and guitar-playing friend John Glover busking on the street. She reported back to the church and a deacon was dispatched to warn of the dangers of playing the 'devil's music'. Lula's reaction to this pomposity triggered a ban on the entire family from attending that particular church.

Stevie's interest in drumming and piano continued, but his musical flair expressed itself above all on harmonica. Progressing from a four-hole toy harmonica to a slightly larger one donated by a friendly barber who spotted Stevie's interest and talent, to a fully-fledged Hohner Chromatic model (more of which in Chapter 9), this time a present from an admiring uncle, he quickly found his way around the instrument and was soon leading the harmonica band at school.

Stevie studied initially at the Fitzgerald School for the blind, though it's not clear how much help he had in instrumental technique at that stage. But certainly listening to the radio, particularly an evening show called *Sundown* on local radio WCHB, supplied him with a wealth of material, from his favourite Johnny Ace track, 'Pledging My Love', to Jackie Wilson, The Coasters, B.B. King, Bobby Bland and a host of others. 'Pledging My Love' is a slow ballad highlighting a rich, round voice over vibraphone-coloured backing track. It's not too far-fetched to compare the vocal style with Stevie's – there's something of 'You And I' in it.

Stevie and John Glover were soon playing the latest hits at their street corner jamming sessions on 25th/26th Streets. Songs they covered included old and recent hits, such as 'Why Do Fools Fall In Love' and 'Bad Girl', as well as numbers by local heroes like The Miracles ('My Momma Told Me To Leave Those Girls Alone') and a young Marvin Gaye ('Sandman'). Stevie would be on bongos and harmonica and John on guitar. Word spread through the neighbourhood about what they were doing, and they were invited to play at local functions, while mixing with other musicians who made up the local music network.

Stevie was certainly in the right place at the right time. Detroit was awash with talented musicians, many of whom had made the migrant journey from south to north. That talent was being tapped not only by local clubs but also an ambitious young record company that called itself Motown, short for Motortown, in recognition of Detroit's motor industry connections.

Detroit

The rise of the automobile industry had brought a massive influx of workers to the Detroit area from around 1913 onwards. Henry Ford needed cheap labour to work his mass-production lines that turned out those new-fangled 'horseless carriages'. By the 1920s, Detroit had become the national centre for the industry, and Ford was actively encouraging movement of workers from elsewhere in the country, especially the south.

Pre-Henry Ford Detroit had been primarily white, with a dusting of Italian and Irish; the African-American contingent was small and unpopular with the white middle classes. Many migrants from the south were now persuaded to leave their farms for a colder climate but brighter economic future, attracted by Ford's offer of $5 a day. But they found only miserable living conditions, a struggle to find food, and a losing battle against disease. Some pushed on even further and crossed into Canada, where racism was less rife. (If Berry Gordy's father thought he was

Detroit was awash with talented musicians, many of whom had made the journey from the south

escaping Ku Klux Klan activities by moving to Detroit he would have been disappointed; in the mid 1920s Michigan boasted the largest Klan membership of any US state – more than three-quarters of a million.)

The city itself was expanding to house the new labour force, but there were physical limits to this expansion. Detroit was absorbing the biggest population increase in the country, housing was stretched to breaking point, and racial tension was lurking just around the corner.

Blacks were obliged to live, socialise, drink, and shop in different places to their white counterparts. The only time they were thrown together was on the auto production line, where there was barely-controlled mutual tolerance. Opinions differ as to whether the mixed workforce was a viable idea; certainly the union, while it theoretically encouraged equal opportunity, in practice came down on the side of whites, who resented the 'invasion' of 'their' assembly lines. If they did co-operate at work, come the end of the shift it would be racist/separatist business as usual. Each would return to their own neighbourhoods and attendant cultural atmosphere.

The heart of the black neighbourhood in Detroit was an area known as Paradise Valley. It hardly

**Little Stevie joins a photo-call with Motown stars of the early 1960s, including, from left to right,
The Temptations, The Miracles, The Supremes, and Martha Reeves & The Vandellas**

lived up to the name: it was not so much a valley as a strip of land to the east of the city housing thousands upon thousands of families – and it was certainly no paradise. Also known as the 'black hole', it was depressing and poverty-stricken, yet still had a lively and cohesive cultural scene, with cinemas and some of the best jazz clubs in the north. These weren't the sort of smooth or cool chic jazz clubs either – the music was anti-establishment and urban and often dance-led. Clubs such as the Chit Chat, the Apex, the Flame, Showbar and especially the 20 Grand were all attracting top touring acts as well as supplying regular work for Detroit musicians.

African-American-owned businesses were not unusual in Detroit: WCBH was the first radio station in the States to be black-owned and staffed; the Concept East Theater established the first black theatre company; and the Broadside Press was a black-owned publishers. There were black union organisations too, as well as black political groupings that were forming the beginnings of black power.

Along the way there was serious race trouble. On one extremely hot day in June 1943 (how often do civil disturbances and high temperatures coincide, I wonder?), 10,000 people fought in the street following the circulation of a rumour that a gang of whites had thrown a black mother and child from a bridge (which turned out to be unfounded, in this instance). The black community ignited, and looting, fire-raising and violence followed in a riot that killed 34 people, 25 of them black. The situation wasn't helped by the fact that the police detained blacks only. An enormous $2m-worth of damage was sustained, mostly in the black areas, leaving many people homeless and with nowhere to buy food.

During the 1950s a new wave of migrants returning from WWII found even worse housing shortages. The number of African-Americans living in the city more than doubled from 1950 to 1970 – the proportion of black people in the local population grew to 44.5 per cent. A further problem in the Fifties was the planning of a new motorway straight through the heart of Paradise Valley, causing displacement and bad feeling as occupants were literally forced out on to the street. This didn't do much to help social stability and reconciliation.

Miracles can happen

In a bid to establish herself in a house of her own, the resourceful Lula somehow managed to save enough money from her employment to put down a deposit on a house in a better area of town, at 3347 Breckenridge Avenue, leaving her old life and relationships behind and finally striking out for her own personal space and freedom.

The children were delighted with the new home and the number of rooms they now had – an enormous change after the confined environment of the 'Projects'. Stevie even had space for his drum kit in the back room, *almost* out of earshot, and was at the same time continuing his on-the-street-corner gigs with John Glover.

John's mother Ruth realised the two boys had genuine talent, as did another admirer, John's cousin Gerald White, who was particularly struck by Stevie's innate musicianship. Gerald's brother was Ronnie White, a member of The Miracles, the group fronted by Smokey Robinson. By the end of the 1950s The Miracles were already popular among the people-in-the-know of Detroit, and had started making some records on Berry Gordy's Tamla label, but neither they nor the Motown brand had made much of an impact at national level as yet. All the same, everyone knew that Berry Gordy

Jr was the man to be seen and heard by, and Gerald nagged his brother continually to get young Stevie an audience with the main man.

Finally (it was 1961 by this time) brother Ronnie agreed to listen to the lad. He suspected that Stevie was just another in the queue of people on the make with no talent or future in the music business, just a lot of front, but he relented and made a date to meet the boy, bringing along another member of The Miracles, Pete Moore. Stevie sang a song he'd written himself, 'Lonely Boy', before switching to harmonica for a solo, and bragging he was a better singer than Smokey Robinson. Well, you do need confidence to get on in show business…

Ronnie White was impressed enough to fix an audition at Motown – although before achieving the holy grail of entering Gordy's office, there was another hurdle for Stevie to clear. First he had to get past Brian Holland, later of the remarkable writing team Holland-Dozier-Holland, who was acting as A&R (artiste & repertoire) manager at that time, talent spotting for the label. He liked what he heard too: Stevie played and sang a Miracles song, and when asked what other instruments he played, he reeled off drums, organ and piano.

This first part of the audition took place on the front porch at Motown HQ, as the offices themselves were thronged with the usual hubbub found inside the expanding label's premises. The Supremes, previously the youngest artists signed by Gordy, were sat downstairs and were curious to follow the proceedings. William 'Mickey' Stevenson, head of A&R ('artistes & repertoire'), was called in and the whole party went up to Gordy's office. Stevie played some more harmonica in front of the boss, who then invited him back down to the studio basement (past the bemused Diana Ross & co) where he wanted to find out if Stevie's multi-instrumental claims had any foundation.

Sure enough, the boy worked his way through all the musical instruments that were lying around, including some Lula had no idea Stevie knew about, such as horns and tuned percussion – Stevie managed to squeeze something musical from them all. (He had studied, or at least messed around with, an enormous range of instruments at school.) Drums and piano, of course, were no problem.

Stevie worked his way through the instruments that were lying around … he managed to squeeze something musical from them all

Supreme Mary Wilson said later: "I especially remember him playing a harmonica he'd brought with him. Of course we were all dumbstruck with amazement… to see someone as young as Stevie was something else."[5]

Stevie himself has described his initial feelings about Gordy: "He was someone who was making a good, positive direction in the black community…" He also added, as if in the voice of the naive boy who auditioned that day: "Anybody who would let me come into their studio and let me play so many instruments had to be a good person."

Good or not, Gordy was convinced Stevie should be signed. It seems he was initially more enthused by Stevie's harmonica playing than his singing voice – and judging from the early recordings you can see why. The other worry about a young boy's unbroken voice is you can never

be sure what's going to emerge the other side of puberty. In this case, of course, he needn't have worried – Gordy would be signing what was to become one of the most distinctive, emotionally expansive, flexible, accurate pop voices the music world has ever heard.

In truth, Gordy didn't really know exactly what to do with this precocious talent – but having seen Stevie's wide-ranging musical skills he was fairly sure that, somewhere down the line, something would have to work commercially. It's worth taking a brief look at Gordy's own background and nature, if for no other reason than to get an idea what kind of boss Stevie would have to deal with.

Mr Motown

It had been a long climb up the ladder for Berry Gordy – from boxing (where he found himself up against Jackie Wilson in the ring at one point) to the army, to running a record shop, to cookery utensil salesman, to assembly line worker, to songwriter, to record company owner. His moderately privileged (or, as they'd say in Detroit, 'big dog') family background and status would have set him off on the right foot, but his character was not that of a passive absorber or follower of predetermined paths: he clearly had to find his own agenda.

His father, Berry Sr, ran a shop in a black neighbourhood, calling it the Booker T. Washington Grocery Store (after the inspirational former African-American slave-turned educator). Berry Sr's formidable wife Bertha, a former schoolteacher, also set up the Friendship Mutual Insurance Company, tailored to serve the needs of the black community. Magazine articles were published featuring "America's most amazing family: the famous Gordys of Detroit have what it takes."[6] Berry Sr and Bertha encouraged all of their eight children either to work in the store or on their own business projects – and all excelled in their chosen fields.

Berry Jr, after a spell of duty with the army in Korea, used his discharge pay to open his own record shop, the 3-D Record Mart, specialising in jazz, blues and R&B. Unfortunately this first enterprise was not long-lived. To make ends meet, the car assembly line beckoned, and for a while Berry was forced to take a job nailing upholstery and attaching chrome strips to Lincoln-Mercury sedans. Domestic bliss was also proving elusive with his wife Thelma, whom he soon divorced.

Berry opted to give up the day job and take the songwriting seriously. Purchasing a two-track tape recorder, and networking at the Flame Show bar – where his sisters had indulged the family entrepreneurial spirit by setting up a photography and cigarette concession – he quickly became involved on the local music scene. He met up again with Jackie Wilson (this time with the gloves off) and they collaborated on 'Reet Petite', a classic R&B hit in 1957.

Berry's writing partnerships flourished and grew to include a friendship with The Miracles' Smokey Robinson. Berry offered to manage the teenage Miracles (previously called The Matadors), and soon produced their first R&B hit, 'Got A Job,' released and distributed by George Goldner's New York-based End Records.

But Gordy, along with his sisters Gwen, Anna and Esther, was already thinking about how he could muscle in on the record company power that was almost entirely in the hands of white-owned labels, who not only promoted white artists above black ones, but often took black music and restyled it in a more 'palatable' form for the white market.

Another crucial contact for Berry on the way up was an up-and-coming singer called Raynoma

Publicity shot of dapper adolescent Stevie: Gordy would have him groomed for stardom from an early age.

Mayberry Liles, who had been pointed in the direction of Gordy for possible management. Not only did she play 11 instruments, she had a fine voice, knew her music theory, and she looked good too. Raynoma (Ray) and Gordy soon became partners – romantically and musically – and formed the Rayber Music Writing Company.

Their first release on Berry's Tamla label was Marv Johnson's 'Come To Me'. Issued in January 1959, it hit Number 30 in the mainstream pop charts, and it set the tone for what would become the Motown sound – what Berry would soon christen "The Sound Of Young America". Bass player James Jamerson, who would become a hugely influential figure, and drummer William 'Benny' Benjamin, plus guitarists Eddie Willis and Joe Messina, all played on the session, which was held in the Rayber studio – basically the couple's house, where the toilet served as a soundbooth and the bathroom as a reverb chamber.

Clearly this wasn't an ideal situation: with Ray, Berry, two children, an office and a studio, the house was bursting at the seams, so Ray was sent off in search of a larger property. She came up with 2648 West Grand Boulevard, situated in mid-Detroit on a tree-lined street, in the heart of the black community. A former photography studio would be converted to a sound studio at the back, and a large sign erected at the front, over a sizeable picture window, which boldly announced the arrival of 'Hitsville USA'. It was here that Stevie, among many other hopefuls, would audition for the label.

"In many ways Hitsville was like growing up in the Gordy family: fierce closeness, fierce competition and constant collaboration."

For the Gordys it was all-hands-on-deck: accounting, manufacturing, and publishing (under the name Jobete) were assigned to various family members to administer. The whole operation became like an extension of the Gordy household. "In many ways Hitsville was like growing up in the Gordy family," Berry Jr later reflected. "Fierce closeness, fierce competition and constant collaboration."[7]

Gwen and Anna extended the Motown family by marrying two musicians crucial to the Hitsville set-up. Harvey Fuqua and Marvin Gay (before he added the 'e') had joined the company after enjoying some success with Harvey & The Moonglows. The two were friends as well as musical associates, so Marvin came along in tow when Fuqua was offered a job as writer/producer. Anna took an immediate shine to Marvin, who was 17 years her junior. When Berry met Marvin he spotted the talent and started giving him piano and drumming sessions in the studio.

One of the first sounds to emerge from the new studio was the Gordy-penned 'Money (That's What I Want)'. Perhaps born out of Berry's frustration at how much work the company was engaged in for minimal return, the song was a minor hit for Barrett Strong in April 1960 – and clearly impressed The Beatles, as they covered it on their second album. (Apparently the line "Your love gives me such a thrill, but your love don't pay my bills" was added by a Motown receptionist, one of many who would apply for a job at Hitsville in the hope of being discovered – Martha Reeves was the most successful example.)

The label's first nationwide success, in 1961, not only highlights Gordy's refined pop sensibilities but shows his perseverance when it came to getting things right. Smokey Robinson had just dashed off a song (in ten minutes, it seems) called 'Shop Around' – reportedly intending it as a follow-up for Barrett Strong. Berry listened, and in his customary style immediately suggested a couple of chord changes, and also that The Miracles perform it themselves, but with the group's other singer, Smokey's wife Claudette Rogers, taking lead vocals.

This original version was released locally, but Gordy obviously felt they could do better. A few weeks later, unable to sleep one night, he phoned Smokey Robinson at 3am, and on an impulse demanded he go down to the studio right away to record a new version. Musicians were raised from their slumber (or whichever club they happened to be at), and a slightly faster, snappier variation was recorded, with Benny Benjamin on (very upfront) brushes, rather than the sticks and rimshots used the first time, and Smokey singing the lead in his lightest of voices. Since no piano player had been unearthed at that rather unearthly hour, Berry played the keyboard part himself. Within a week the single was in the shops, reaching Number Two on the pop chart and becoming an R&B Number One. It was Motown's first gold record.

Smokey Robinson was soon on a roll, not just fronting The Miracles but writing and producing for Mary Wells, whose 1962 hits included 'The One Who Really Loves You', 'You Beat Me To The Punch', and 'Two Lovers'. 'Two Lovers' contains many of the trademark Motown musical features: a strong drum track (including one of the classic Motown fills), a seductive (and echoed) vocal, guitars clanking on beats two and four, a distinctively hooky bassline, slick horn and vocal arrangement, congas for extra exotic percussive colour, and a 'no frills' attitude towards the harmony.

Another common feature of early Motown songs is that they'd all be two-and-a-half minutes long, almost to the second – and definitely never more than three minutes. Berry reckoned shorter records had more chance of being played on the radio. The immediacy is the thing here: although there are usually interesting off-beat rhythmic features further back in the mix, the vocal and drum track lay first claim to the listener's attention, and provide an instant 'feel good' factor.

Various writing and production teams worked with different combinations of artists on a variety of songs, and 'quality control' meetings would take place every Friday morning at Motown to listen to and evaluate the week's work, creating a ferment of creative energy (that "fierce competition and constant collaboration") which projected the records into the charts.

The Funk Brothers & the snakepit

Studio A, in a downstairs room at Hitsville, has almost passed beyond legend. The snakepit, as it was called (ostensibly because of the masses of cables that weaved across the floor, wall to wall – though also perhaps a reflection of the often less-than-comfortable working conditions the musicians had to endure), was open pretty much 24 hours a day in the peak years. An in-house studio made sense to Gordy – it meant more creative time could be spent at no extra cost (other than paying the musicians, and that was minimal). New techniques were constantly being employed, and if the piece of gear required for a sound wasn't available, it would be built by the Motown studio engineers themselves.

In the early days, the takes were recorded onto three-track tape, before being mixed to mono. Normally track one was for the rhythm section instruments – drums, bass, percussion, guitars, piano and/or organ; track two would be for any other instrumental input, usually either brass or strings; which left track three for the vocals. The big advantage of 'multi-track' tape is that the tracks don't have to be recorded simultaneously. So the vocals were rarely recorded at the same time as the band – they would be worked on later.

With the three tracks complete, the final mono master (stereo was a few years off yet) would be mixed, balancing the individual channels through the mixing desk, while monitoring them from three separate speakers. Interestingly, the producer would often not be present at the mix in those days, leaving it to the studio engineers to sort out. The result would be played to Gordy, who would send it back downstairs sometimes as many as 20 times, till he felt the right sound had been achieved. Listening was often done on small car radio speakers, since Gordy reckoned that most of his potential audience would first hear the songs that way, so it had to have maximum impact while driving. The idea of having a 'real world' speaker set-up in the studio for checking a mix is now standard practice.

The choice of musicians on those studio sessions was down to A&R boss Mickey Stevenson, who had overall responsibility for matching up artists with producers, making sure songwriting

Unsung and underpaid, the Funk Brothers would contribute to countless Motown sessions for anything between $5 and $10 a time

deadlines were met, and organising the musicians. One of the first musos on the scene was pianist Joe Hunter, who started out as bandleader. In the excellent film *Standing In The Shadows Of Motown*, Hunter recalls how he first met Gordy: "Berry showed up down at Little Sam's [a popular Detroit club] one time and he walked over by the bandstand while we were playing, and he said to me, 'Will you have time to talk to me?' I says I got more time than money. He explained to me what he was about, he wanted to set up a record company, and he needed good musicians. I thought it was a wonderful idea and he wanted to know did I know anybody to fill the thing … He called the first rehearsal over at Claudette's house … that was late 1958."[8]

Hunter admits that his favourite pianist/composer is Rachmaninov (he used to practise copying the great man's left-hand parts), although he worked the clubs as a bluesy jazz player. A later Motown pianist, Johnny Griffith, was also originally a classical man, but toured with many top-flight jazz singers before being lured into the snakepit. Guitarist Joe Messina also had a fine jazz pedigree, having worked with people like Charlie Parker. Stevenson set up a jazz label called Jazz Workshop, precisely in order to attract top-flight musicians and tempt them with the offer of recording their own albums, while using their talents on the pop tracks.

Along with the bass and drum team of Jamerson and Benjamin, the pool of players called themselves the Funk Brothers. Unsung and underpaid, the team would contribute to countless Motown sessions for the remuneration of anything between $5 and $10 a time. At a period when the standard union rate for musicians was set at $52.50, you can see that the Funk Brothers took quite a pay-cut for the (mostly elusive) Jazz Workshop recording promise. But it did mean Gordy had a great band who could not only play the majority of the Motown arrangements with one hand behind their backs, they could also get stuck into a groove and make it swing when required.

Another musical weapon in the Hitsville armoury was the touring live show – another of Berry Gordy's groundbreaking ideas. Tours had always been part of the job for most bands and singers, but usually they would be responsible for organising such concerts themselves. Berry recognised the crucial link between live shows – being seen and heard in the flesh – and the purchase made in the record shop the next day. So he initiated the concept of the record-label-supported tour, in the shape of the *Motortown Revue* (or Review), later abbreviated to the *Motown Revue*. (You can see one of the Motown tour buses on Stevie's *Fulfillingness' First Finale* album sleeve – in-between Stevie with his harmonica and Martin Luther King.)

Typically Berry would organise a tour lasting up to ten weeks, featuring the likes of The Miracles, Marvelettes, Contours, Mary Wells, Martha & The Vandellas and Marvin Gaye. The tour would take in Washington and the Southern states (which still practised racial segregation), ending up with ten days at the Harlem Apollo Theatre in New York City. If you were successful there, right in the heart of African-American showbusiness, then, as the song goes, you could make it anywhere.

The rest of the tour followed a regular 'chitlin circuit', a succession of venues mostly run by black promoters for black audiences. These tours were not without incident: in Birmingham, Alabama, there were shots fired in the artists' general direction following a performance in front of a mixed-race crowd.

The Motown singers and musicians themselves were on the whole young and green, mostly with no previous experience of the rigours of touring. Stage experience was lacking too, something Berry would soon get around to remedying. The first tour set out in October 1962, and returned with a financial smile on its face. Even the artists made some money, as Berry had arranged for their earnings to be banked as the tour progressed, arguing that this would protect the younger performers from their own spending power. As he claimed in the local *Detroit Free Press*, "We try to help artists personally with their investment programs so they don't wind up broke. We are very much concerned with the artists' welfare."

Minor setback

After Stevie's impressive Motown audition, Gordy's next step was to draw up a contract that would deal with Stevie's position as a minor. He proposed setting up a trust fund into which money from record sales would be put until Stevie was 21, at which time he could access the fund.

The job of negotiating, or even understanding, the details of the contract on Stevie's behalf was left to Lula, who was invited into the Motown office one day while Stevie was let loose downstairs to check out the studios, the musicians, and the instruments. Stevie didn't care about the wheelings and dealings of a contract, all he wanted was to get into the 'snakepit' and make music with the like-minded friends he was making there.

(It has to be said that this feeling wasn't completely mutual at first. Young Stevie got up the noses of a few of the musicians, by virtue of his persistence and ever-presence. On one of his first visits he spoiled a take by walking straight into the studio, oblivious of the red 'recording in progress' light outside. Earl Van Dyke, who replaced Joe Hunter as Funk Brothers keyboard man and musical director in 1963, revealed the general attitude when he recalled: "Stevie liked to hang out with the guys, you know... him being a musician. We could never really get rid of Stevie..."[9])

Lula's experience in financial matters was not vast, but she didn't feel happy with the idea of an inaccessible trust fund, with only expenses being paid to Stevie, so she walked out of the contract meeting. When he found out what his mother had done, Stevie was distraught. Having had the carrot of a music career dangled in front of him, an 11-year-old boy is not exactly going to be cool-headed about having it taken away. But Lula was steadfast in her decision. She'd always been very supportive of Stevie's musical ambitions and development (she would even get involved in his songwriting in years to come), but at this point in time she'd just managed to steer her life so that it was in pretty good order, and she was reluctant to complicate matters with a record deal and its inherent practical difficulties, like having to reconcile touring with Stevie's schooling.

Stevie went into a sulk that continued for days. It was highly unusual – he wasn't the sort of boy to have long-term gripes over issues. Disagreements between mother and son were usually fairly easily and quickly repairable. But this was different. Two days were spent in relentless verbal persuasion, and though Lula was weakening she still wasn't happy about what amounted to handing over control of a part of her son's life.

That's when Stevie started the drumming... From his room over the next few days came an incessant, furious, percussive tirade that began at dawn and continued unabated till dusk. When Lula came home the third day to find quiet reigning over the house, she suspected it might be over, but as soon as Stevie heard her footsteps in the hall he renewed his onslaught, even increasing the intensity of the frenetic performance. Lula had had enough, and decided there and then to relent, realising just how much it meant to the boy. She went into Stevie's room to tell him, and found him a shadow of his usual self, exhausted by his days of exertion. All he was able to say was a breathless, "Thank you, Mama."[10]

A five-year deal was worked out, in conjunction with the Michigan Department of Labour, in order to comply with the child employment laws. A small weekly allowance would be paid to Stevie, as well as his expenses, and a $200 monthly allowance paid to Lula. Meanwhile the royalties and performance fees, administered by Jobete (Gordy's music publishing arm) and ITM (International Talent Management), would be placed in the trust fund. At the signing of the contract, Stevie's surname was put down as Morris, as Lula was worried that any Judkins connection could enable his wayward father to dip his hands into the kitty, something she was anxious to avoid.

And that was that, done and dusted – first step in what would turn out to be a long and convoluted history of contractual negotiations. It was also the start of the lengthy association between Stevie and Berry Gordy, not to mention the team of musicians down in the studio. By all accounts Stevie was as curious as a toddler with a new toy, spending many hours with Benny Benjamin in particular, who left his mark on Stevie's own drumming style. In turn it's often claimed it was Stevie who gave Benjamin the enduring and endearing nickname 'Papa Zita' – possibly after a Spanish-Cuban phrase the drummer would sometimes utter when playing.

All the while Gordy was trying to figure out a way to translate Stevie's precocity into hit records. Finding the right musical angle to channel his talents was a time-consuming challenge, but Gordy was used to finding solutions to problems. His whole approach to making records, and creating pop stars, was innovative in its day: he claimed it was based on his experience of car assembly lines.

"At the Ford plant, cars started out as just a frame, pulled along on conveyor belts until they

One of Stevie's earliest television performances, on the UK's new pop show
Ready Steady Go! in December 1963. It was also the first time Stevie's shared
a bill with The Rolling Stones, who starred in the same episode.

emerged at the end of the line brand spanking new cars … I wanted the same concept for my company, only with artists and songs and records. I wanted a place where a kid off the street could walk in one door an unknown and come out the other a recording artist – a star."[11]

If that concept sounds somewhat detached and impersonal – we're talking about temperamental artists here, after all, not machines – it has to be remembered that Gordy's emphasis was always on Motown being one big family: a black organisation set up to challenge the status quo of white-owned record label dominance in the market place.

Stevie joined the *Motortown Revue* as opening act for the last nights at the Apollo, billed as: 'Little Stevie Wonder' (the name was Gordy's idea) – 'The 12-year-old who plays piano/drums/organ/ bongos/harmonica, and sings too!' He'd spend the set springing around the stage from instrument to instrument, a ball of restless energy that electrified the dreaded Apollo audience (they could be vicious with below-par acts), ensuring the ultimate success of the tour.

The live shows continued to provide evidence (if it were needed) that Stevie could really whip up an audience. Tricks such as throwing his glasses, then his bow tie, into the audience, coupled with his need to hear and feel an audience response, resulted in some wild shows – Gordy was often heard barking at Clarence Paul to get Stevie off the stage when he was hogging the limelight. The company had to be careful where they sent him to gig, as restrictions in his contract, as well as state laws, barred the underage Stevie from playing nightclubs, and certain theatres.

Practical arrangements also still had to be made regarding Stevie's schooling. The Detroit board of education, acting on a tip-off from some of his teachers, raised the touring-versus-education question at the end of the 1962-63 academic year. Stevie had been running into a spot of trouble at the Fitzgerald Elementary school, with some kids calling him bigheaded, others 'Stevie Wonders' – a name he disliked intensely – and it was clear a certain amount of peer jealousy was being stirred up.

The school board, in cahoots with Stevie's father Calvin Judkins, threatened to call a halt to the boy's musical career. Stevie remembers it as a very difficult time: "I just couldn't keep up my regular studies at school, because I was on the road. There was no person qualified to tutor me while on tour. My teachers told me I should stop pursuing music and continue my education until I was 19 years old … legally they could keep me in school until that time. I'll never forget that day. I was miserable. I remember going to the bathroom and crying, praying that God would allow me to remain in the industry. But I just knew it was impossible."[12]

The pessimism wasn't necessary. There are two versions of what happened next. According to one telling of the story, Lula (inventive as ever) placed an advertisement in the newspaper explaining her situation and asking for assistance, which bore fruit in the shape of a contact at the Michigan School For The Blind, in Lansing, 150 or so miles away. The alternative story is that the initiative was taken by a concert promoter, who was so disappointed not to have Stevie appearing in the *Motown Revue* that he took it upon himself to sort out an arrangement that would be acceptable to all concerned.

Whichever is the accurate account, a deal was struck with Dr Robert Thompson at the Michigan school which meant Stevie would attend that institution for two weeks of the month, and have a private tutor to coach him the rest of the time, either at home or on the road. Thompson recommended Ted Hull, a partially sighted teacher with a post at the Penrickton Center For Blind Children in Detroit.

Ted went up to meet Esther Gordy in September 1963 – Esther was at that time a vice-president at Motown, having quit her job as aide to the Governor of Michigan in order to develop the management side of the family business, ITM. She approved of Ted, and he approved of her, and he was hired, promising to pitch up at a press conference the next day in the Graystone Ballroom. Stevie met Ted that day for the first time, and formed a relationship that would last the next seven years.

The primary reason for the press conference was to celebrate the fact that Stevie's 'Fingertips Parts 1 & 2', co-written by producer Clarence Paul and staff writer Henry 'Hank' Cosby, released on May 21st, was now heading both the pop and R&B singles charts – the first live recording ever

Ted Hull was a caring, conscientious tutor, but life on tour with Stevie came as something of a culture shock

to do so. And what's more the live album recorded in Chicago had become a best-seller too, making what was at the time an unheard-of double Number One.

This blind, black, under-privileged teenager, a coiled spring of irrepressible energy, had clearly touched a nerve in the black community, and was already making a name for himself further afield. Suddenly everyone wanted to know about the new boy genius.

The other event worth celebrating was Berry Gordy's purchase of the Goldstone Theater itself. He'd bought the venue, on Detroit's Woodward Avenue, in June that year, in a move that demonstrated the power of his enterprise. For $123,000 the Graystone was restored to African-American hands, having been abandoned by black audiences during the previous two decades (the likes of Duke Ellington and Cab Calloway had played there in the 1930s). Gordy's acquisition of the Graystone not only meant there was once again a large entertainment venue accessible to black audiences in Detroit, but symbolically it was a re-establishment of African-American rights.

Stevie headed the bill (at the age of just 13) in a series of concerts there in July 1963, alongside The Temptations and The Supremes. A review in the *Michigan Chronicle* read: "The young people were neatly dressed and well-behaved at the matinee and the older crowd at the evening performance was just as attractive and mannerly." (Were they expecting a riot, perhaps?)

Mickey Stevenson explained that concerts like this, "gave us a chance to get the youngsters off the streets and see what our image was about … inspiring them a little to maybe live up to that imagery."[13]

Woodward Avenue was also the traditional racial dividing line in central Detroit. It was on that street that the black community aired its grievances on June 23rd 1963 in a demonstration that came to be known as *The Great March To Freedom*. They certainly had grounds for complaint: earlier that year the Detroit commission on community relations revealed that 10,000 buildings would be demolished in the urban renewal projects, already underway, and 70 per cent of these premises were inhabited by African-Americans – earning the plans the nickname 'Negro Removal'. Martin Luther King addressed the large (and peaceful) crowd, and Gordy taped the proceedings for later release.

School of pop

Stevie's schedule for a lot of this period looks exhausting. It seems as if Ted Hull was a caring, conscientious tutor but, almost inevitably, a strait-laced one, and life on-tour with Stevie came as something of a culture shock.

Ted tells of one particular instance of a *Motown Revue* trip. He and Stevie arrived at 9.20am for a 9.30 departure, and the other artists would turn up in dribs and drabs, with Marvin Gaye being the last to show. Clarence Paul was another late arrival. The rest of the 50 or 60 people boarding the bus read like a who's who of mid Sixties pop: Martha Reeves & The Vandellas, The Supremes, The Temptations, The Four Tops, The Contours, Smokey Robinson & The Miracles, and Mary Wells. Then there was the band, led by pianist Choker Campbell, and Beans Bowles, the road manager (and flute player on the studio 'Fingertips').

As Bowles remembers it, "We were always overcrowded. And he [Gordy] booked way too many dates. The strain was bad. We had a bad accident in November 1962, my driver was killed. And we were lucky not to have others."

But Stevie became used to being on the road. The company there was always good; Martha Reeves was especially close to him – they would work late into the night on songs and dance steps that Stevie could perform. Junior Walker became another ally on the long drives when Stevie needed to share an idea. The two formed a close friendship, with each able to tease the other mercilessly.

The number of overnighters on Motown Revues steadily increased – it was back on the bus after the gig and straight on to the next town. With a tour lasting anything up to 90 one-night stands, that inevitably sapped some energy, though it seemed Stevie could outlast everyone when it came to

In school, Stevie was able to keep a lid on his more 'playful' tendencies ... It was a strange kind of double-life he lived

staying up late. The pattern of little or no sleep that he developed at this time became a permanent fixture, and would test the endurance capabilities of anyone engaged to work with him.

Despite the rigours of the road, the schedule of schoolwork was adhered to. Hull was firmly disciplined, and stuck to the four-hours-per-day timetable, starting at ten o'clock every morning. Because of the individual attention paid to him, Stevie found himself ahead of his school friends academically, although it seems some subjects were of more interest to him than others (he particularly enjoyed physical activities, including wrestling and skiing).

When he was in school, his behaviour was by all accounts exemplary; in the relatively unfamiliar school environment he was able to keep a lid on his more 'playful' tendencies. He was also sporty, and sang in the choir. It was a strange kind of double-life he lived.

Back on the bus, things were less goody-goody. He was introduced to marijuana one night by the touring band, and next morning complained of an intensely painful headache. Gordy guessed what had been happening, and gave the whole bus a lecture on how they should behave towards young Stevie in future.

As Ted soon discovered, these were not school picnics. Some members of the entourage were more indulgent than others. "There might have been a little weed around," says Bowles, "but no coke. Who had the money?" Clarence Paul may have the answer: "Marvin and I did our fair share of cocaine, beginning in the early Sixties. We were into it early on. Other artists, like little Stevie, hated the stuff." Guns were not unusual accessories either: The Four Tops and The Temptations, as well as the Funk Brothers, carried them as protection, and gunshots were not uncommon after – or even during – some gigs.

Ted Hull, being a rare white face on the tour, would find himself in strange and sometimes threatening situations. Segregated washrooms/toilets presented a problem, as did single-race restaurants and hotels. It's a strange picture to conjure up: the white, bespectacled tutor with his teenage black charge, using braille playing-cards while the big-stake games would be further back on the bus. Often during the overnight journeys there would be a pleading from the back for Stevie to stop playing his harmonica, which he would do at all hours, night and day.

One of Stevie's favourite tricks was to find out physical details about someone, perhaps passers-by in the street, and call to them through the open window of the bus, much to their confusion; or being told in advance what a girl might be wearing and then surprising her by saying something like, "That's a beautiful red dress".

It seems Stevie was aware of the pleasures of the opposite sex from quite an early age – and there was ample opportunity to enjoy their company over the years on the road. One report has him losing his virginity to The Soul Sisters (R&B duo Tresia Cleveland and Ann Gissendanner), another recounts the episode in a hotel, après-gig, and après Ted Hull's bedtime, when one of the musicians arranged, and paid, for young Stevie to get off with a girl.

So Stevie's education was perhaps broader than he (and Ted) had anticipated. In terms of his musical career too, although consistent success was still elusive, this period was spent constantly learning his trade – both on the road and in the studio.

CHAPTER 2
SIXTIES RECORDINGS

"You must have bad times to know what the good times are."

By the time Stevie signed with the company in 1962, the Motown hit machine was only just starting to get into gear. That year was the kickoff point for the careers of a significant number of Motown artists, including The Supremes, The Temptations, Mary Wells, and Marvin Gaye. But Berry Gordy still had to decide exactly what to do with the talents of young Stevland Morris.

The easy part was Stevie getting to know the musicians, having them jam with him and show him the ropes in the studio. Gordy was naturally impressed with the boy's harmonica-playing and multi-instrumental capability, and he liked the general air of exuberance and confidence in Stevie's personality. The problem was musical direction. Little Stevie didn't quite seem to fit the Motown mould – and that youthful, headstrong attitude made him something of a loose canon, not easily controlled by producers and management. Quite apart from the worry about how his voice would develop and change over the next few years.

But they pushed ahead with some demos anyway – various 'standards' with a string of producers – most of which were never widely heard. A notable rapport soon began to grow between Stevie and producer Clarence Paul. Coming from a musical family in North Carolina, Paul had sung with various gospel outfits and made some hit records before (as with Gordy) the Korean war intervened. He wound up in Detroit, where Gordy found his musicianship invaluable and assigned him to songwriting and production projects at Hitsville.

With Stevie in need of a father-figure and musical mentor, Paul was soon the clear favourite for the role. Not everybody was totally happy with this choice of collaborator for an impressionable teenager – both Lula and Esther had voiced their doubts over Paul's penchants for wine, women and song (well, they didn't mind the song part, just the other things). But Clarence and Stevie would continue to work closely together for the next few years. As guitar and vibes player Dave Hamilton confirms: "Clarence shaped Stevie. I remember when Stevie would be over at Clarence's house and Clarence would be teaching him to sing those standard tunes like 'Masquerade', those tunes that people would be amazed to see a kid his age singing. [Clarence] was a hell of a singer himself."[14]

But singing was put on the back burner for Stevie's debut recordings. While trying to figure out a plan of action for the voice, Gordy and Paul decided to feature Stevie's instrumental skills on an album called *The Jazz Soul Of Little Stevie* – a very unusual move for the singles-obsessed Motown company. Paul arranged the horn charts and, to the accompaniment of a big-band sound, Stevie showcased his harmonica, bongo, drum and piano skills. He managed to sound fresh and inspired (if not always consistent) on harmonica, over some underwhelming backing tracks that smacked of Sixties TV/movie music. Having put in all that effort, the powers-that-be sat back and listened to the results – before admitting there were no singles to be extracted. No single meant no hit. No hit meant there was little point in releasing the album, so it was shelved, for the time being at least.

Motown's next idea was to try hitching a ride on the coat-tails of one of Stevie's major role models, Ray Charles. The album *A Tribute To Uncle Ray* was a mixture of Charles songs and originals, again recorded using the big-band arrangement approach, but this time with Stevie in full voice on tracks such as the exuberant 'Hallelujah I Love Him So', 'The Masquerade', and 'Drown In My Own Tears' – a testament to Stevie's ability to empathise with subject matter he could have understood little of at that age, and to translate that to sung emotion.

Gordy and Paul still weren't convinced by the results. Again no single poked its head above the parapet, and no single meant no hit, etc etc. They were increasingly sure, though, that there was something worth nurturing – Stevie had learned to mark his style on a track, in spite of the often ill-suited big-band arrangements.

Pretty music

On August 16th 1962, Motown released Stevie's first single, 'I Call It Pretty Music (But The Old People Call It The Blues)'. Written by Clarence Paul, and announcing the official arrival on record of 'Little Stevie Wonder', it disappeared into a pool of molten vinyl, to reappear only rarely on budget compilations long after Stevie became famous.

Motown was disappointed with the single's failure. Stevie was devastated. But at least the opening commercial move had been made – and Stevie was the first 12-year-old kid on the block walking around with his own record under his arm.

Another single came and went in October that year: 'Little Water Boy', a co-write with Paul, still didn't capture the attention of the market place. But the third single, 'Contract On Love', seemed to be getting closer to a finished sellable product. It had handclaps on every beat, a bouncy Hammond organ part, excellent backing vocals courtesy of The Temptations, and Stevie sounding good in his 'boy' upper range (technically C#4) on the bridge – yet it still didn't quite manage to turn the key in the Top 40 lock.

There are signs that the session was under-prepared too: the musicians seem confused over the chord on one of the stops, and Stevie comes down to a note on the bridge that doesn't sit well with the harmony underneath. Still, at least it sounds like a pop record, which showed that it could be done, and it caused the greatest stir yet – even if that's not saying very much.

The next six months were frustrating ones... at least until Berry Gordy decided to gamble on that live recording of 'Fingertips'

Presumably the record company thought it worthwhile, at this stage of controlled exposure, to release the two albums that had been gathering dust on the shelf: *Jazz Soul* and *Uncle Ray* were released in September and October 1962 respectively.

And then... nothing. The next six months were frustrating ones on the record front – at least until Berry Gordy decided to gamble on that live recording of 'Fingertips', and Stevie's career went through the roof.

Suddenly nationally famous, the next step was to capitalise on the dramatic success of 'Fingertips' and prove Stevie could be more than a 'one-hit wonder' (so to speak). As it turned out, as if to show just how fickle the pop market can be, none of his next six singles even broke into the Top 30. The immediate follow-up, 'Workout Stevie Workout', was obviously conceived as an attempt to recreate the energy of the live 'Fingertips' in the studio. The groove is certainly happening, with a snare-dominated New Orleans-ish drum pattern, a slightly bizarre baritone sax part, superbly and funkily executed, gospel-tinged backing vocals chanting the chorus, and some frenetic harmonica blowing –

all this nearly drowned out by the insistent good-time handclaps. It should have been a recipe for a hit single, but the song itself was slack and uninteresting in structure, and the hook lacking in character. The crumbling of the top range of Stevie's voice is also evident. The single limped to Number 33 in the pop charts – not a disaster, but not the follow-up Gordy must have hoped for.

The next single, 'Castles In The Sand', did little except confirm the perilous state of Stevie's voice. Released early in 1964, you can hear that the lower register is beginning to appear and solidify, but inadvisable forays into the upper boyish range leave the listener uncomfortable. The track is interesting, though, for its use of a recording of the sea on the intro, an atmosphere-inducer that must have been unusual to contemporary ears (sound effects on pop records didn't become commonplace till later in the decade).

It has to be said that, at this point, the record company were floundering around trying to find suitable material for Stevie – either to match his one-off chart topper, or at least do his talent justice. An attempt at a standards album, *With A Song In My Heart*, failed dismally. Tunes such as 'Make Someone Happy', 'Smile', 'Without A Song', and 'When You Wish Upon A Star' are all given the hackneyed strings/backing vocals thing that doesn't do anyone any favours. At least the sleeve notes score highly for effort, claiming: "The result is a moving display of musical technique and forcefully sensitive rendition..." Hmmm.

Another mistake was an extension of the 'Castles In The Sand' ethos – a whole beach album, which completely missed the boat. Surf music had peaked the summer before, and by the time of the release of *Stevie At The Beach* (June 1964), the trend had been all but wiped out – largely thanks to the US invasion by The Beatles and the UK beat bands.

While the recording side of his career was frustratingly slow, the live shows at least provided Stevie with an outlet for his frighteningly active adolescent energy. With all the touring and side projects – such as his inexplicable beach-movie cameos – Stevie was spending decreasing amounts of time at home (which was now Greenlawn Avenue, in a smart, predominantly white, part of north-west Detroit, where he'd moved with his four siblings).

Motown was by now beginning to make waves in the UK and the rest of Europe, so a trip to Paris was arranged, where Stevie was to top the *Motown Revue* bill. But this visit would coincide with the onset of several teenage problems. The prime cause for concern was Stevie's voice: it was painful for him to speak, let alone sing. His voice was also well-and-truly on the break, deepening all the time – Wade Marcus, the musical director for the tour, found himself transposing songs as they travelled, compensating for the elongating vocal cords. Stevie's boy voice had always seemed fragile at the top, and now it was just not functioning.

Stevie was upset to find his spot was being moved to earlier in the show, as his set seemed to be losing the impact required to end the night. He took it as a personal snub from Motown. Relationships weren't eased when a journalist from London claimed (completely erroneously, as it turned out) that there were in fact ways to restore Stevie's sight but the record company was keeping this information from him because the singer's blindness was too good a selling point. The atmosphere was inevitably charged.

After the tour Stevie was investigated by doctors, who discovered two nodules on his vocal cords. He had to undergo throat surgery, followed by what must have been quite a difficult two weeks of silent recuperation.

During his awkward, voice-changing period, Stevie's harmonica playing was a reliable constant

Bye bye Little Stevie

The one positive development in Stevie's career at this period was the disappearance of the 'Little' part of the stage name, much to Stevie's relief. But the direction was still far from clear. Even at the weekly A&R/production/quality control meetings, there would be a dearth of volunteers to work on Stevie's projects. Stevie himself certainly wasn't tempted to abandon his career, though: "I felt bad because I wasn't successful in writing or singing, but that didn't discourage me. It never made me feel like giving up ... it made me try even harder. You must have bad times to know what the good times are."[15]

If Stevie was having bad times, the rest of the pop industry, and Motown in particular, was on the up. Mary Wells had her massive Number One with 'My Guy', a record that The Beatles would champion when she came to the UK to tour with them. The Supremes broke through with 'Where Did Our Love Go', a Holland-Dozier-Holland song that featured Diane (later Diana) Ross on lead vocals – her distinctly individual and charmingly naive/sensual voice, allied to a song with a teeny-bop angle, captured the summer mood, topping the chart in July 1964. More was to follow soon.

But the biggest pop news at the time was of course the British invasion. The Beatles, a musical and cultural phenomenon that swept across the USA in a way that has never been equalled since, had no less than six Number One hits in 1964, including 'She Loves You', 'I Want To Hold Your Hand' and 'A Hard Day's Night'. In this two-way cultural exchange The Beatles drew from the Motown songbook themselves by recording 'Please Mr Postman', Gordy's 'Money (That's What I Want)', and Smokey's 'You've Really Got A Hold On Me'.

The Beatles, and later The Rolling Stones, generally raided the larder of rhythm & blues, merging it with a pop simplicity and English whimsicality. What wasn't perhaps so characteristically English was the aggression and edge of these bands' sounds, particularly the Stones – though of course this has to be gauged against the mellow standards of the day, rather than the heavy rock and punk band sounds of more recent times. (Another interesting example would be a track like 'Bits And Pieces' from fellow invading Brits The Dave Clark Five: I always remembered a really strong, forceful drum track on this – it was the band's signature sound – but we've become so used to drum-heavy pop tracks that it now sounds positively weak by comparison to today's mixes.)

"I felt bad because I wasn't successful ... but it made me try harder. You must have bad times to know what the good times are."

While both sides of the Atlantic were listening to each other, the technology of record-making was changing too. The three-track tape machine at Hitsville was nearing the end of its days. Frustration at not being able to remix elements of the backing track once they were recorded led to a demand for more tracks. The only multi-track machines commercially available were four-track, which was not enough to solve the problem, so Berry Gordy commissioned his studio engineer Mike McLean to design and build an eight-track version.

With the three-track monitoring arrangement the 'logical' step would have been to add five more, but in a move that defined the path for stereo recording, Mike proposed a two-channel monitoring system, with the outputs of the eight tracks sent to varying positions in the stereo field. He also devised pan (panorama) pots for the mixing desk, to place each track precisely in the stereo picture.

From 1965 onwards, mixing a stereo master from eight-track multi-track became the norm. The level of instrumental complexity in a tune was constantly on the increase, though, and eight tracks could be exhausted fairly quickly. The solution was to 'bounce', to do a mini-mix of perhaps four tracks down to two tracks, freeing up two tracks to record more instruments/vocals/effects. Eventually two eight-track machines would be used in tandem (on the Temptations' 'My Girl', for instance), before the arrival of full 16-track recorders.

All this enabled a degree of unprecedented experimentation: for example two basses might be recorded, one electric and another an upright bass, each with different musical roles. And Motown became pioneers of using synthesiser effects in pop, on tracks such as The Supremes' 'Reflections' and 'The Happening' – an oscillator setup was designed by Russ Terrana, and experimented with by the Holland-Dozier-Holland production team.

Everything is alright

By the summer of 1965 Motown must have been getting pretty itchy over Stevie Wonder's future in the music business. Four more singles had come and gone – 'Hey Harmonica Man', 'Happy Street', 'Kiss Me Baby' and a live recording of 'High Heel Sneakers' (with a tune called 'Pretty Little Angel' cancelled along the way). 'Hey Harmonica Man', with its almost country-blues feel, was the only one of this batch to bother the pop Top 40, peaking at Number 29. But it was now two years since the huge success of 'Fingertips', and even some people at Motown were beginning to doubt if Stevie's early promise would come to much more.

It was clear the right combination of writer/producer still hadn't emerged. Clarence Paul was worried, as his partnership had been largely unfruitful. Still, time was on Stevie's side – with an adult voice developing, and some creative ideas of his own also beginning to find expression, he was sure there was still a way to create and maintain a career.

He was encouraged in his own writing endeavours by both Clarence Paul and Hank Cosby. In hotel lobbies or bars where there was a piano, Paul and Stevie would work on tunes and ideas. They even carried around a keyboard that worked on batteries – it sounded more like a squeezebox than a piano, but was workable enough to try new ideas on. As Paul later recalled: "You had to get Stevie in a mood to work. You had to kind of push him, and the more you pushed him the harder he worked."[16]

One of the early ideas they hatched on the road became the b-side of 'High-Heeled Sneakers', a song they simply titled 'Music Talk'. As Paul recalled, it "was one of them things that we made up riding on a bus. Stevie, Ted and I just grooved along doing some 'music talk'."[18] But it was the next single that would bring Stevie back into the hit-making fold. It was his big international breakthrough, as well as being his first co-writing success – 'Uptight (Everything's Alright)'.

In an admission that the USA was listening to and being influenced by music from the UK, Stevie has since said that the track was inspired by the Rolling Stones' 'Satisfaction'. Released on November 22nd 1965, 'Uptight' certainly shares the raw energy of the Stones' track, as well as a marked similarity in the harmony, and the fact that it's structured around a two-bar riff. But whereas 'Satisfaction' has more than one section, 'Uptight' sticks doggedly, like a bull terrier with a plastic

bone, to the same pattern from beginning to end, happy to keep a bassline and drum part substantially the same from post-intro to fade.

Credited jointly to Stevie (peculiarly using the surname Judkins), Hank Cosby and fellow Motown writer/producer Sylvia Moy, it's clear from the kickoff that there is more of a pop sensibility at work here than has been heard on Stevie's releases to date. It's worth looking in some more detail at the song's arrangement.

First, the drum track. This is as straight-down-the-line as it gets, snare crashing down on every beat and hi-hat on (mostly) eighth-note feel, interspersed with fills that just scream, "Look what I can do", and "Look, I did it again", and even "Look, I can do it where it most definitely should not be". In fact the first fill of the song (last beat of the second bar) is a very tasteful snare roll, but the full monty gets rolled out two bars later when the two-bar 16th-note runaround from snare to toms is revealed in all its glory.

So who's playing here? The bass certainly belongs to James Jamerson, and the drums are often credited to Funk Brothers regular Benny Benjamin – but from the sound of it, I'd be pretty surprised if that wasn't an excited teenager behind the drum kit.

It could be that Paul had been a conservative influence on the music, despite his supposedly supportive stance towards Stevie's creative input

In short, this is precisely what Stevie should be doing – getting involved in writing and instrumental roles, not just singing half-baked standards with, quite frankly, second-class arrangements. (Personally speaking, I can't help wondering why it took so long.)

It could be that Clarence Paul had been a rather conservative influence on the music (if not the lifestyle), despite his supposedly supportive stance towards Stevie's creative input. Certainly Paul's lack of involvement on this recording seems to have had a liberating effect, and co-producers Cosby and Mickey Stevenson obviously picked up on the new freedom and energy.

There's an interesting underpinning of the drum track too, an extra tom overdub, over on the right, same side as the drums (a silent count of 1-2 then dom-dom-dom-dom-dom-*dom*, all eighth-notes) – which sonically ties the drum part in with the bass, providing a driving low-end propulsion. Incidentally, it's apparent that eight tracks (plus bounces) are in use by this time: drum tracks, extra drum overdub, bass, extra bass overdub, horns, guitars, backing vocals (which from now on I'll generally refer to as BVs), it's all piled in there. As far as the stereo picture is concerned, the guitars are over on the left, balancing the drums, while bass and vocals steer a course through the middle.

The intro sets up a bass riff, which is then joined by a guitar, and you'd naturally think that the song would be based around that riff, but strangely it never reappears. Was this maybe an afterthought, added to spice up the introduction (which would otherwise just be stark drums), or even give it more of an instantly hooky 'Motown' signature. The sound of the bass on the intro is also very different from the bulk of the track – it's played with a pick (which means it's probably not Jamerson at that point, as he used fingers) and the level is pushed into distortion. The intro guitar is equally close up – and perhaps one more take would have solved the awkward rhythmic feel – and is very unlike the regular guitar clank in the rest of the song.

Once the brass comes in, the bass sound changes and a far more jazz-tinged line appears, starting on the root note (C♯) then dipping down to almost the lowest bass note (F) before clawing its way back up, half-step by step by half-step, and so on to the root. The number of slight variations over the next 2:53 is a bit like a climber trying out a variety of routes to ascend a mountain. It never seems completely at ease, which implies this is a rough take that was preferred for its energy.

Once the huge double-tracked brass fanfares are done (again quite rough in the tuning department), the chorus kicks in for maximum exposure and audience hooking. The first thing you notice is Stevie's voice: backed by female BVs pitched higher than his voice, it sounds fairly settled in range with no vestiges of the 'Little' Stevie hanging around. A bit hoarse/tired perhaps but the essence of the adult voice is all in place. Happiest emoting in the area just above the middle of the keyboard (roughly C3 to A3), with notes above that for special starburst climactic effect, at last the voice suits the lyric.

Suitably enough it's a boy-and-girl story – he's from the rough side of town, while she's the spoiled/snooty rich girl:

"I'm a poor man's son, from across the railroad tracks,
The only shirt I own is hangin' on my back,
But I'm the envy of ev'ry single guy
Since I'm the apple of my girl's eye."

He doesn't have money but he can give her his love: "She says baby, ev'rything is alright, uptight, clean out of sight."

The title causes some confusion, because the word 'uptight' later took on the meaning of nervous, edgy, uneasy – basically not cool. But in the early 1960s it meant something very different, more like excellent, first-rate, tip-top, or in the more recent vernacular, 'wicked'.

The image of right and wrong side of the railroad tracks gives a bluesy reference to the lyric, even if the next line adds a very unbluesy reference:

"The right side of the tracks, she was born and raised
In a great big old house, full of butlers and maids."

Stevie hadn't quite arrived at that level of luxury but he knew enough about both sides of the financial coin to be able to inject a real sense of identification into the vocal.

A sense of how adept Stevie already was at setting a lyric to syncopated rhythms was already evident – witness "railroad tracks" and "hangin' on my back". He's also developed a penchant for emphasising words that shouldn't really be held, and inserting pauses where you wouldn't expect – for instance he sings, "Since I'm the… apple of my girl's eye" and "My money's low and… my suit's out of style". It's almost like the gap in a funk groove that leaves you hanging in the air before dropping you on the next beat.

Other glimpses of future Wonder include the second verse "*great* big old house", where the upper climactic limit is approached before being exceeded on "*never* never never make my baby cry", and the (surely improvised) "*way* out of sight".

In other words, after some intriguing transitionary vocal outings – particularly the rarely-heard 'Don't You Feel It' from late 1964 – 'Uptight' can be called the first fully-fledged Stevie Wonder vocal performance.

Just to return briefly to the Stones comparison, Stevie's chords here are the same on top as the 'Satisfaction' riff (C♯, B/C♯), but because the movement in the bass is so different from the Stones' E, D/A, he manages to get away with it.

Not a lot develops through the song: the horns come back midway and the 'girl' verse leads to the chorus, then to the outro. Horns and chorus blare and a few nice BV 'woohs' reflect the level of genuine fun being had by all. Certainly makes a change from the rather forced 'yeahs' that had routinely, un-enthusiastically, appeared on previous Stevie records.

Politics and riots

'Uptight' reached Number One in the R&B chart and Number Three in the pop chart (14 in the UK), so it's no surprise that the same overall concept was retained by the producers for the next single, 'Nothing's Too Good For My Baby' – using the same drum pattern (even the same fill), though this time without the underpinning from the toms, while horns and piano on the right balance drums and guitars on the left.

It's pretty much a one-chord song, with the same harmonic structure as 'Uptight', though there is a bridge that has some uncharacteristic rocky chord moves. Stevie is not credited as a writer here – which means someone else on the team was also listening out for the latest sound.

By this time there was a defined market for 'soul' music – the term itself had even been copyrighted by Gordy when establishing a label to promote the music, though he obviously failed to impose a monopoly on its use. Soul can be defined as black secular music with its origins in the gospel music of the church – during the late 1950s gospel music had found its way out of church, particularly through the work of Ray Charles. Tracks such as 'Georgia On My Mind', 'Hallelujah I Love Him So', and 'Drown In My Own Tears' (which Stevie covered) set the palette of piano-dominated rhythm section, horns, and above all a soulful vocal.

Stax, a new label based in Memphis with an Atlantic distribution deal, was also carrying the torch for black artists such as Otis Redding, Aretha Franklin (daughter of the Rev C.L. Franklin, a Detroit preacher with a touring gospel 'caravan') and Wilson Pickett. Stax was the first black-run (though not black-owned) label to challenge the Motown sound. Those in the know appreciated the unfussy production values, which refused to pander to a white pop market. Instead it was a sound suited to the new stirrings in the black political arena; with Black Power just around the corner some of the Motown acts were beginning to sound (and look) too overtly commercial for some black tastes.

Berry Gordy decided to launch Soul Records in late 1965 to feature the work of Junior Walker (whose hit 'Shotgun', with its massive tambourine, funk guitar and earthy vocal, was the label's first hit), Jimmy Ruffin (whose 'What Becomes Of The Brokenhearted' is a legend of a soul song), and Gladys Knight & The Pips.

Stevie's next single, on the other hand, followed a different musical tack altogether, even if the lyrics reflected his growing politicisation as an artist. For his version of 'Blowin' In The Wind', the

Bob Dylan song that had charted for Peter, Paul & Mary back in 1963, Stevie was reunited with Clarence Paul, whose studio involvement had been on the wane, despite retaining his position as live musical director. The Dylan reworking had been a live hit in Stevie's shows for a while, but Berry Gordy was dead against it being released as a single – apparently he hadn't even wanted the song on the recent *Uptight* album (the 16-year-old's sixth album in less than four years). To risk rocking the boat of hit singles with a protest song seemed to make no sense to Gordy.

It's true the track's gospel/country/soul treatment was not the freshest arrangement on the block, and Clarence Paul's sharing of vocal duties, by prompting Stevie with the lines on the second verse, is slightly uncomfortable. I guess it might have worked on-stage, but falls rather flat on record.

Stevie does have a feel for the song, though: "How many years can a man exist, before he's allowed to be free?" is sung with the conviction of a young man ready and able to embrace the cause of the burgeoning civil rights movement.

The track marks the starting point of Stevie's appetite for songs with a social commentary which, despite his cold feet, Gordy was persuaded to release. An R&B Number One and pop chart Number

He sings with the conviction of a young man ready to embrace the civil rights movement

Nine in June 1966 certainly vindicated the decision. 'Blowin'…' reached the UK chart too, albeit just inside the Top 40, as opposed to 'Uptight' which made the UK Top 20.

Despite the odd cover version, Stevie was continuing to write with Cosby and Moy at this point: "What would happen is, Henry Cosby would do some writing with us, he would come up with a chord pattern for my melody, then maybe he'd help Sylvia Moy with the lyrics to the tune. Sylvia did a lot of writing on the early things. I would come up with the basic idea, maybe a punchline, and she would write the story."[18]

But the next in the trail of single releases, 'A Place In The Sun', brought a new writer to the Wonder enclave in the shape of Ron Miller, who'd been employed at Motown since 1961. Co-written by Bryan Wells, and drawn from the forthcoming *Down To Earth* album (which had Clarence Paul back in the production chair), the song is mid-tempo and more than slightly cloying, especially with the string thing going on, but skilfully written all the same. There's another 'freedom' line in there too, which might have appealed to Stevie: "Like the branch of a tree, I keep reaching to be free…"

The next single, at the end of 1966, was also a barely disguised political comment: the track 'Someday At Christmas' (he would release an album of the same name a year later) is memorable less for the music than the inclusion of lyrics such as: "Someday at Christmas, men won't be boys, playing with bombs like kids play with toys." That's the anti-war part, here comes the civil rights section: "Someday in a world where men are free…", before the pessimistic conclusion, "Maybe not in time for you and me."

It was a time of growing social unrest in several US cities, despite the hippy movement's proposals of peace and love. The Detroit riot of 1967 was triggered by a combination of the Vietnam war and deteriorating race relations, and the five-day conflagration resulted in 43 deaths, over 7,000 arrests, injury to hundreds more, and $50m damage to homes and property.

In the Detroit of the 1960s several problems were reaching intolerable levels. Firstly police brutality and generally contemptuous attitude towards black citizens was commonplace. In the 12th Street area, around the corner from Hitsville, four-man police units, or 'Tac squads', would patrol looking for bars to raid or prostitutes to arrest or just black youths to question regarding ID. Most of those stopped would be verbally abused as a matter of routine – and that would be getting off lightly.

The *Detroit Free Press* conducted a survey of local concerns, which confirmed police behaviour as the major issue. The second biggest problem was housing: by the late 1960s, despite the movement of some of the black population into formerly white areas, black residents generally had to pay more than their white neighbours for equivalent accommodation. And with the building of motorways and bulldozing of housing – the so-called 'urban renewal' – the heart of the black community was physically ripped out.

At the car factory things were no better. The assembly lines had been automated and the subsequent job losses were mostly shouldered by young black workers. Even though Detroit boasted a lower rate of unemployment than many inner cities, job prospects were gloomy, and patterns of boredom and depression began to emerge. Dissatisfaction with inequality pushed many towards the black militant movements. A Black Power rally in early July threatened the white powers-that-be in Detroit that if conditions didn't improve, they would "burn you down".

The national civil rights campaign was also mobilising, and already splintering. When James Meredith (famed for being the first African-American admitted to Mississippi University) was shot by a sniper during his one-man 'March Against Fear' in June 1966, he quickly re-adjusted his non-violent stance, regretting he had not armed himself. Martin Luther King, Stokely Carmichael and others continued his march, but dissenting voices refused to sing the line "black and white together" from the anthem 'We Shall Overcome'. King spoke in Detroit, expressing his dismay at the use of the slogan "black power" instead of the less separatist "freedom now".

Come July 23rd 1967, in the small hours of a hot, steamy Sunday morning (stifling weather yet again), Martha & The Vandellas were at the Fox Theatre on Woodward Avenue performing 'Dancing In The Street' when the news came that they would have to stop and go home to safety as events outside were turning ugly. Police had raided a 'blind pig' (an illegal drinking hole) on 12th Street, which doubled as the United Civil League For Community Action. After a tip-off from an undercover officer, they sledgehammered their way in, deciding to arrest all those present (instead of just the owners, as was customary). An angry crowd quickly gathered outside, and soon bricks, beer cans, and stones were flying.

By the end of that Sunday, 12th Street was in flames, and the first life had been lost. President Johnson called in troops to quell the 'civil disturbance'. By the second day, full-scale gun battles raged in the streets, crossfire casualties and deaths followed, and by the Thursday whole segments of the city had been destroyed.

Hitsville miraculously escaped the flames, though the buildings all around were razed. The Chit-Chat club, for instance, was not as fortunate as the Motown building – the venue that gave gigs to the Funk Brothers, allowing them to try out ideas that would appear in the studio the next day, was burned down in an arson attack. Other black-owned businesses important to the community were destroyed, particularly Joe Von Battle's record shop, and Edward Vaughn's Forum 66 bookshop, which it was claimed the police firebombed.

In the aftermath of the riots the community was overwhelmed by a sense of desolation. Depression and then bitterness enveloped the city when it became clear how much rebuilding there was to do. Berry Gordy offered his services, realising the responsibility of his position as a successful black businessman. He initiated a fund-raising scheme, putting forward The Supremes to head the campaign. Gordy also had the idea of a more educational arm to the Motown label, which would issue a series of largely spoken-word recordings in the mould of 1963's 'Great March To Freedom' speech recording – a concept which eventually became his Black Forum series in 1970.

Stevie himself was clearly shaken by the events in Detroit and elsewhere. He tried to maintain his natural optimism and idealism while resolving to find a way to address political issues, both within and outside the medium of music.

Made to love

No doubt one of the tracks booming from the jukebox in most 'blind pigs' at the time would have been Stevie's new single, 'I Was Made To Love Her', released in May 1967. Although down in tempo compared to 'Uptight' (it starts at 100bpm, but soon gets excited), the track certainly packs a punch – largely thanks to the force of the vocal and Jamerson's free-but-disciplined bass approach.

But there are several other elements at work here, such as a rock/pop approach to chord structure, and a straight, driving, rock drum groove, which combine with a guitar that tries to be plain but just can't bring itself to be.

With a career that stretched back to the touring days of Marv Johnson at Motown, Funk Brothers' guitarist Eddie Willis had a background in the blues, and it shows here. The arrangement is much more sophisticated than its predecessors: gone are the 'clank' guitars, replaced by the mid-range edge-of-distortion riff that takes over the track after the initial phrase and continues to fill throughout. The best-sounding of these is on the line, "Like a sweet magnolia tree", where the guitar is driven just far enough to hurt.

We hear all the material from which the song is built within the first six bars, two of which build the hooky riff and four establish the chordal pattern. Over this is a fantastic harmonica solo that sets the track up a treat – the phrasing takes the blues thread and bends it all around the 2nd and 3rd notes of the scale, basically introducing the vocal melody. BVs, strings and celeste (an instrument most commonly associated with Tchaikovsky's 'Dance Of The Sugar Plum Fairy' from the *Nutcracker Suite*) are in on the act, and across the other side of the soundstage from the guitar is a Wurlitzer electric piano, unfussily stepping through the changes.

But first let's take a closer look at that bassline. It's sometimes hard to concentrate on the rest of the track here because the bass is so ear-catching, and so remarkably played. The slower tempo offers the restlessly inventive Jamerson space to inject some fast (16th-note) runs into the melée. Most of the movement is re-enforcing eighth-note lines, especially in the area of the fourth bar of the cycle, which houses the hooky riff, but in the first bar those little skips mirror and emphasise the adolescent energy generated by the vocal.

The song itself is a product of that same youthful dynamism: it was reportedly written in ten minutes (all of those verses?) and tells the story of teenage sweethearts. The writing credits this time are split between Stevie's mother Lula (her first credit, though not her last), Stevie, Moy and Cosby. The inspiration was drawn from Stevie's first real love, a girl called Angie Satterwhite. It's a charming

On the back of the success of 'Uptight', Stevie undertook a three-week European tour, starting with this date at the Titan Club in Rome, Italy, in November 1966

lyric, if that doesn't sound patronising, full of the first flush of youth and it-will-last-forever positivity:

> "I wore hightop shoes and shirt tails,
> Suzy was in pigtails,
> I knew I loved her even then.
> You know my papa disapproved it,
> My mama boohooed it,
> But I told them time and time again,
> Don't you know I was made to love her…"

Every device in the book is used to describe the love – poetic references drawn from nature (sweet magnolia trees, mountains), even humour ("I was knee high to a chicken when that love bug bit me"). But what's most noticeable is that the vocal tracks are getting stronger all the time – hear the raunch on "disapproved it", and the upper extension on "boohooed it".

You can also hear an early example of the soon-to-be-typical breath intake and exhalation, conveying a keen sense of immediacy and urgent desire to communicate. The story goes that Cosby and Stevie were inspired by the way a particular Baptist minister would use his voice and breathing in an emotive way to rouse his congregation, and they deliberately attempted to incorporate that technique into Stevie's studio vocals.

The endless four-bar repetition is given a rest midway with a breakdown section that introduces double-time tambourine and an even funkier bassline. Bearing a marked resemblance to the shape of the line on 'Uptight' (F down to A then up again chromatically), this time the 16th-note syncopation starts to sound like the bass player who would later pick up musically where Jamerson would leave off – Jaco Pastorius.

The intricacy of the bass generally offsets the simpler, rock-style chord sequence. The third bar of the cycle passes through two major chords back to the root (D♭ and E♭ then F) in a raw, unsophisticated 'move your finger up the frets' way. Jamerson completely subverts that direct approach by filling in the spaces in-between, stepping through D on the way to E♭. So suddenly what would have been a tired trudge uphill becomes a light skip. From the breakdown onwards, the strings return and it's a sprint to the finishing line.

The single duly raced to the upper echelons of the charts, achieving a more-than-respectable R&B Number One and pop chart Number Two, also charting in the UK at Number Five. Another single, 'Until You Come Back To Me (That's What I'm Gonna Do)', was issued in the UK in 1967, though it failed to reach the Top 40 – and strangely it wasn't released in the States at all, at least until Aretha Franklin had a hit with a slightly sped-up cover in the 1970s. Stevie's version turned out to be the last time Clarence Paul's name would appear as writer or producer on one of his singles. A crafted, Bacharach-ian tune (rather weirdly produced – is that BVs in the distance over there?), it's a very musical affair, if not as immediate as some of Stevie's bigger hits of the era.

It also brings to mind one of Stevie's side-projects at the time – one that displays a puzzling sense of artist direction and record company/producer steerage – namely the 1968 'Alfie' single and accompanying Cosby-produced instrumental album, released under the name Eivets Rednow (Stevie's name backwards, see?) on the Gordy label, rather than bearing the usual Tamla logo.

Burt Bacharach and Hal David's song 'Alfie' (the theme from the 1966 Michael Caine movie) had been a hit for Dionne Warwick in the US and Cilla Black in the UK, and it shows Stevie's appreciation of Bacharach's tune-crafting that he included another of his songs, 'A House Is Not A Home', on the same album. Stevie himself contributed four tracks to the LP, including 'Bye Bye World'.

Considering that Stevie and Cosby had just worked on the singles 'I'm Wondering' and 'Shoo-Be-Doo-Be-Doo-Da-Day', both Motown groove specials – particularly 'Shoo-Be' with its funky swung beat (and featuring an early outing for Stevie's later-beloved clavinet keyboard) – you might wonder why Stevie would be interested in recording a saccharine-sweet album of harmonica tunes.

The answer is complex: listening to some of the tracks it sounds as if he maybe *wasn't* entirely committed to or inspired by the project. It turns out in fact he had been expecting to make an instrumental album with Wes Montgomery at the time, but the famed jazz guitarist died just before the recordings started, so Stevie saw it through on his own.

It's also undeniable that, for all his soul and later funk leanings, Stevie has always had a soft spot for the occasional rather 'cheesy' easy-listening tune – whether his own or someone else's. He clearly liked the 'Alfie' theme, for instance, and was still performing it on-stage decades later. Harmonica-led instrumentals have always held an appeal for him anyway – interestingly Stevie even today expresses a desire to record a jazz harmonica album, sensing unfinished business perhaps.

End of an era

The assassination of Martin Luther King in 1968 was a tragic blow to the nation, and it hit everyone at Motown particularly hard. Stevie, who'd met King two years earlier at the *Student Christian Freedom Rally* in Chicago, was especially affected by the news. He'd heard the report on the car radio on the way back from his school, and fell silent for the rest of the journey. As Lula said at the time, "They always shoot the good ones."[19]

Motown swiftly offered its services, organising a benefit gig involving Stevie, Gladys Knight & The Pips, The Supremes, The Temptations, and an 11-piece band, which raised over $25,000. Gordy

> If it was the end of the 'golden age' of Motown hit-making, it was just the beginning for artists willing to embrace technological change

pledged again to pursue his Black Forum series, and King's 'Why I Oppose The War In Vietnam' speech was eventually released in 1970 (earning the company a Grammy in the process).

In a decade profoundly altered by the assassination of key figures (John Kennedy, Malcolm X), the murder of Robert Kennedy was equally shocking for Stevie – he was staying at the same hotel in Los Angeles at the time, where the senator was campaigning for president when he was shot. For a teenager, Stevie had already seen his fair share of funerals – the previous year, when Otis Redding died in a plane crash, Stevie went to the memorial service alongside Aretha Franklin, James Brown and Little Richard.

Politicians were under pressure to do something about the country's growing unrest. President Johnson had commissioned a report following the 1967 Detroit riots and other inner-city disturbances, which delivered the stark warning that the country was moving towards two societies, "One black, one white – separate but unequal". Johnson himself decided not to run for president again, declaring there was "division in the American house", but in his final months in office (shortly after King's death) he signed the Civil Rights Act of 1968, legislation that sought to end housing and employment inequalities and discrimination.

Meanwhile over at Motown, all was not peace and harmony by any means. In March of 1968 Gordy moved the Motown operation to 2547 Woodward Avenue in Detroit – partly for space reasons, partly for a smarter address. But this move, plus the buying out of local competitive labels, and the fact that the era of being on first-name terms with the executives was over, provoked a distinct feeling that, despite its stated intentions, the Motown corporation was more concerned with profit than civil rights, or indeed individual rights.

As far as the distribution of wealth among its artists was concerned, rumblings of dissatisfaction had been heard for some time. Mary Wells had left Motown in 1964 after being offered a better contract elsewhere; in 1966 Clarence Paul had organised a meeting at his house to try and co-ordinate musicians and writers to pursue fairer deals. Mickey Stevenson left the company to join MGM – many felt he wanted to escape the meanness of the financial climate at Motown, though it could also have been that the company didn't share his faith in the potential of his wife Kim Weston as a singer.

The low-point was undoubtedly the dispute with Holland-Dozier-Holland. The H-D-H songwriting team had been responsible for an extraordinary bevy of Motown hits for The Four Tops and The Supremes, but when the river of hits dried up around 1968, Gordy filed a lawsuit for breach of contract. H-D-H counter-sued with a range of accusations from fraud to conspiracy and deceit, and the bitter dispute would run and run into the mid 1970s.

It seems the opposing interests of 'family' versus 'hit factory' were causing the fabric at Motown to crumble. The gap between the label and the studio musicians was ever-widening too. Once close to Jamerson and Van Dyke, now Gordy was at arm's length. In fact the snakepit regulars had never even felt comfortable with the working methods of the Holland-Dozier-Holland partnership: H-D-H were untrained musicians, who had an ear for melody, but disregarded the importance of chords, and instead used the studio technology to build up their songs in a patchwork kind of a way. The seasoned Funk Brothers began to feel rather alienated – it was a far cry from the jazz-influenced, recording-as-a-performance attitude of the early years.

If it was the end of the 'golden age' of Motown hit-making, it was just the beginning for artists and producers who were happy to embrace technological change. Greater possibilities were supplied by the addition of two Ampex tape machines in the studio, and new sounds were emerging every day.

Perhaps Stevie's most sonically forward-looking track of this period is 'You Met Your Match', released as a single in June 1968. The clavinet is now fully incorporated into the band sound, there's less emphasis on the guitars, the bass and drum groove is funky, the BVs are wittily arranged and perfectly performed, and the brass, while mysteriously mixed (disappearing into a reverb signal only), are at times punchy.

The song is based around blues changes, another foretaste of later development, though it lacks

The not-so-mysterious Eivets Rednow recorded an instrumental album of harmonica-led tunes in 1968

an 'earworm' hook of a melodic line. It was valuable as Stevie's first experience of producing in the studio (along with Don Hunter, who also co-wrote the track with Stevie and Lula), but the single underperformed in the charts.

At the end of 1968, Stevie's sound was back on the more familiar Motown rails, and his career boosted by his biggest international hit so far. 'For Once In My Life', as originally written by Ron Miller and Orlando Murden, started life as a slow 'standard' type of a song, in a Frank Sinatra/Tony Bennett style, which Stevie was not keen on. He and Cosby took the original writers' idea, sped it up and, making full use of the three Funk Brothers guitarists, made a track that polarises opinion. I would count it as a great pop song, full of detail and a stunning vocal, others consider it a schmaltzy diversion along the road to maturity.

It certainly introduces the kind of 'inner accompaniment' lines that resurface in Stevie's work much later on. Always inherent in the harmony/chord structure, they're most audible as string lines that descend/ascend in half-steps – descending in semitones above a minor chord, forming a min/maj7th, a min7th, and a min6th.

There's an excellent harmonica solo that stretches nicely, making the most of the space. I just wish the backing vocal choir had stayed at home that day. The piano part is probably Earl Van Dyke, and it finds him at his most barrelhouse – during the first verse in particular he revels in the groove, which sits in that intriguing slot between straight and swing (there's a similar feel on the later 'Boogie On Reggae Woman').

The recorded sound is more 'natural' than previous singles, the production less gimmicky, although there are still quirky Motown touches such as the jaunty piccolo. If Stevie was unenthusiastic about the song and its production, you'd never guess it by the vocal: the jealously guarding "This is mine, you can't take it", and the way the vocal intensity builds through the song, are signs of a maturing talent. 'For Once In My Life' was released in October 1968, and was only held off the Number One spot by Marvin Gaye's spectacular 'I Heard It Through The Grapevine'.

Broader visions

In August 1968 The Beatles had released the single 'Hey Jude', which held the top spot in the US charts for nine weeks and sold six million copies, give or take a few. Abbey Road, London, might be an awful long way from Hitsville, Detroit – physically and culturally – yet something of what The Beatles had been doing over the last three years or so was about to permeate aspects of Stevie's work.

Ever since *Revolver* and the extraordinary 'Tomorrow Never Knows', with its frighteningly contemporary ambient soundscape, The Beatles' albums stretched the boundaries of available technology (they were on four-track longer than Motown) further than anyone thought possible. They weren't alone of course – as has often been pointed out, *Sergeant Pepper* probably wouldn't have existed without The Beach Boys' *Pet Sounds*, and there were others pushing the envelope: The Velvet Underground & Nico, The Pink Floyd, battering at the gates of conformity, while Hendrix and Cream were starting to extend the limits of what the term 'rock music' could contain.

On Beatles' albums, anything from string quartet to barrel organ to mellotron, by way of specially built electric harpsichords, would be pressed into service by the band and producer George Martin. An improvised orchestral climax, starting at the bottom of your instrument and ending at the top? No problem. A freeform psychedelic Stockhausen-esque musique concrète assemblage? Fine. Perhaps a song about the Wild West called 'Rocky Raccoon'? Certainly sir. The range of musical styles they fearlessly embraced was wider than the Mississippi, and a reflection of a time when it was suddenly possible to imagine doing anything.

The release of 'Hey Jude', a McCartney tune with a refrain that runs around the block several times more than you might expect, undoubtedly found its way to Stevie's turntable/transistor radio at some point. The vocal freedom over the outro, the just-in-range falsetto, the simplicity of the chord shapes and the intensity of feeling all surface on Stevie's next single, 'I Don't Know Why I Love You'. The radio stations preferred the b-side – 'My Cherie Amour' – but it's 'I Don't Know Why' that reflects the influence more immediately. (The track even bounced back across the Atlantic when it was covered by The Rolling Stones the following year, though that version wasn't released until 1975's *Metamorphosis* odds-and-ends compilation.)

Starting with an ominous low clavinet/bass phrase that's a million miles away from familiar Motown riffy intros, 'I Don't Know Why' goes straight into major chord rock land, triads (three notes at once) in a raw unadorned state, accompanied by a strumming guitar, while a rough-hewn Stevie vocal intones in desperation. A rockier/bluesier guitar joins in – or at least it's as rocky as guitars from that studio get (it's said the snakepit was so small that the guitars were plugged straight into the mixing desk, with no amps to provide overdrive or distortion). It sounds like the same guitar style as 'I Was Made To Love Her' – probably Eddie Willis again.

From simple beginnings the song builds up towards fifth gear on the chorus, the voice straining for the top note; then the "oh darlin', darlin', darlin'" that signals the next verse, with the voice in its highest register (an octave higher than the first verse), at which point it's almost like a fusing of McCartney and Jagger – unfunky phrasing, but nonetheless impassioned. French horns swoop, high strings dip their toes into (chromatic) psychedelia, and Stevie is consumed with breathless fervour, barely hitting the notes in a real bare-knuckle fight.

Co-production here is once again by Don Hunter, who was co-writer again too. Hunter appears to have struck up a good musical rapport – he seemed to know where Stevie is coming from. He certainly let him off the leash when it came to keyboard parts and vocal expression, and was perhaps more in touch with the changing world outside.

If the regular Motown record-buyers were not quite ready to fully embrace the stark emotion and atmospheric rock sounds of 'I Don't Know Why...', they were very comfortable with the lyrical, easy-listening b-side, 'My Cherie Amour' (which in fact was soon repackaged as the a-side). The way Ted Hull recalls it, the song was born out of frustration with the company: originally written in a one-hour piano period in his final school year, Stevie insisted on presenting the tune to Gordy, who grudgingly admitted it had "a little potential". It was then handed to the production team to whip into shape – Sylvia Moy and Hank Cosby shared the writing honours with Stevie, and Cosby again landed the producer's role.

'My Cherie Amour' could also be a nod in the direction of The Beatles, this time the McCartney tune 'Michelle', with its French exotique romanticism. Stevie and McCartney had met years before, after a London date – Stevie had even played the Cavern in Liverpool – and in 1982 of course they would link up to record 'Ebony And Ivory' together at George Martin's Air studio in Montserrat.

It seems the two have always had a mutual respect and admiration of each other's talents. McCartney recalls The Beatles' reaction to hearing Little Stevie's "truly remarkable" 'Fingertips' back in 1963: "We were very interested in this prodigious talent," McCartney admits; and like everyone else they were keen followers of what he went on to do next – particularly the classic 1970s albums we'll be looking at shortly, which McCartney calls, "inspirational".[20]

Stevie was quite an anglophile too, if you believe the interviews – he told the UK's *Melody Maker* on one of his regular trips: "I'm almost a native of England. I like the people here very much, they're so relaxed." (A couple of Stevie's end-of-the-Sixties singles, like 'Yester-Me, Yester-You, Yesterday', even did better in the UK charts than at home in the US.)

The instantly memorable 'My Cherie Amour' was written when Stevie was 16 (not long after the release of 'Michelle' on *Rubber Soul*), inspired by a breakup with his "sweetheart" – it was originally titled 'Oh My Marcia'. The song seems to mark an important step in the growing-up process, as Stevie later recalled: "I was young and carefree. I didn't think about anything, not even the money I was making. I didn't take anything seriously. I changed with 'My Cherie Amour' – I suddenly realised it was time I calmed down and started behaving responsibly."[21]

From the outset, the hooks are there to reel-in the listener. The flutes and Stevie's 'la-la-la'-ing over the intro set the mood for a rhythm track that follows Cosby's preference for a smoother, more natural sound. If the intro chords sound a bit lumpy and mechanical, the groove that follows is

Major 7ths are everywhere in 'My Cherie Amour' ...It was clearly young Stevie experimenting with a new style, and the public seemed to like it

slickness personified. Brushes are used on the drums in a light 16th-note groove (with ever such a slight swing), strengthened by some congas that take a while to settle into a pattern but, like the rest of the rhythm section, get there in the end.

The guitars and piano only start to hit their stride mid-song as well, almost as if they're not quite sure what to do with this mid-tempo groove; occasional efforts at doubling the feel towards the end of the first verse don't lead anywhere fruitful, but the lack of colour and energy on the backing track (apart from the over-prominent and filmic strings) highlights the sophistication/over-sweetness of the way the melody sits on the chords. There's no attempt at rock-mock toughness here – the sound of smooth jazz is built into the structure, largely down to the copious use of major 7th chords.

Major 7ths are loved and loathed in equal measure by musicians, viewed either as a badge of easy sophistication, or the preserve of sugary lounge pianists. You take a triad (root, 3rd and 5th) then stick a major rather than minor 7th note on top, and honey instantly oozes from the speakers and all over the floor. These chords are so associated with well-being that you have to remind yourself this song is about unreciprocated love rather than fulfilment. Perhaps their use here represents how things *could* have been...

Major 7ths are everywhere in 'My Cherie Amour', in almost every bar in fact. And it's not as if they're disguised or hidden – the melody usually falls on the 7th. This was clearly young Stevie experimenting with a new style, and the public seemed to like it.

Another new chord that enters his vocabulary here is the one at "pretty little one that *I adore*" –

On TV in his late teens. Still adhering to strict Motown dress code, despite the 'summer of love' era – Stevie could never be accused of jumping on the hippy bandwagon

it's one that will come back as reliably as a boomerang in Stevie's work, most famously in the second bar of 'You Are The Sunshine Of My Life': in both cases an F9 with a ♭5. What Stevie was doing at this period was flexing various songwriting muscles – the studio was like his musical gym.

Stevie's voice is completely comfortable now. Apart from the normal emoting quality of the high notes, no trace of strain remains, and indeed in the mid-range the full mature richness has developed – you can hear it in the second verse at "You've never noticed me".

There's another factor that it's possible to overlook when talking about Stevie as a singer, and that's tuning. The human voice is capable of infinite gradation of frequency – there are no frets or keys to guide your vocal cords, so it's easy to slip above or below the pitch of a note. These days there are automatic pitch correction programs that take care of any unwelcome deviation, but applying one of these devices to Stevie's vocals would be an unrewarding task. There's just nothing to fix. In all the recordings there's not an instance of bad pitching – there's expressive pitching, using slides or pitch variation (vibrato), but no off-key notes as such. And in case you're thinking he might have simply recorded dozens of takes in the studio before getting it right, I should add that the perfect pitching applies to his live albums as well. A remarkable achievement.

Working it out

When Stevie graduated from the Michigan School For The Blind in June 1969 it meant that Ted Hull's role as tutor was over, after six years of duty. Having become increasingly involved in road management tasks as well as the teaching, Ted was not sorry to be returning to a relatively normal life. But a few final matters had to be sorted out first.

Stevie was talking about enrolling in college: he told the press he was going to the University of California to study composition and arranging. Ted wasn't encouraging – perhaps he felt Stevie was more of an instinctive rather than an academic musician – and he expressed his concerns in a family meeting at Motown, which didn't go down well.

The other problem at this point involved Gordy fending off Stevie's demands to buy a synthesiser. Gordy considered this an over-extravagant luxury, comparing it to something like a speedboat (!), and he told Stevie he would have to wait. In the end, though, Gordy relented, just as he had with tape recorders back in the early Sixties, and Stevie got his synth... only for his brother Timothy to spill a can of Coke over it. Ouch.

The synthesiser would soon open up new instrumental possibilities and a path to a whole new sound vocabulary, but in the meantime Stevie was enthusiastically learning all about the biggest and most versatile instrument of all: the recording studio. For years he'd been dabbling in a bit of everything – overdubbing vocals and keyboard parts, the odd bit of drumming, even some co-production. But the time had come to combine all the expertise he'd been acquiring.

Here again there may have been a Beatles influence. With the 'fab four' splintering in late 1969, Paul McCartney had recorded an album of songs on his new home four-track machine, playing all the instruments himself. Released in April 1970, the *McCartney* album was a mixed bag, but contained some excellent tracks, particularly 'Maybe I'm Amazed' and 'Every Night'.

It's probably no coincidence that one of Stevie's first truly solo recordings was an open tribute to The Beatles, which he released as a single only. Stevie took 'We Can Work It Out' from the *Rubber Soul* period and completely revamped it, tearing away the old-world elements and displaying a virtuosity in the studio (as well as musical arranging, assisted by Wade Marcus) that's not far short of stunning. The distorted clavinet leads into the foray with an attitudinous buzzing that proclaims confidence, as indeed does the whole track.

Having earned his first full production credits with the single 'Signed, Sealed, Delivered' in the summer of 1970, Stevie was now in full flight, ready and able to realise his ideas without a father-figure of a producer looking over his shoulder.

One of his freedoms may have been to choose his own sounds: the title track from the *Signed, Sealed, Delivered* album is notable for the sitar-like timbre of the intro – probably played on an electric sitar-guitar – another feature inspired by The Beatles and now transplanted to a Motown context. Its sound reflects the still-fashionable interest in Eastern influences, from religion to music to joss sticks to exotic cigarettes. Stevie wasn't handed the production reins for the whole *Signed, Sealed* album though – Hank Cosby was still around, to an extent, while Don Hunter took the lion's share of production credit. But things were changing. The 'Signed, Sealed' single had reached Number One in the R&B chart and Number Three in the US pop chart – not bad for a first solo production.

Stevie was intentionally pushing his production further away from the Motown model, perhaps drawing more on the Stax label sound – a tighter, funkier style of southern soul that had emerged from Memphis in the 1960s. It was centred on the house rhythm section of Booker T & The MGs, who provided rhythm tracks for the likes of Otis Redding, Sam & Dave and Wilson Pickett. (Isaac Hayes was a Stax songwriter and producer of Sixties hits before carving his own direction of orchestral soft-soul in the 1970s.) Sam & Dave's 'Hold On I'm Coming' reveals the balance of Memphis horns and super-tight backbeat drum track, as well as links to the approach of 'We Can Work It Out'.

Though Stevie was starting to look outside of the Motown mould, it's interesting to note what elements remain from the old Hitsville arrangement regime. On 'We Can Work It Out' there's the typically insistent drumming, and familiar clanking guitar on beats two and four on the right side of the stereo mix (if indeed that is a guitar – it's possible it could be a very short clavinet hit in exactly the right guitaristic register). There's a typically nimble and funky bass in there too.

But it's the up-front fuzz clavinet that emerges as the novel anchoring element here, playing mostly single-note riffs along with the bass. As all guitarists who have ever plugged into a fuzz box know, single notes and open intervals (4ths and 5ths) work well using fuzz, whereas with other intervals (such as the so-called 'consonant' intervals like the 3rd and 6th) the sound gets too mashed up – as you can hear in the track's intro – and sounds unpleasant to many ears.

Much of the arrangement effort goes into the BVs; the not-always-keenly-enthusiastic shouts of 'Hey!' are just the start of a dialogue/duet between lead and BVs (in a John/Paul fashion). Strange that one of the changes Stevie makes to the song is to straighten out the chorus hookline, which in the Beatles' version is syncopated. The original has the "We" on the first beat of the bar, with some 16th-note syncopation. What Stevie does is to iron out those skips, but move the whole phrase forward (by an eighth-note) so the emphasis falls on "can" and "it", thereby re-inserting an eighth-note syncopation. The effect is cleverly displacing for the listener – and it demonstrates a very pattern-based way of thinking. (It's also possible that Stevie realised the Beatles' setting was almost identical to the way 'Signed, Sealed, Delivered' works rhythmically.)

For someone who, a few years earlier, had been trying to veer away from the top range of his voice, the BVs are pitched ultra-high. The chorus is high enough (hitting C4) but the line during the harmonica solo (you certainly can't say it's *behind* the solo) stretches a few steps higher still, to E♭4.

The crunch comes just before the drums return after the second intro: Stevie's low register is intoning "Work it out with me baby…", meanwhile his shrill backing vocals (some two-and-a-half octaves higher) sound like Chaka Khan on the *Feel For You* album.

Another vocal part mimics a lead guitar, then after the last verse the two backing lines run together, and the lead vocal joins the stratospheric ululations. As a display of vocal technique, the last verse lead is incredible: where Brian Wilson would have needed falsetto and then some, Stevie covers the ground with relative ease.

As far as the other instruments go, drums are tightly played, the half-open hi-hat dirtying up the groove nicely, and the funky clavinet chugs along in the mud-splattered gutter.

Which leaves the matter of the bass and guitar. All the available authorities, except one, hold that Stevie played every instrument on this track. But bassist Bob Babbitt seems to disagree. The man who gradually took over the intimidating Funk Brothers' bass chair from James Jamerson, and had

You can almost hear Stevie breaking free from the musical cocoon of his youth

been working with Stevie live ever since 1966, certainly played on 'Signed, Sealed' in 1970, but in the biographies for the movie *Standing In The Shadows Of Motown* he reveals that the first session he did for Motown was Stevie's 'We Can Work It Out'.

This makes a lot of sense, as the bass is definitely an electric, but it lacks Jamerson's jazzier (chromatic) leanings, and the playing is not so hard. It does have a solid rhythmic feel though, jumping strings and octaves with ease. Which begs the question – if the bass isn't played by Stevie, could it be the guitar is also another musician? Worth a trip to the betting shop, I think.

Just as 'My Cherie Amour' flexed Stevie's 'sweet harmony' muscles, this tune flexed the vocal cords and studio 'chops'. You can almost hear Stevie breaking free from the musical cocoon of his youth, every song another twist that weakened the constrictions of the now-unnecessary Motown protection, as he prepared to take on adulthood in a typically fearless manner. The next decade would reveal the true extent of that fearlessness, and would see Stevie pushing himself, and the whole of pop/soul music, in some exhilarating new directions.

By the end of the 1960s Stevie's clavinet was already becoming a distinctive musical and visual trademark

CHAPTER 3
INDEPENDENCE &TRANSITION

"I wanted to see what would happen if I changed. It challenged me to give the public something other than what it was used to hearing."

The 1971 album *Where I'm Coming From* is the crossover point in Stevie's career; from here on we can start to think in terms of his albums as 'the work', rather than concentrating on individual tracks or singles. While Motown's perceptions of the industry meant they persevered as a singles production machine, the outside world had moved on. The notion of a concept album, or even just a collection of tracks that added up to more than the sum of their parts, was very familiar by the start of the Seventies: from The Beatles' *Sergeant Pepper* and *Abbey Road*, to Frank Zappa & The Mothers Of Invention's *Freak Out!*, to The Who's *Tommy*.

Berry Gordy's reluctance to let Motown become involved with politically provocative songwriting had softened over the previous couple of years of social turmoil. Some of the label's established artists also felt pop music could influence its audience on a socially relevant level. For instance The Temptations' 'Cloud Nine' (produced by Norman Whitfield, the new-broom-sweeping-clean at Motown) dealt with escapism through mind-altering drugs, while The Supremes' 'Love Child' and 'I'm Livin' In Shame' tackled the issue of single mothers. Edwin Starr, a comparative newcomer to Motown's stable of writers in 1970, released the anti-Vietnam song 'War' (another Whitfield co-write) with its chant of "What is it good for? Absolutely nothin'!", and reached Number One in the pop charts. Political comment in music almost seemed obligatory in the early Seventies.

The man who first combined the concept album with social issues was Marvin Gaye. His string of hits with Tammi Terrell (including 'Ain't Nothing Like The Real Thing', and 'You're All I Need To Get By') had been interrupted when Tammi died from a brain tumour in 1970 at the age of 24. During her two-year illness, and after she died, Marvin entered a period of depression (to which he was always prone). He stopped performing, and even considered abandoning music for a career as a professional footballer.

The project that rekindled Marvin's interest, and revived his career (for his first comeback at least), was the 1971 album *What's Going On*. But it wasn't the easiest of projects to get started. It took a few false starts – Marvin wasn't happy with the initial efforts – before he produced this career-changing and era-defining body of work. Funk Brother keyboardist Johnny Griffith recalls the session where things began to turn around: "One day Marvin came in an hour-and-a-half late with a bucket full of fried chicken. He said, 'We're gonna do something different this time'."[23]

They surely did. What Marvin came up with was Motown's first concept album, which in its internal musical linking was a groundbreaking step in pop music. All the songs were presented as an entity: the track 'What's Going On' ran into 'What's Happening Brother', and so on. Songs about the Vietnam War, pollution ('Mercy Mercy Me (The Ecology)'), and urban deprivation ('Inner City Blues (Make Me Wanna Holler)') were all combined to form a seamless whole. The arrangements were lush, loose, orchestral and sophisticated, but wide-ranging in their sources – the saxophone lent a jazz edge, the percussion an African resonance – and above it all soared Marvin's free-roaming, impassioned, persuasive and seductive soul/gospel voice.

Gordy – who'd recently decided to relocate Motown HQ and studios from Detroit to Los Angeles, a move that would stun the Funk Brothers – further illustrated that his judgement had gone west by stating his dislike of *What's Going On*. He held misgivings about releasing it all, even though it would go on to break all Motown sales records when it eventually, inevitably, hit the shops.

The exhaustive sleeve notes for Gaye's album listed all the musicians involved, at last crediting

James Jamerson individually for his contribution on bass, along with Joe Messina and Robert White on guitars, Johnny Griffith on celeste, Chet Forest on drums, and Marvin himself on piano. By this time, sadly, drummer Benny Benjamin had already passed away; he'd missed Gaye's 'Grapevine' session through ill health, brought on by drug abuse, and he died in 1969. Jamerson's performances were also suffering the effects of alcohol, and the disorienting move to Los Angeles finally broke his career – this album was his last great contribution (Bob Babbitt played on some tracks too).

Where I'm Coming From

With the Funk Brothers no longer the united hit machine they once were, and the Motown 'family' atmosphere finally dissolved in the shift to LA, Gordy also had to face the fact that Stevie's contract with the label would end soon, when Stevie turned 21. He was also aware that, whether or not he actually believed a 21-year-old could cope with being given total artistic control, the days were long gone when he could dictate terms to an artist like Stevie – which perhaps explains his flexibility when the time came.

Stevie spent the last 12 months before turning 21 working on the album that would become *Where I'm Coming From*

Stevie spent the last 12 months before turning 21 working on the album that would become *Where I'm Coming From* – an album whose theme, or 'concept', would be primarily social issues. He'd started co-writing with Syreeta Wright (whom he married in September 1970), and would go on to produce the album himself, as well as playing all the instruments, and singing pretty much all the vocals.

Production was something he knew he enjoyed and could do successfully, having already turned out a hit for The (Detroit) Spinners in the shape of 'It's A Shame'. Interestingly, *Where I'm Coming From* (which I'll refer to from now on as *WICF*) combines arrangements born in the 'new' era of electronic keyboards, alongside traditional string, horn and piano parts. Perhaps Stevie still felt comfortable in the clothes of acoustic arrangements, or maybe, with the slower tunes in particular, he had yet to discover a sympathetic alternative setting.

WICF is a musically disparate affair, but as a first step out of the fold it's a plucky excursion. Stevie later admitted that the album was, "kinda premature to some extent, but I wanted to express myself. A lot of it now I'd probably remix."[24]

From the first track, 'Look Around', the sound is mostly in 'Shoo-Be-Doo'/'I Don't Know Why' territory. The keyboard here is less like a clavinet and more like an RMI Electra-Piano (as used by The Doors, Edgar Winter and Sly & The Family Stone), which I believe was kicking around the studio at the time. With the top line sent to a delay unit that spins it back to the other side of the mix, we can hear Stevie is already extending his range of studio techniques.

The musical ground is unorthodox too: the rhythm is three beats to a bar, with a distinct classical edge to it. No rock'n'roll here – the influence is more 1770 than 1970. Same goes for the answering BVs that appear at the end of the chorus over on the left (that's why the lead vocal is panned unexpectedly right). All in all the part arrangement is rather mannered and formal, if cleverly done. By the time the second chorus comes around the lead is also harmonised with BVs, finally balancing the counterparts in a wall of vocal tracks maybe six parts thick.

It's a very strange choice for an opening track, especially one that signals the start of an era of independence: the instrumental backing track hasn't weathered the years well, and just sounds plain weak. (The Stranglers must have liked it though – it's very 'Golden Brown'.)

Then again, perhaps the track that follows – 'Do Yourself A Favor' – wouldn't have made the same impact without the muted and reserved flavour of the opener. The contrast couldn't be greater: with 'DYAF' the listener is slammed up against the wall of a furiously wah-wah-ing clavinet (in the key that will turn out to be *the* funk key for Stevie – E♭), as it embarks on more than six minutes of rock/funk extravagance. We're now a very long way from the old three-minute Motown pop template.

The guitar-mimicking clav (which sounds more like a bullfrog on acid by the end) and the Hammond organ (with swirling Leslie cabinet in full throttle after the second chorus) call to mind Jimi Hendrix and Stevie Winwood (of Spencer Davis/Traffic fame) playing on Hendrix's *Electric Ladyland*. (The Electric Lady studios will, coincidentally, figure very shortly in Stevie's story.) By this time Cream had also reached a worldwide audience with songs such as 'Sunshine Of Your Love' and 'Strange Brew', from 1967's *Disraeli Gears*, extending the possibilities of instrumental prowess and musical statements within a rock set-up. The Eric Clapton guitar style (quite different to the Hendrix approach), the energetically powerful drumming of Ginger Baker, and the slightly out-of-reach lyrics were at the centre of the late-Sixties rock phenomenon, and left a deep impression on most contemporary artists – not least the idea that it was OK to stretch out a track.

On 'Do Yourself A Favour' Stevie's intention seems mainly to jam, albeit with himself. And so what if there's two minutes of groove in which nothing really happens except some strange Lennon-esque voices counting up to ten... we're having a good time, aren't we?

The other factor that points to Hendrix is the appearance of lengthy periods with few chord changes, and the penchant for extended soloing over a riff. The song is tonally static, and with some change of emphasis on the chorus, that's how it's going to stay. The shape of the bassline brings Jamerson to mind again – there's plenty of reiterating the root and then the line plunges down that interval Jamerson was so fond of (a 6th), before climbing back up again to the root. Some things just refuse to go away.

It's a moot point whether a solo of some sort, in a Hendrix/Clapton style, would have held the attention more, but the slightly shambolic collective exploit suits the feel of the 'band' breaking free of its chains, unconstrained by record company execs. The "get your funky self together" backing vocal, with its possibilities for misunderstanding, would probably not have passed an executive/quality control meeting – nor possibly would the final nursery rhymic episode (shades of the 'Mary Had A Little Lamb' quote in 'Fingertips'?).

The lyrics fall squarely into the socio-political category, with the chorus praising the value of education as a solution to society's problems, as listed in the verses in quite an abstract way. It seems as if Stevie and Syreeta are trying too hard in the drug-fuelled imagery stakes: "Suffocate the new high/Ride the thorny mule that cries/Dig your grave and step right in." (It makes "semolina pilchards" sound positively sensible.) The song is basically warning of the dangers of hell on earth, and the need to "get yourself together."

While Motown were still keen to mould him into an all-round family entertainer, complete with dinner jacket and lace cuffs, Stevie was proving he had more adventurous musical ambitions

The title of the next track, 'Think Of Me As Your Soldier', is strangely ambiguous. Although in the lyrics the singer is purely declaring his endless love and promising to dedicate himself to his woman, as a soldier would for his country, the album's sleeve (showing what seems to be Stevie himself bedecked in an army uniform – bearing in mind this was still at the height of the Vietnam war), it's hard not to think there's some other angle here. Stevie later hinted at his apparent feelings of guilt over the fate of many of his contemporaries: "Sometimes I wish that I could have been all the soldiers that were killed in Vietnam – I guess you could call it a sacrificial wish."[25]

The race issue is tackled in 'I Wanna Talk To You', a fairly excruciating piece of music, but an entertaining recreation of a dialogue between a (young) black man and an (old) white man, highlighting generational as well as racial conflicts. Stevie adopts a persona for each character – the black man has a gospelly piano/bass free-time musical setting, while the white man has a rock riff on clav and bass and drums to express his point of view. The exchanges soon break down into snapped lines back and forth: (white man) "You can have dinner with me next week and mow my lawn"; (black man) "You cain't tell me nothing white man". Eventually the two sides are locked in a communication bypass rant, illustrating primarily the entrenched attitudes of white society, but also pointing out the occasionally self-pitying black stance: "Who can I blame/for the way I am/I ain't never had one soul to help me".

Another possible, if less likely, interpretation of the track is that it represents Stevie haranguing the record label in a final outburst of rebellious youth.

'Take Up A Course In Happiness' feels as if it came from the pen of a transcendental meditation teacher (oddly enough, Syreeta was one); and I'm afraid musically the same comment applies here as with 'I Wanna Talk'. Here it's a shameful mock big-band affair, (sorry to say this) a 'Maxwell's Silver Hammer' – a vaudeville disaster of a track: "And your bridge of dreams comes tumblin' down", cue lush strings in a downward stagger (towards the door of the studio maybe). Nothing can save this from itself, not even the ultra-loud finger clicks and 'Penny Lane' feel-good chorus. Thankfully, and perhaps unexpectedly, the next track finally brings a song to enthuse over.

'Never Dreamed You'd Leave In Summer' is the first of the great ballads – or at least it could have been without the interference of an over-enthusiastic arranger. Things get off to a pretty good start:

"It's completely different – it's more me than anything I have ever done before"

voice and piano and the bass sound that pervades the album state the simple chords, and then a daring harmonic move (first two chords are C, Fmaj7, then the move to D) ushers in the oboe and strings. From there onwards the listener's musical filters have to be activated so as to concentrate on the song and vocal and eliminate the superfluous.

It's a straightforward lyric of love loss, with a seasonal angle, and some strong vocal embellishments; the second verse "I never dreamed you'd leave in summer" is delicious in the way it extends upwards first of all (to the ♭9) and then returns via a circuitous route to the melody note. The very last 'stay' note is also superb, held over six bars (with the assistance of some added reverb), a device that re-occurs on many of the later ballads. With a bit of imagination you can hear Sinatra singing this song in his 1950s prime, with a more appropriate Nelson Riddle arrangement.

The other significant tracks on the *WICF* album are the final cut, 'Sunshine In Their Eyes', and 'If You Really Love Me', a single that did well in the UK, less so in the States. The latter has a 'colla voce' (piano follows the voice) irregular-beat section alternating with a chorus that's worthy of the name. 'Sunshine In Their Eyes' is a strange creature: a cringe-worthy sentimentality pervades the first half, which is a real shame because just under that cake icing of a surface lies a freshness in the musical elements that deserved better. The ease with which the verse harmony twists, like an olympic swimmer turning at the end of a pool length, is worthy of an Antonio Carlos Jobim song (more of which in the 'Latin' section, Chapter 8). At the same time the tune is too hymnal – it's probably intentional, judging from lyrics like "a prayer is heard", but sounds at cross-purposes with the (almost Eighties-style) rock beat underneath it.

And then there's the children's voices... Ah yes, the children: "He can't wait to see the day/ There's sunshine in our eyes"... The lyric is full of good intentions, drawing attention to the plight of deprived kids – unfortunately the youngsters on the record weren't quite up to learning the tune.

An *Abbey Road*-style segue links the first section to the next, which highlights wider problems with society, before we're off on a *Hair*-type 'far-out' passage, replete with horn section (again the mixing is bizarre: why would you record blaring horns unless you wanted to hear them?), and a strangely good-time feel for such a weighty lyric. The track seesaws between this and the previous section, finishing with a rave-up over the second segment, which approaches a climax and fades.

It's an ambitious plan, and you can't fault Stevie for giving it a go, but the tensions between lyric and music, poetic expression and sentimentality, simplicity of idea and complexity of arrangement, are too great for the track to hold together. Having said that, the end fade-out is an exhilarating ride, Stevie improvising with abandon over some earthy baritone parts and a chord sequence that cycles round in the same satisfying way as 'She's So Heavy' from *Abbey Road*.

Stevie was clearly searching for an identity with this album. He's quoted as saying at the time, "It's completely different – it's more me than anything I have ever done before ... A lot of the things on my new album deal with the social problems. I have been influenced by the things that have happened in the world."[26]

Musically, though, the huge diversity of approaches is problematic. While breadth of influence can be a healthy attribute, all the disparate elements (funk, Hendrix, Beatles, Sly Stone, soul ballads, classical language) need to be bound into a firm musical entity in order to sound cohesive. It's like when planets revolve in a solar system, kept in their own orbits by the gravitational pull of the sun at the centre. Take away the gravity and the smaller planets dart around on their own disordered paths – as the influences do here. While elusive on this record, that gravity would gradually emerge during Stevie's maturing process over the next few years – an evolution that would require a change of scenery, a few new instruments, the confidence of financial security, and the major influence of a couple of new musical associates.

Keyboard man

So far, the Wurlitzer electric piano (or Wurly), the clavinet, and the RMI Electra-Piano have been mentioned with regard to new keyboard instruments. While you could say Stevie had quickly formed a clavinet style of his own, the electric piano on 'Where I'm Coming From' didn't provide the quality of sound required to support the sensitivity of vocal expression. The keyboard bass notes on the record also sound inflexible, probably because the RMI had no velocity sensitivity (which makes notes sound loud when hit hard, soft when tickled), and this made it appear clumsy and lumpy.

But the means to solve these problems was close at hand. The world of keyboard instruments had been transformed at the end of the 1960s with the appearance not only of the first manageable synthesisers (such as the Moog, which we'll discuss later), but also the Fender Rhodes electric piano, which was starting to make its mark on-stage and in the studio.

The Fender Rhodes has its roots in World War II when Harold Rhodes (born 1910), responding to a request to provide therapy for wounded soldiers, came up with the idea of a 'bed piano' – literally fitted across the bed of an immobilised patient. Having been a piano teacher before the war, with a chain of schools across the States, Harold started work building a tiny 30-key piano from, among other things, the hydraulic aluminium pipes from the wings of a B-17 bomber. With the tuned strips of metal cut down to about the size of a xylophone, and the whole thing able to fit in a small suitcase, thousands were manufactured, and Rhodes was awarded a Medal Of Honor for his efforts. Come the end of the war, various companies were interested in manufacturing the piano commercially, but Harold decided to have a go himself and designed what he called the Pre-piano. It was the era when electrically amplified instruments were just breaking through, so he added a microphone 'pickup', amp and speaker. After some further refining of the design, he established US Patent number 2972922, and the familiar Rhodes keyboard was launched.

Whereas the earlier Wurlitzer – designed in the 1930s by Ben F. Meissner and featured by Ray Charles on his 1959 recording of 'What'd I Say' (and made even more famous a decade later by Marvin Gaye on 'Heard It Through The Grapevine') – used the idea of striking a vibrating reed with a felt hammer, in the Rhodes a regular piano mechanism makes the hammers hit tuned 'tines', thin rods of metal that operate like tuning forks.

Rhodes was tied into an agreement with Fender, but boss Leo Fender wasn't a fan of the instrument's sound, which meant that nothing much happened till 1965 when CBS bought Fender out for a hefty $13m. (Pre-CBS Fender did release a piano-bass version, a 32-key affair that Ray Manzarek used to play with The Doors.) The Fender Rhodes proper started production in a form called the Suitcase 73 (because it had 73 keys), which also featured a mono tremolo, a 50-watt amp and built-in speakers. By 1969 the tremolo was stereo and the output beefed up to 2x50W. A year later, the 88-note version was launched, along with the Mark 1 Stage versions – basically the same pianos minus amplification. Which neatly brings us up to 1971, a year away from the first appearance of the Rhodes on a Stevie Wonder track.

So what does a Fender Rhodes sound like? Nothing like a piano for starters – the tone is fatter in the mid-range, with less upper harmonic action than an acoustic piano. One of its first appearances on record was Joe Zawinul playing with Cannonball Adderley on the tune 'Mercy, Mercy, Mercy'. (For more recent comparative examples, Jamiroquai's album *The Return Of The Space Cowboy* – itself a nod in the direction of both Stevie and Sly Stone – showcases the Rhodes, while 'Where It's At' from Beck's *Odelay* features the Wurly.)

Aside from the difference in tone of the attack – the Wurlitzer being sharper, the Rhodes having more mid-range thunk – the main thing that distinguishes the two keyboards is the way each of them sustains. The Rhodes is a clear winner in that department. The keyboard feel is very different in each too: the more weighted (but variable) Rhodes feel has more of a soft, spongy key-bed than the lighter/faster Wurlitzer – which is why the jazz piano-players who picked up on the Rhodes at the end of the Sixties took to it more easily.

Herbie Hancock and Chick Corea, as well as Joe Zawinul, all played the Rhodes with the groundbreaking Miles Davis on his genre-demolition record *In A Silent Way*. Even the purist Keith Jarrett was coerced into getting acquainted with a Rhodes for the Davis album *Live Evil*, where he made use of a badly adjusted tine to build a solo, itself an illustration of the dynamics coaxable from the instrument.

The story of the clavinet also stretches back to the 1950s. Ernst Zacharias designed an instrument called the Cembalet, for the German company Hohner, as a portable (and amplifiable) alternative to the harpsichord. He then built the Pianet, which, like the cembalet and Wurly, was reed-based. But for his next project he used the working principles of a clavichord – a smaller, quieter version of the harpsichord, dating back to at least the 17th century.

The harpsichord has a leather 'quill' that plucks the instrument's strings on the way up, brushing past them on the way down, lending the instrument its sharp, though not velocity-sensitive, sound. The clavichord hits the strings from underneath and stays there – any further pressure simply bends the string (which makes it a fantastic instrument for playing the blues, incidentally), but the sound is so quiet as to make it a 'drawing room' keyboard only. The clavinet, launched in 1964, uses the same principle, but by fitting pickups the problem of audibility was solved.

Various early clavinet models preceded the popular C (not the A and B, as you might expect, but the I, II and three-legged L models). The C was in turn superseded by the D6, a fully portable, amplifiable version. Here's a snippet from the Hohner D6 owner's manual: "The Clavinet D6 keyboard range of five octaves is suitable for a big proportion of piano music, beginning with lute and organ music of the 14th century, covering all baroque piano music up to the classical period. It is also suitable for a section of piano music of the romantic period because intonation depends on keyboard pressure. Although this instrument can play very melodiously, it is also possible to produce very incisive single notes, with very special appeal to the jazz pianist. Rock music has tremendous impact with the Clavinet D6, provided ample amplification is available." Quite so. Tone controls allowed for variation in timbre and a damper muted the strings for a dull, short sound. But I'll bet the manufacturers never envisaged a track like 'Do Yourself A Favour'.

Here come the synths

The world of synthesis is all about imagination, and probably a certain amount to do with serendipity. In the late 1960s, synths were just starting to trickle into musicians' hands. The first designs had been largely built for academic composition studios, such as the RCA synthesiser installed at Columbia University in the late Fifties. Composers like Milton Babbitt and Morton Subotnick were already creating electronic music, albeit very much in the exploratory contemporary classical field.

The idea of electronic instruments was not new, of course: from the theremin in 1917 (spotlighted half a century later on the Beach Boys' 'Good Vibrations'), the ondes-martenot in the 1920s, the trautonium and electric organs such as the Hammond in the 1930s, many exotically named and ingeniously designed creations anticipated and paved the way for the arrival of the synthesiser.

The modern synth is a musical instrument (best not to call it a machine) with three significant

Stevie married Syreeta Wright on September 14th 1970.
She would co-write several of his songs of this period, including 'Signed, Sealed,
Delivered', 'If You Really Love Me', 'Love Having You Around' and 'Do Yourself A Favour'

characteristics: first of all it's capable of producing an electronically generated sound; secondly you can alter various parameters of that sound; and third, you can move it from one room to another without the aid of a forklift truck – which couldn't be said for many of its predecessors.

The key to the new breed of synths that appeared in 1968/69 was the principle of voltage control. Putting an oscillator under the control of a keyboard (to establish pitch), or an envelope generator (to regulate how long the sound lasts), or a filter (to vary the harmonic content) through a new type of circuit board, all made it possible to build smaller designs.

The first batch that appeared were modular synths, constructed in separate, functional blocks, or modules, linked together by short patch leads (cords). The system built by Don Buchla at the San Francisco Tape Music Center Inc in the early 1960s included a pair of sequencers, modules that store patterns of notes in some sort of memory. While Buchla's design concept was rooted in the contemporary music field (there was no keyboard, just some ingenious touch pads), the modular synths made by Robert (Bob) Moog had a more intuitive feel, better suited to a keyboard player.

One of the first musicians to explore the possibilities of the modular Moog was Walter (later becoming Wendy) Carlos, with an album of J.S. Bach compositions titled *Switched-On Bach*. The record caused uproar on its release in 1968: suddenly every record company wanted their synth record, and every band their synth. The Beatles had their Moog (as heard on *Abbey Road*), Mick Jagger had his (a modular version from 1967, which after years of neglect was sold to Tangerine Dream), and studio demands for fresh sounds resulted in plenty of orders. Musical instrument retailers were probably the last to catch on, but certainly by 1971 you could walk into a music store and purchase a Minimoog, the first neatly packaged synth to appear.

The idea behind the Minimoog was to produce a compact, easily programmable and gig-worthy synth, without a patch cord in sight. The Model D Minimoog, introduced in the summer of 1970, was the realisation of that concept: it had three oscillators, which gave it its notable 'fat' sound, a 44-note

Stevie was so interested in learning and taming the beast that he had the front panel of his ARP 2600 synth labelled in braille

keyboard (three-and-a-half octaves), two envelope generators and two wheels – one for pitch-bend and one modulation for controlling expression. It retailed for the considerable sum of $1,495 (nearly as much as a sports car at the time, or indeed a speedboat) and despite some tuning stabilisation problems, became the player's synth that the rest of the competition had to beat.

And there was certainly competition around. Hard on the heels of Moog was the ARP Instrument Company. Alan R. Pearlman (ARP, get it?) was producing the model 2500 modular system in the mid 1960s. Interested in the educational aspects of synths, he dreamed up a synth that was integrated in one physical package but modular in the sense that you could override the preset routings with patch cords – plugging things into other things, then those things into even more things, and so on. The front panel was helpfully illustrated with the signal flow, so you could follow the path, and a row of sliders and switches gave access to the variable functions. In manufacture by 1970 (if not necessarily selling), the asking price for the ARP 2600 was higher than the Minimoog, at $2,600. The ocscillators were more stable, though, and the patching possibilities more inspiring. Joe Zawinul, soon to become one of the most innovatory synthesiser players, using the instrument to its fullest potential, had several of them, as did Pete Townsend of The Who and Edgar Winter – and, of course, Stevie Wonder. Stevie was so interested in learning and taming the beast that he had the front panel of his 2600 labelled in braille.

Another synth maker active at the end of the 1960s was the British company EMS, formed by avant-garde contemporary composers Peter Zinovieff and Tristram Carey working from a computer music studio in Putney with electronic designer David Cockerell (who went on to work for Electro-Harmonix and Akai). The studio incorporated a DEC (Digital Equipment Corporation) computer, modular synths, sequencers and computer-controlled filter banks – all pretty advanced for the time. Their first neatly packaged cut-down portable synth began life as the VCS3 (known as the 'Putney' in the US), their particular variation on the theme of synth design being a matrix panel that used pins to route signals and patch/bypass modules. The later Synthi AKS came in a black plastic attaché case, with a touch keyboard and sequencer. It's probably easier to list the few bands that *didn't* own one at the time – users included King Crimson, Pink Floyd, The Who, Brian Eno (on keyboard duty with Roxy Music), The Moody Blues, Tangerine Dream, Jean Michel Jarre… best to stop now.

So say you were to purchase one of these new-fangled synth devices at the time, and get to know how to program it, how then could you use it on a track? The first limitation of early synths is that they were monophonic – they could only play one note at a time. If you wanted to produce more, you would need to have a massive modular set-up worth about the same as a fair-sized house. Most synth parts at the time varied between a lead line sound for solos or fills in a backing texture, or sound effects that weren't necessarily very musical but lent an atmosphere that was exciting and futuristic.

If you were Stevie Wonder, the multi-instrumentalist, toying with the idea of overdubbing as many self-generated parts as possible on top of your own drum/piano tracks (and by now there were 16 tracks to play with on the multi-track machine), the first immediately obvious sonic gap to fill is in the bass. Because a bassline is normally monophonic, it's a perfect candidate for 'keyboardisation'. And as it turned out, the Minimoog makes an ideal bass machine – though it's hard to say exactly what it was about the sound that worked. Even Bob Moog has struggled to explain it: "I believe the Minimoog sound comes from a balance of several factors: the warm, low-order distortion introduced by the VCF and the VCAs [filters and amps], the rapid attack times of which the contour generators are capable, the small amounts of noise in the oscillators that keep them from locking together at very small frequency differences, and the frequency response of the instrument as a whole."[27]

Happy birthday

May 13th 1971 must have been a hugely significant, indelibly momentous day in the life of Stevie Wonder. It seems, looking back, as if a whole Rubik's cube of circumstances was clicking into place when Stevie turned 21. He had developed into a young man who clearly had his own take on things, he was in touch with the current black political thinking that other Motown artists were beginning to explore, and he knew his own mind well enough to reject the record company's attempts to mould him into an all-round entertainer along the lines of Sammy Davis Jr.

As a successful recording artist, he would have some money coming his way (though not as much as he'd figured, as we'll see). He was an educated man, who'd had an incredible musical upbringing – his presence on all those studio sessions, soaking up the playing styles of James Jamerson, Benny Benjamin, Earl Van Dyke et al, had given him an insight into successful pop production processes. His experiences on the road with the *Motown Revue* and under his own steam had introduced him to not only the satisfactions of performing but also the rigours of the touring schedule. Already married and well-travelled, he was comparatively mature. Altogether, he had more than earned his artistic and financial freedom.

Although the reception given to *Where I'm Coming From* was not great, either in public or critical terms, and that caused a large dent in his confidence, Stevie had weathered those periods before, and had come through the other side with musical enthusiasm intact.

The tools that would shape the sound of Stevie Wonder's next three albums and beyond were also magically appearing. With the multi-track capabilities, plus the keyboard and synthesiser technology, the scene was pretty much set, but the final piece of the jigsaw had still to be slotted into place. As is often the way, it would happen more or less by chance, when Stevie hired a studio in New York to start work on his next album, and he met composers/producers/artists all-round boffins Robert Margouleff and Malcolm Cecil.

Before that, though, there was a huge financial question still to be sorted out...

The night before Stevie's 21st birthday, Berry Gordy threw a party at his home to celebrate. Stevie and Syreeta attended, with no mention made of contracts or business. But the next morning, Gordy flew back to LA to discover a letter from Stevie's lawyer on his desk informing him that Stevie wished to end his contract with Motown and be paid the monies due to him. (Opinions differ on how much that was expected to be, but the (just-short-of) $1million handed over must have been a fairly small fraction of the revenue received by the label over the previous ten years – even taking into consideration the traditionally low Motown rates, the studio expenses, and relatively poor sales of *Where I'm Coming From*.)

Gordy was offended by the brusque manner of the business dealing, and an embarrassed Stevie sacked his lawyer over the way he'd conducted the affair. But he still insisted on ending his relationship with the label. Ewart Abner, then a vice-president at Motown (later president, before quitting to become Stevie's personal manager in 1975) recalls Stevie telling them: "I'm 21 now. I'm not gonna do what you say any more. Void my contract." And with that Stevie and Syreeta packed their bags and headed for a New York hotel.

Bob, Malcolm, and Tonto

Back in those halcyon days it was normal for long periods of writing to be done in the studio, so Stevie had booked himself in at the Electric Lady studio in Greenwich Village – the studio Jimi Hendrix had built in New York in 1968 (when he realised he was spending $300,000 a year in studio time for writing, rehearsing and recording). The building was originally the site of the Village Barn, a big-band dance hall that Hendrix initially imagined he would keep as a music venue. The completion of Electric Lady in August 1970 established the practice of artists, rather than record companies, owning the studio, thus providing them with the necessary comfort, technology and coffee to realise their ideas. Tragically Hendrix didn't live long enough to reap the rewards of his investment – it was just a month after the studio opened that he was found dead in London.

Various habits would strangely pass from Hendrix to Wonder (not the druggy ones, mind you); Hendrix was a compulsive studio worker, not only recording as many as 43 takes of a track (as with 'Gypsy Eyes'), but recording far more songs than he ever issued – after his death, around 300 or so unreleased tracks were found on tape. His working hours were erratic and long, stretching around the clock when he was engaged with a project. He and Stevie also shared a love of music technology – Jimi had kitted out the studio with the best gear available.

Stevie discovered the same passion for work, irrespective of time of day or length of session – or need for sleep, for that matter. Paul Wiffen, who worked for Stevie (programming and engineering) in the mid 1980s, recalls the experience of turning up for a session booked for 7pm: "We'd go out for dinner… then finally he would show up, sometimes it would be one o'clock in the morning." Stevie was always a bit of an insomniac, and three or four hours sleep would be enough for him when he was recording. Working 24 hours straight through in the studio was not uncommon.

Stevie created a huge catalogue of songs (and parts of songs) over the next few years – and with the help of Cecil and Margouleff he would soon forge the new style he was already imagining. He told Seventies biographer Constanze Elsner: "It was a completely different thing that was in my head. I don't think you can gradually leave a kind of music. You can't mix one concept with another. It has to be an abrupt change where you say, 'OK, this is what I want to do from now on and all the other stuff belongs to the past'."[28]

Stevie first became aware of Robert Margouleff and Malcolm Cecil when he heard their album *Zero Time*, recorded under the name Tonto's Expanding Head Band. On it they explored the creative opportunities that orchestrating a bank of synthesisers could provide. The work clearly left its mark on Stevie's musical imagination.

Malcolm Cecil's career had started in the north east of England, as a double bass player with Mike Carr's Emcee Five (Carr was a well-known local piano/vibes/organ player), alongside a young guitarist by the name of John McLaughlin. Cecil also played with Ronnie Scott and Stan Getz, and worked with the BBC Radio Orchestra before moving to the States in the late 1960s. Ending up on the west coast with no gigs he gravitated towards the technical side of things, installing an Ampex MM1000 (a pioneering 16-track tape recorder) into a blues studio called Sunwest, creating LA's first 16-track studio. Still not able to sort out his union card, he decided to move to New York, landing a job as chief engineer at Recordmart. From there he moved to Media Sound studios, where Robert Margouleff, a photographer and Moog expert, was working.

Margouleff picks up the story: "I had been fooling around with synthesisers since the mid-Sixties. I got my first in 1966 – it was serial number three or four from the Moog factory; definitely one of the first ever made. Bob Moog used to come and sit on the floor of my studio to fix the keyboards because the pitch would drift. By the time Malcolm and I found each other at Media Sound in 1970, he was already an accomplished jazz musician, but also running the studio operation and maintenance department for Media Sound. We made a deal: he'd show me how to be a recording engineer if I'd show him how to use a synthesiser."[29]

Together the pair began to assemble the largest synth yet devised, by adding more and more modules to the Series 3 Moog. The behemoth became known as Tonto (The Original New Timbral Orchestra). In 1971 they recorded what they were doing under the name Tonto's Expanding Head Band. Margouleff explains how their rather outlandish experimentations came to the notice of Stevie

Stevie's new-found musical independence was reflected in his less formal stage-wear...

Wonder: "We put out an album called *Zero Time*, which was on Embryo Records, a vanity label owned by Herbie Hancock and distributed by Atlantic. We didn't even think that what we were doing was music in the pop music sense. But there was a big spread on us in *Rolling Stone*, and the bass player in Stevie Wonder's band, Ronnie Blanco, saw it and picked up the album and then brought Stevie to meet us.

"Back at that time, we were making a lot of noise and a lot of people were coming to us. The reason we became so indigenous in the business is the fact that we worked with everybody, whereas most of the other synthesiser players, like Subotnick and Wendy Carlos and Beaver & Krause, mostly worked for themselves. We put ourselves in a major recording studio and worked for everyone who wanted to come through the doors – we made ourselves a ubiquitous comestible."[29]

It's worth looking quickly at the kind of thing Cecil and Margouleff were producing at the time, to help appreciate their influence on Stevie's work to come. *Zero Time* has been described as "the first purely electronic album to take the synthesiser to the limits of its liberating capabilities while

As an avid technophile, getting his hands on Tonto would have been a thrilling prospect

still making music that laymen could enjoy listening to."[30] Consisting of six tracks, the album starts with a minor blues, 'Cybernaut', which is musically conventional but sonically innovative. A thick bass sound lays down the two-bar bass riff, with a lead line and mallet-like percussive accompaniment. The arrangement builds in complexity with more voices entering, and the synth sounds open up, before the textures thin again, leaving the tuned percussion to fade. The next track, 'Jetsex', starts in a more abstract fashion, with a heartbeat sound/passing car/giant insects/boiling kettles that come and go. 'Timewhys' is a faster, more motif-based, orchestrated piece... and so it continues – a combination of tunes, to keep things friendly, and some alien synth sounds that borrow from Subotnick's vocabulary.

So what would Stevie Wonder have heard that appealed so much? A method of building texture and colour through the use of a whole new palette of synth sounds – a vast, seemingly infinite variety of "sounds limited only by your imagination" (as the ads say).

Let's face it, you either get synths or you don't. There are plenty of musicians who love pianos but have no stomach for electronics, preferring the sound of acoustic instruments. Stevie has seemingly always been an avid technophile, and getting his hands on, or getting others to harness, the power of Tonto would have been a thrilling prospect.

Malcolm Cecil recalls their first meeting: "Stevie showed up [in a pistachio jump suit] with the Tonto LP under his arm. He said, 'I don't believe all this was done on one instrument. Show me the instrument.' He was always talking about seeing. So we dragged his hands all over the instrument, and he thought he'd never be able to play it. But we told him we'd get it together for him."[31]

And they did. They installed Tonto in Electric Lady studios. "We never stopped working from that moment, night and day," says Margouleff. "He'd do the playing, we'd do the programming, and we started to accumulate a huge library of songs."[32]

Cecil describes the ever-expanding scale of the apparatus: "When Tonto got to be nine feet long, and we were running from one end of the instrument to the other towing a trolley behind us with the keyboards on it, we decided there had to be a better way to lay the instrument out..."[33]

Because Tonto was in a constant state of development, exact specifications are difficult to ascertain, but what they probably had was a synth set-up able to produce six timbres simultaneously, based around the Moog (and later another Moog Series 3), plus four Oberheim SEMs, two ARP 2600s, a cornucopia of EMS and Serge modules, and several sequencers, including an adapted EMS 256. (Robin Wood of EMS remembers going out to New York to deliver and install the sequencer, probably after *Music Of My Mind* but before *Talking Book*.)

Meanwhile back at the office...

It was obviously common knowledge in the industry that Stevie's contract at Motown was up, and other record companies were not slow in coming forward to tempt him to join them. Through working at Electric Lady, Stevie had bumped into Richie Havens, who introduced him to his lawyer, Johanan Vigoda. He had previously done work for Hendrix and had a reputation for, shall we say, firmness in business matters. So he was assigned to negotiate with Atlantic and CBS, while simultaneously continuing to talk possible renewal terms with Motown.

Stevie was happy to carry on working and wait for the deal to be fixed – presumably he also felt it helped to have some new material under his belt to strengthen his position even further. He needn't have worried. In the end Vigoda struck a vastly improved, and highly flexible agreement with Motown, demanding Stevie's complete creative control over content of the records, and even the formation of his own record production and music publishing companies (which would become Taurus Productions and Black Bull Music Inc respectively – the names inspired by Stevie's interest in astrology: his star sign is Taurus, the bull). Stevie would deliver product to Motown to manufacture, distribute and promote.

Six weeks of negotiations ended with a 120-page signed contract, agreeing all of the above and paying Stevie a lump sum – it's not clear exactly how much, though bearing in mind the competitive interest from other labels, it would likely be substantial.

The cash was undoubtedly welcome at that point too: Stevie and the team had already notched up a bill of $250,000 at Electric Lady (you'd think he might have learned Hendrix's lesson), but for that they'd recorded around 40 tunes from which to choose tracks for a forthcoming album.

Stevie recalled the period later: "I decided to go for something besides a winning formula. I wanted to see what would happen if I changed. It challenged me to give the public something other than what it was used to hearing."[34]

The 'something other' would of course turn into its own 'winning formula' – one that was conceived in Stevie's head and brought to fruition with the help of the Tonto team. By early 1972, the album *Music Of My Mind* was ready for delivery.

CHAPTER 4
THE 'CLASSIC' ALBUM YEARS, 1972–1976

"Stevie Wonder made a mark in music, which is that popular music can be art too."

HERBIE HANCOCK

So began a frighteningly intensive period of creativity. Four of Stevie's greatest, most musically satisfying and culturally significant albums – *Music Of My Mind*, *Talking Book*, *Innervisions* and *Fulfillingness' First Finale* – were all released within the space of an astonishing two-and-a-half-years, from early 1972 to mid 1974. These were followed in 1976 by his most commercially successful album, *Songs In the Key Of Life*.

The first four 'classic' albums had basically the same production team of Stevie, Robert Margouleff and Malcolm Cecil, with the same scrupulous attention to every detail – be it the shape of a song, or the doubling effect on a voice, or the synth line behind the main synth line, or the way one side of an LP shapes up in its own right.

Released from the artistic constraints of Motown, and with his two attentive assistants in tow, the new string of albums achieved an instantly recognisable sound character for Stevie – both in the quality of the recording and the choice of instrumental and vocal colours. The quality and honesty in the recording, and (for the most part) the lack of gimmickry, are the reasons the albums from that period are still not only enjoyably listenable 30 years on, but considered among the finest pop albums of the 20th century.

Indeed, like the mature work of The Beatles, Stevie's records from this period helped cement the idea that some pop music could be more than fashionable, disposable ephemera, and could possess lasting qualities reserved for the best in any music field. Herbie Hancock expressed it well when he said: "Stevie Wonder made a mark in music, which is that popular music can be art too."[35]

Not that the idea of rock as art was Stevie's invention, but from his cultural background and history in the business – where Berry Gordy had his eye firmly on the buck – it was a large step for Stevie to take (as it was for Marvin Gaye before him) out of the singles market and into the album-as-art fraternity.

Exactly how much co-producers Cecil and Margouleff had to do with the formation and arrangement of the songs of this period is kept within the walls of Electric Lady studios, but certainly the overall care in the recording and the hugely expanded and personalised synth sound palette are their responsibility.

The four main 'classic' albums credit Stevie as the producer, with Cecil and Margouleff associate producers, engineers and programmers. Which begs the question, what is a producer for? There's no short answer to that (apart from a few unprintable epithets), because every studio situation, every band/singer-producer relationship is unique, just as the capabilities of each personality vary. One singer or musician might be very good in an organisational sense, in terms of knowing the song and what they want to do vocally, but might just need some emotional assistance when gearing up for a take; someone else might need help with writing and arranging. The producer might be strong on the engineering and studio side, and less up on the musical nuts and bolts – or vice versa.

Brian Eno, who produced Bowie, Talking Heads and U2, among many others, often saw his role as encouraging unpredictability, famously saying: "When you go into a work situation, you come in with an idea but eventually it goes off course. Look closely at the thing when it goes off course – it might be better than the original place you wanted it to go."[36]

During the 1960s the role of the producer changed as the possibilities of overdubbing and shaping sound in the studio increased. No longer technicians in white coats, sometimes Svengali figures with an air of mystery (often in a cloud of smoke), the famous producers are divided into two camps: those who forged a specific sound – like Phil Spector and Norman Whitfield – and those who were enablers, following ideas and making things possible – like George Martin with The Beatles. The bottom line, whatever happens on the musical input front, is to provide the best circumstances for an artist to record, and then make sure that the recorded performance is as technically perfect as possible, within the limitations of the equipment.

Given that the production team for *Music Of My Mind* (*MOMM*) was in a state-of-the-art studio, the instrumental sounds on tape were bound to be more faithful than the Motown set-up. Even though standards at Hitsville had gradually improved, there was always a quality to the acoustic of the room/mixing desk/reverb that instantly stamped a recording with the name Motown. For Stevie's recordings, that would no longer be the case.

Music Of My Mind

The sleeve notes on *MOMM* state: "The album is virtually the work of one man. All of the songs are composed, arranged and performed by Stevie Wonder … on pianos, drums, harmonica, organ, clavichord, clavinet, and ARP and Moog synthesisers. The sounds themselves come from inside his mind." (There's more, but it starts to get a little sticky…)

Later remarks by Margouleff, however, suggest that he and Cecil were involved in more than just engineering and programming with Stevie, especially when compared to other artists they'd collaborated with, like The Isley Brothers: "Working with The Isley Brothers was much more business-like than working with Stevie. With Stevie, it was like living inside this world; it was a lifestyle, and we were really part of every aspect of the creative process, shaping the songs and getting sounds and all."[37]

The drift of that statement suggests more of a contributive musical involvement than merely getting a sound onto tape. Cecil and Margouleff were certainly educating Stevie in the realm of synthesis, and he was probably educating them with what could be done by overdubbing self-played rhythm sections.

What's immediately apparent from the start is the equal attention given to every sound on a track

There's no holding back with the synth on *MOMM*. Full-blown structural orchestrations appear as early as 'Superwoman' and continue to sprinkle the album with aural delectation, culminating with the dark yet uplifting 'Evil'.

'Love Having You Around', the opener, sets the parameters for one type of track. Instrumentation is (distorted) clavinet, Rhodes, drum kit, and in all probability synth bass. That's the basic rhythm track, to which was added lead vocal and BVs and then a sort-of-vocal 'bag' track. The 'bag' was something Stevie had picked up in a studio in Detroit – acting like a resonator, the player mouthed the shape of the words down a tube attached to the keyboard, and the effect was a robotic 'played' vocal – not unlike the guitarists' 'talkbox' used during the Seventies by Joe Walsh, Jeff Beck, Peter Frampton et al.

What's immediately apparent from the start is the equal attention given to every sound on a track.

Gone are the days of huge, pointlessly inaudible brass sections. The whole texture is pared down, but at the same time (and this is the trick) beefed up. A prime example of the maxim 'less is more'.

What's also obvious is the level of musical organisation: at one point the clav and Rhodes play answering phrases back and forth, and at another the whole thing falls apart for a breakdown, only to be revived by a blistering trombone solo, courtesy of Art Baron (who once worked with Duke Ellington). So while it may sound jammed and spontaneous – and no doubt some of it is – there's a deeper level of arrangement going on that provides the solid basis for the proceedings on top.

The same goes for the track 'Happier Than The Morning Sun' (another Beatles nod, perhaps, as in 'Here Comes The Sun'?), which has a simpler-than-it-sounds clavinet track mixed with the low end of a synth. The clav track is cleverly chorused so as to appear as if it's two takes, panning from left to right, sounding rich and full – almost like a 12-string guitar – and thoroughly unlike the thin electric piano on 'Look Around' from the last album. At last it's time to bask in opulent sonic surroundings, instead of making allowances for sound deficiencies. And we've only just started...

'Superwoman' features a full-on synth section, as well as pushing the compositional envelope by following a narrative through almost two separate songs (I'll come back to this in Chapter 9). 'Seems So Long' is a jazzy ballad of a song, though that description might give the wrong impression completely. It's jazzy in that the feel is swung, and it's a ballad in that it's a song of lost love/starting new love, but the instrumental colour lends so much more.

The drums are swishy-cymbal dominated, the bass synth grounds it, a lush and smooth Hammond organ inhabits the middle ground, synth horn-like lines circle the edges, and a bizarre free-form softly-wailing synth line wafts in and out and round the whole thing. Add to that a synth guitar that could be Wes Montgomery (perhaps a homage to their earlier doomed duet), and that's quite a recipe for a track. The great thing is it works too, particularly as the vocal is so good. Again a different colour, recorded using a close-miking technique so Stevie could be more intimate, it purrs along on top of the track.

A word about the use of compression here. The Motown engineers had been particularly keen on the use of limiting/compression to get as much level as possible at all times onto tape. (You could say they were bludgeoningly unsubtle at times.) That's the reason why on some of the older records you can hear the intake of breath louder (it seems) than the sung note. Too much compression can also make the sound harsh and metallic. On *MOMM* the effect is used more sparingly, enough to give a presence to each sound and bring it to the 'front' of the speakers. It helps, of course, that the track is not too busy in terms of the number of instruments; the more crowded the picture, the harder it is to make individual elements audible.

Compositionally, the songs are as adventurous as anything on *Where I'm Coming From*. The fondness for having two grooves available, and switching from one to the other, is continued here on 'Sweet Little Girl', where the blues/rock feel and harmonica (at one point it's almost like John Mayall & The Bluesbreakers) carve a straight path, using even eighth-notes, while the bordering-on-sleazy spoken section, imploring his girl for some love action, turns up the late-night feel by sliding into swing. There's even some X-rated (and pretty un-PC) harmonica playing, as well as some very entertaining lines, like: "I've given you cookies and candy, and the woofer [sic], and still you don't wanna be good; come on honey sugar, you know your baby loves you, more than I love my clavinet".

With the exception of 'Superwoman', the songwriting ideas are fairly contained. The simple-but-

effective 'I Love Every Little Thing About You', and 'Girl Blue' don't have an ounce of spare flesh about them. 'Girl Blue' is interesting for several reasons: the synthesised percussive elements mixed in with the unconventional drum part (more like David Byrne in the 1990s than Stevie in 1971); the song's use of a descending bassline on the verse and ascending one on the chorus (perfect symmetry); and the visual imagery of the lyric, aided this time by his wife's sister, Yvonne Wright, who also co-wrote 'Evil'.

One question that comes up at this stage is the physical problem of how they synched the drum track with the synthesised percussion and the keyboard tracks and so on. The fact that everything stays in time so well suggests that (although there's bound to be a little driftage) a guide click would have been laid from the synth set-up for Stevie to play along to, ensuring the track remained steady enough to overdub further parts. This method is completely commonplace today (using click-tracks and MIDI synching etc), but in 1971 it would have been unusual, because in most band situations it wasn't required – you'd just play along with the drummer, and you had to live with human tempo fluctuations.

It also takes a while to get used to the feel of playing with an inanimate click, learning how to maintain an elasticity to the groove despite being held to a strict grid. It seems that, however it was done, Stevie never had a problem with building up a real rhythm section feel – the method was probably sorted as early as 'We Can Work It Out'.

Another problem no longer in need of a solution was the bass part sound. From 'Superwoman' onwards the synth bass sits comfortably and provocatively under the track, with just the right amount of attention-grabbing activity.

It should be pointed out that in the world before samplers and digital recording, a keyboard/synth bass sound would never exactly match the timbre of a Fender Precision or an upright bass – but that was the whole point. For a while in the Eighties and early Nineties you might have thought that the definition of synthesis was being able to imitate acoustic instruments, but not so – the original concept was always to imagine and program *new* sounds.

"The Moog itself is a way to directly express what comes from your mind, hence the album's title … I'm just trying to be myself."

For instance, what you might call the 'oboe' on the track 'Evil' is just a useful verbal hook – the sound is thin and reedy so you tend to grab the nearest description for convenience. It's not that the sound is imitating an oboe – though it may be tapping into the oboe's historical emotional resonances (just to confuse things).

As Stevie said after *MOMM* came out, synthesisers allowed him, "to do things I've wanted to do for a long time, but which weren't possible. They've added a whole new dimension to music. The Moog itself is a way to directly express what comes from your mind, hence the album's title … I'm not trying to be different. I'm just trying to be myself."[38]

Even if the public backlash was not as extreme as when Bob Dylan went electric (times had a-changed, after all), you couldn't say the new synthesised Stevie was an instant hit with record-buyers. *MOMM* reached Number 21 in the album charts in the States, and the singles – an edited version of the eight-minute 'Superwoman', and 'Keep On Running' – caused minor ripples in the singles charts. If the public expected to hear the familiar Stevie/Motown sound, they would be disappointed. That was gone forever.

With the move out west, and Berry Gordy now busy with The Jackson Five, Detroit was well off the map. The Seventies saw the end of the Hitsville old guard: Martha Reeves & The Vandellas split up, Gladys Knight & The Pips jumped ship, Smokey Robinson left The Miracles, and The Temptations never recovered from the departure of Norman Whitfield, who went to work for another label. The original "sound of young America" was history, in every sense.

But despite all this, Stevie was happy to remain (albeit loosely) within the Motown organisation – a case of the devil you know, perhaps. Stevie also felt he'd made his point by threatening to quit, and had since been granted all the freedom he required.

"I basically wanted to stay at Motown. I've been with them since the beginning, and I felt that I would like to be one of the pioneers of seeing it change, get into a new direction. I knew the company, and I knew the people, and all I had to do was somehow convince Gordy, and part of my convincing had been done when I split."[39]

Listening now, it's hard to appreciate how experimental *MOMM* was at the time, but judging solely by the synth ingredients it must have been considered quite wacky.

But because all the songs are tonally based, and conventionally structured with verses and choruses, it allows some leeway for weird synth programming and other rogue elements – such as 'bag' vocals, breath noises etc – without the tracks lurching into avant garde alienation.

The fact is, the technology was providing Stevie with the means to hear his songs as he imagined them, synth parts included. There must have been a certain amount of unplanned, experimental stuff added in the studio too: because it was the first time he had worked with synths, he would have been trying out all manner of oddness cooked up by Cecil and Margouleff.

Was it overcooked? To my ears, no. The more abstract synth work, while it imparts an eerie atmosphere, is in no way odd or disaffecting to a 21st century listener. We're quite accustomed to sound manipulation now.

Stevie would never be quite so adventurous with synth colours again – he basically established the fact that his taste is for musical rather than 'sound design' keyboard parts (*Secret Life Of Plants* excluded – see Chapter 11). He also knew he had found recording methods that worked, production values that meant something, and if the record company was worried about the lack of singles, well, just let them wait for the next album.

In fact the record company had already been cashing in on Stevie's back catalogue. *Stevie Wonder's Greatest Hits Volume 2* contains all the hit material from 1968-71, including 'Shoo-Be-Doo...', 'For Once In My Life', 'Signed, Sealed...', 'We Can Work It Out', etc etc. A three-LP collection entitled *Looking Back*, tracing the complete story so far, was released in the UK only.

But it seems Motown didn't exactly exert themselves in the promotion of the new *MOMM* album. And strange though it may seem, Stevie had no personal manager at that point in his career. Why that became important is because suddenly he was asked by a PR company, Wartoke Concern, to be support artist on a Rolling Stones tour – some 50 dates over eight weeks. Stevie accepted and assembled Wonderlove, his live band – they rehearsed for a day and then they were off. With no management, and no record company support to speak of, it must have been pretty lonely out there in the world of rock'n'roll. The Stones were touring *Exile On Main Street*, a splendidly rough album, certainly one of their rawest, with tracks such as 'Tumbling Dice', 'Just Want To See His Face', 'Rocks Off', 'Turd On The Run', 'Sweet Black Angel' – the Stones at their 'blackest'. For Stevie, though, it represented a chance to take his music to a new, predominantly white rock audience.

As it turned out, it wasn't an easy experience. The radio stations along the way had little or no interest in playing tracks by a black artist, his name never made it to the ad hoardings (almost unbelievably now), there was a spat with the drummer mid tour, and it seems the Stones were personally fairly hostile. But despite all this, the crowds went bananas over a set that included 'Fingertips', 'Superwoman', 'Heaven Help Us All', 'Shoo-Be-Doo...' and 'Signed Sealed...'. And to cap the evening off, Jagger and Wonder would duet spontaneously on 'Satisfaction'.

The exposure took Stevie into a position where, with the next album, he would not merely be classed as a pop or soul artist, but welcomed by the mainstream rock audience and viewed as someone with genuine cross-genre appeal. He was at last about to fulfill the potential that had been apparent ten years earlier.

Talking Book

The helter-skelter recording period in New York, which yielded *MOMM* and some of the next album, *Talking Book*, resulted in something of an administrative nightmare too. So many sessions, some using other musicians, were held at such erratic times of day and night that the amount of paperwork and form-filling grew completely out of hand. I don't suppose a desk job ever appealed to Stevie anyway, but he certainly lacked support on the business/promotional side of running his own production company. In the end it fell to Motown arranger Gene Kee (who'd incidentally arranged 'Alfie') to hotfoot it to NYC and clear up the administrative backlog.

Stevie certainly had a lot on his mind at the time. The man was busy. When he wasn't on the road in 1972 (his live appearances included joining John & Yoko for a benefit gig at Madison Square Garden in August), Stevie was in the studio working on *Talking Book*, which was finished in the autumn and released on October 27th.

Three days beforehand, a relieved record company had issued 'Superstition' as a single (for the full story of this track see the 'funk' section, Chapter 5) – it was a slow burner, but eventually provided Stevie with his first pop Number One since 1963's 'Fingertips'. It's not hard to understand why 'Superstition' was a hit: a completely compulsive groove, a killer clav riff, and a hooky chorus line, all assembled in perfect listening order, is an irresistible combination. And when you kick the album off with what will become one of the most covered (and 'lounged') songs ever – 'You Are The Sunshine Of My Life' – things are starting to look quite promising.

It's strange that the first voice you hear on *Talking Book* isn't Stevie at all, but singer Jim Gilstrap – he and fellow Wonderlove backup vocalist Gloria Barley (though some claim it's Lani Groves) sing two lines apiece at the start of 'You Are The Sunshine' before Stevie joins in. A nice touch, showing a rare generosity in someone of Stevie's star status, deliberately limelighting his backing singers in this way. (Stevie later presented Gilstrap with a gold disc as further evidence of his appreciation.)

'You Are The Sunshine' was in fact recorded earlier, at the time of *MOMM*, though apparently deemed unsuitable for the mood of that album. It may also have been held back for more personal reasons: the song was apparently a paean to Gloria Barley, who happened to be Stevie's new love interest (what is it with piano players and singers?), at a time when he was still married, albeit shakily, to Syreeta Wright. When it was finally released as a single in February 1973, the song provided Stevie with his second consecutive US Number One.

Talking Book might lack the experimental slant of *MOMM*, and some of it might sound middle-of-the-road to certain ears, but the muted expression is sympathetic to the album's theme of lost love, which invades 'Maybe Your Baby', 'You And I', 'Tuesday Heartbreak', 'Blame It On The Sun' and 'Lookin' For Another Pure Love' – basically half the album.

The break-up of his marriage to Syreeta, which followed the Stones' tour, was responsible for the bleakness of certain tracks: Syreeta even provided lyrics for the last two of the tracks just mentioned. Sister Yvonne supplies the words to 'You've Got It Bad Girl', but the other tracks are Stevie's alone, including the overtly political stance of 'Big Brother' (see Chapter 7 for more on this and other socio-political tracks).

The lyric-writing is generally more focused on *Talking Book*, and there are some excellent lines – for example: "Heart's blazing like a five-alarm fire" (from 'Maybe Your Baby'); "Shattered dreams, worthless years, here am I encased in a hollow shell" (from the closing track, 'I Believe (When I Fall In Love It Will Be Forever)'). It does get a bit gawky at times as well: "Tuesday heartbreak seem to be a drag, when you know that you love her especially…"; and depending on your taste/current mood you will either find 'You Are The Sunshine' nauseating or naively charming, or even nauseatingly charming. Remember, though, it is a pop song...

The involvement of a mixture of musicians, as well as various backing vocal teams, seems to make the sound of the album wider and less enclosed than *MOMM*. For instance, even though overdubbing your own vocal to provide BVs can work, and has a unique sound, a blend of vocal characteristics makes for a broader texture.

Sax star David Sanborn makes an appearance, as does guitar superstar Jeff Beck, alongside Buzzy Feiten (former guitarist with Paul Butterfield's band). Congas are by Daniel Ben Zebulon, and Scott Edwards plays bass on the opening track. Add the horn section (on 'Superstition', and on the single version of 'Sunshine') and you have a fair amount of outside input.

Robert Margouleff might have had less to do in the synth department, but he compensated by taking the (in)famous cover photograph of Stevie in African regalia – in touch with the earth – which defined a mood and stage of personal development.

The break-up of Stevie's marriage to Syreeta was responsible for the bleakness of certain tracks

There are generally fewer complex synth arrangements on *Talking Book*: the monster Moog is pressed into service on the ballads 'You And I' (see Chapter 7) and 'Blame It On The Sun', with a drifting sine-wave timbre that will be a familiar returning element right through to *Fulfillingness' First Finale*. There's also a gorgeous synth sound on 'You've Got It Bad Girl' – rich, warm, everything a Moog should be. The three synth voices are panned left, right and centre, played with a degree of expression (through grace notes and pitch bend) that was already earning Stevie his reputation as humaniser of the machine.

Elsewhere the synth is heavily used for basslines, and on 'Maybe Your Baby' the emphasis is on the heavy. The impact that the first chords make, ditching the sweetness of the previous song, is down to the mixture of clav and bass synth that bear the weight of the rhythm track. Stevie's keyboard bass style is certainly taking shape. As if the sound is not 'phat' and alluring enough, extreme pitch effects (portamento) and subtle pitch-bend are used to inflict further meanness to the track.

The chorus of clavinets on 'Maybe Your Baby' is by far the loudest element, as on 'Superstition', and with a restrained drum track, the funk is fully engaged. Vocals are piled up to the ceiling on this one (with some experimental pitch-shifting in evidence), which sonically is almost a continuation of 'Love Having You Around'. (There's a fair chance Prince was well aware of tracks like 'Maybe Your Baby' in his formative years.) Despite the darker moods contained on *Talking Book* it ends, as it starts, with an optimistic song – 'I Believe (When I Fall In Love It Will Be Forever)'.

It's possible to see threads running through albums now – the mean funk track, the ballad, the socio-political angle, the pop song – and on this album the Latin colour continues to emerge. These are the threads that will be looked at in greater detail in the upcoming chapters – including a section on the songs that occupy their own unique, unclassifiable category. Before leaving the funk, though, I ought to mention an album that's often stated as an influence on Stevie's work of this period.

The career of Sly Stone is discussed some more in the next chapter, but at this point it's worth mentioning *There's A Riot Goin' On*, which made a huge splash at the end of 1971 with its mixture of funk, dark lyrics, and black political overtones. Gone was the positivity and innovation of earlier albums like *Stand*. Aside from being in a drug-fuelled downward spiral, Sly was also a studio-holic, recording for days on end at some points.

With the world seemingly crashing around him (there really was a mini riot in Chicago when Sly was due to play there), and his band disintegrating acrimoniously (legend has it bassist Larry Graham hired hitmen to attack his boss), Sly made the *Riot* album mostly by himself, adding overdubs using anything that came to hand (noticeably clavinet), with just a few additional sessions from other bandmembers.

His track 'Brave And Strong' pitches in with a depiction of Black Panthers forced by police to strip and line up: "Frightened faces to the wall/Can't you hear your mama call?/The brave and the strong survive./Survive!" With four bars of drum intro, followed by a scream, leading to a funk groove, it's hard not to think of 'Superstition'. The slow grind of 'Poet' matches Stevie's 'Maybe Your Baby' – the lyric of which even touches on what Sly must have been going through, even though it's the love-lorn Stevie speaking:

"I feel like I'm slippin' deeper,
Slippin' deeper into myself,
And I can't take it,
This stuff is scarin' me to death."

It has been suggested that *Talking Book* is Stevie's response to *Riot*, which is probably overstating the case. The two men are very different – there might be a shared musical influence, in the funk development, and a willingness to go deeper emotionally than with previous material, but that's really where the similarities end.

Margouleff and Cecil have pointed to *Talking Book* as the peak of their collaboration with Stevie, but for me that would be a hard call. Certainly *TB* combines successful commercial tunes and relevant lyrics with a widening of harmonic vocabulary, more especially on the slow and mid-tempo tunes, but the peak? I'd say they reached that on the next album...

Innervisions

In early 1973 Stevie used mostly musicians from his own Wonderlove band on Syreeta's second album, *Stevie Wonder Presents Syreeta* – it featured Reggie McBride on bass, guitarist Mike Sembello, Ollie Brown on drums, and 'Superstition' trumpeter Steve Madaio. The main focus of his energy at this time, though, was assembling tracks for his new project, initially titled *The Last Days Of Easter*.

With an agenda covering not only the hypocrisy of a political system that had returned Nixon to the White House, but also a general need for social and spiritual change, the album would display a dark edge, as well as an interest in religious matters that had barely surfaced in his work to that point.

Innervisions would display a dark edge, as well as an interest in religious matters that had barely surfaced in his work to that point

Cecil and Margouleff were naturally on the production team again, and it's the first time the name of Stevie's future studio collaborator Gary Olazabal appears, credited here as 'tape operator'. Recording work this time was divided between Media Sound studio in New York City and the Record Plant in Los Angeles.

Among other duties, Cecil and Margouleff were responsible for a song catalogue called the 'blue book', which listed the vast number of songs or fragments that had been collected over the past few years, and to which new tracks were being added all the time. There are no credited co-writes on this album, though (which along the way lost its Easter connotations and was retitled *Innervisions*). Stevie took time to hone the lyrics, as it seems he still lacked confidence in his ability with words. On the evidence of the finished album, he needn't have worried – it's probably his most cohesive work.

The first thing you notice about the sound of *Innervisions* is that the drums and percussion are generally higher in the mix, which supplies a sense of momentum to the proceedings, as does the way the tracks are mastered, with a feeling of continuity and flow from song to song. Between 'Living For The City' and 'Golden Lady' a solo piano segment actually modulates from one song to the next, setting up the change of key and mood. The end of 'All In Love Is Fair' is another similar example.

The ordering of the tracks is crucial – you couldn't put this album on random/shuffle play on your CD player, the result would be too unnerving. Or is that just familiarity? No, I feel there is definitely a sense of drama in the construction that would be lost.

It's also a mark of the completeness of the album, and the importance of each track to the whole, that the 1999 compilation *At The Close Of A Century* includes every track from *Innervisions* except

'Jesus Children Of America', such is the quality of the songwriting (and one wonders whether that track's omission has as much to do with the worry over US 'moral majority' offence at the title than any quality control consideration).

Right from the intro to 'Too High', the listener is on fairly familiar ground: Fender Rhodes, synth bass, drums and exquisite backing vocals form the habitual yet un-formulaic sonic palette. Amazing the way bass and Rhodes blend, almost sounding like one instrument – the reason is that the synth supplies all the front end and the piano sits subserviently behind it. With its stark drug abuse warning, it's clear Stevie is on a mission to highlight and then change some problems in society.

The next track, 'Visions', considers the ideal society, which it seems can only exist as a vision in the mind. The instrumental setting here is unusual: three guitars – one electric (David 'T' Walker), two acoustic (probably both Dean Parks) – pick a reassuring backdrop. It almost sounds the way you'd expect ancient Greek music to be: airy and harpy and modal, with a good view of Mount Olympus. Meanwhile Malcolm Cecil himself dusts off his double bass to provide the foundation. (There's more on the song 'Visions' in Chapter 10.) With Stevie on inconspicuous Rhodes, and the lack of any percussion, the resulting freshness is welcome; it also points to the fact that the clavinet does have its limits in terms of acoustic guitar emulation.

The clavs on 'I Believe…', though excellently played, are stiff compared to the fluidity of 'Visions'. But the clav sound hasn't lost its funk potency – the immediacy of 'Higher Ground' (more of which in a moment) is largely due to the rocking clavinet track.

Elsewhere Stevie's keyboards of choice are mainly Rhodes and acoustic piano, often both together. Tonto is conspicuous by his absence on all but 'Golden Lady' and 'Living For The City' – on which Stevie more than compensates by being very involved indeed (as we'll see in Chapter 7).

Two songs speak directly of spiritual matters: 'Jesus Children Of America' tackles the innocence of children, depth of religious understanding and belief, sects, junkies, transference of pain, and transcendental meditation – which is probably enough for one tune. But there's an open-endedness about the song's message that is attractive rather than irritating or preachy.

More disturbing is the lyric on 'Higher Ground', which takes the idea that the writer is on his second life, having lived one life of sin. And while he's aspiring to the "higher ground", he warns others guilty of warring and lying to do the same: "I'm so glad that I know more than I knew then/Gonna' keep on tryin'/Till I reach my highest ground." All this to a hypnotic, round-and-round (symbolically circular?) backing track. The Buddhist re-incarnation aspect and the warning, "Cause it won't be too long", are the album's strongest indicator that something new and rather strange was happening to Stevie's mood.

In an interview with *Rolling Stone* in April 1973 he surprisingly pronounced that he felt he was going to die soon, and around the same time ended another interview with the morbid, "I'll be here until I die". It's easy with hindsight to read more significance into these comments than they deserve, but Stevie did seem to have a sense of foreboding during the period leading up to the release of the *Innervisions* record. It could be that, as a 23-year-old who had seen more than his fair share of public and private death, personal mortality was becoming a reality. But he could have had little idea what a close brush with mortality he was soon to face himself.

On the way from Greenville, South Carolina, to Duke University, Durham, in the early hours of August 6th 1973, just three days after *Innervisions* was released in the States, Stevie and his cousin/driver John Harris were involved in a car accident. Stevie was asleep, seatbelt on, in the passenger seat, and while John was attempting to overtake a logging truck (a common sight in that area) something went awry, and the car went into the back of the lorry. One of the logs slid off the truck, through the windscreen, and straight into Stevie's forehead.

An ambulance arrived and took the heavily bleeding singer to a nearby hospital. After initial treatment he was transferred to the Department of Neurosurgery at North Carolina Baptist Hospital, where he was diagnosed with a broken skull and severe brain contusion. Surgery was ruled out, and for an extremely worrying five days Stevie lay in a coma.

Lula flew in from Detroit and, very disturbingly, found her son's head had swollen to three times its normal size. Berry Gordy was rung by the hospital and told that Stevie was not expected to live.

That's when Ira Tucker, Stevie's publicist/road manager/Man Friday, arrived at the hospital. He found a sombre scene, with everyone being quiet and reverential around Stevie's bed. Ira suggested to the doctors that maybe a 'loud' strategy might be more appropriate for trying to get through to the comatose patient – Ira knew Stevie always enjoyed listening to music at relatively high volume.

After some yelling, with no response, Ira started singing 'Higher Ground' at full volume into Stevie's ear. Eventually a slight movement of the fingers was noticed, followed by a genuine tapping in response to the song. A gradual recovery ensued, with the complication of some sensory losses, such as the inability to taste and smell – which must have raised questions as to how the rest of his brain was affected. Ira brought Stevie his clavinet to assess his musical facilities, and incredibly, after some initial nervousness, Stevie was soon playing as before.

The whole episode left Stevie feeling he had been given a second chance on life

The physical side of things healed quickly (leaving just some scarring above his right eye), and as far as anyone could tell there was no neurological damage – the accident just left him prone to tiredness and headaches.

You might think he'd take a few months off after something as traumatic as that, but the lure of music and performing was such that by September 25th Stevie was back on-stage as a guest of Elton John, performing 'Superstition' and 'Honky Tonk Women' at the Boston Gardens. Nothing like getting straight back in the water to calm the nerves.

The whole episode of his dark moods, then the accident and its aftermath, left Stevie feeling he had been given a second chance on life, and he resolved to use the experience to improve himself. In the meantime, the *Innervisions* album and 'Higher Ground' single had both reached the same chart positions – Number One in the US R&B chart, and Number Four in the pop chart. If anything, all the publicity surrounding the accident had helped sales.

'Living For The City' followed as a single release in October – another R&B Number One, this time Number Eight in the mainstream chart. A break from touring was compulsory, but by early 1974 Stevie had rehearsed up a new Wonderlove band and a few choice gigs were undertaken, first in Cannes, the *MIDEM* festival, then back at Madison Square Garden for a show that included the nine-month pregnant flautist Bobbi Humphrey, Sly Stone, Roberta Flack and Eddie Kendrick (of the

Temptations) in a finale of 'Superstition'. Sly was apparently a trifle too enthusiastic and was led firmly away by Stevie when he looked in danger of stealing the show.

Stevie himself stole the show at the 1973 Grammy awards ceremony, held in March 1974. Lula was present as Grammy after Grammy came Stevie's way. There were five in all: Best Male R&B Vocal Performance, Best R&B Song for 'Superstition', Best Pop Male Vocal Performance for 'You Are The Sunshine', and finally two Album Of The Year awards for *Innervisions* – one as the artist and another, alongside the equally deserving Cecil and Margouleff, as co-producer.

Stevie had found industry as well as public recognition through an album that combined accessible yet personal music and pertinent lyrics. In the words of *Rolling Stone* reviewer Lenny Kaye: "His concern with the real world is all-encompassing, a fact which his blindness has apparently complemented rather than denied … On *Innervisions*, Stevie Wonder proves again that he is one of the vital forces in contemporary music."[40]

Fulfillingness' First Finale

Success certainly seems to breed success: the Midas touch was spreading out to other projects like aftershocks of an earthquake. Syreeta's album was released in June 1974, and in the same year Stevie produced and sessioned on Minnie Riperton's album *Perfect Angel* (from which her hit single 'Lovin You' came); he wrote a song for Rufus & Chaka Khan that would earn him another Grammy ('Tell Me Something Good'); he produced tracks for the Jackson 5; and finally (pause for breath) one of his old songs, 'Until You Come Back To Me (That's What I'm Gonna Do)', in a new version by Aretha Franklin, would turf his own 'Living For The City' off the R&B Number One spot.

Plus, of course, there was another album to work on. It was originally envisaged as a double, but when Motown refused to budge on the scheduled release date, Stevie decided to abandon that idea (for the moment), and he duly delivered *Fulfillingness' First Finale* in time for a July launch.

He must have been under a fair degree of pressure, not only to equal the achievement of *Innervisions*, but take the music further still into his personal world. Stevie had hundreds of songs stashed away for a rainy day, but he rejected most of them, preferring to push himself to create something he felt was fresher and better. He was also determined to produce a new sound to express those ideas.

As the elaborate title suggests, *Fulfillingness' First Finale* was Stevie signing off the pre-accident stage of his life and embarking on stage two. The cover art continued the theme by portraying scenes from his past, including images of Little Stevie, his first drum kit, JFK, his graduation with Lula, Martin Luther King, past album artwork, and the *MotorTown Review* bus, all framed within an Africanised Escher-type keyboard/staircase. The sleeve concept was by Ira Tucker and the artwork by Bob Gleason (who also did the movie poster for *Halloween*).

By retaining Margouleff and Cecil as assistant producers, Stevie was making a decision not to destabilise the structure that had supported him on his recent successful run. The consequence was that his sound would not in fact change significantly, keeping a consistency with the past rather than breaking away. Musically the album is more of a consolidation than a departure, although several new areas of musical influence are incorporated, digested and reworked.

The overtly political 'You Haven't Done Nothin'' (more of which in Chapter 7) stormed straight to the top of both pop and R&B charts, with his 'Big Brother' track from a couple of years back tacked on as perhaps an over-obvious b-side choice. Then 'Boogie On Reggae Woman' (more of which in Chapter 5) made R&B Number One and Number Three in the pop chart – it had an old song on its b-side too, from even further back: in the US the choice was 'Seems So Long', and in the UK 'Evil', both from *MOMM*.

'You Haven't Done Nothin'' takes the funk materials and applies them to social criticism, while 'Boogie On' is a song that combines reggae-ish groove and bluesy piano with one of the toughest diamond-glaze bass synth tracks ever.

Clarence Paul once stated that the groove (ie drums, bass, rhythm section piano/guitar/clav) was always the first element to arrive in Stevie's compositional process, everything else came later. And indeed it's easy to mark out Stevie's albums in terms of grooves or rhythmic feels, and the way they combine/contrast to form a satisfactory whole.

For instance we can look at the consecutive grooves on *Fulfillingness' First Finale*, track by track:

'Smile Please' – mid-tempo 'Sunshine'-style/Latin-influenced/congas, bongos
'Heaven Is 10 Zillion Light Years Away' – mid-tempo rock/soul/slight swing/clavs as guitars
'Too Shy To Say' – slow ballad/piano/pedal steel guitar for extra colour
'Boogie On Reggae Woman' – up-tempo reggae-funk, piano/auto-wah Rhodes
'Creepin'' – slow groovy ballad/Rhodes/dreamy synths
'You Haven't Done Nothin'' – slowish earthy clav-based funk/horns
'It Ain't No Use' – mid-tempo ballad/soul/Rhodes/BVs build
'They Won't Go When I Go' – extremely slow/gospelly/BV and synth colours
'Bird Of Beauty' – up-tempo funky samba/rhodes/clav
'Please Don't Go' – mid-tempo cool funk/piano/huge BVs

Compared to *Innervisions*, which had more entries in the up-tempo category, the general tone of *FFF* appears to be more thoughtful and slower-moving.

Lyrically there's an awful lot of frustration about: 'Creepin'' has the singer wondering if his nocturnal obsessions are reciprocated; 'Boogie On' is sexual desire made all too real; 'Too Shy' relates how good she makes him feel, yet he can't find the words. Elsewhere there are songs of loss, religious salvation, persuasive songs about belief in God, and... the benefits of smiling.

In terms of strength of musical material, I'd argue this album is less consistent than both its predecessors. And would I be right in saying that, with notable exceptions, the energy level in Stevie's voice is more subdued? There seems to be slightly less conviction and confidence in the delivery – which would be understandable given the shocking personal experiences of the past year.

But there are still some stunning, unforgettable songs and musical events here that are unequalled in Stevie's work. I'm thinking of the whole of 'They Won't Go When I Go' (see Chapter 6), both of the hit singles, and 'Creepin'' – as much for the glowing, effervescent timbre of Minnie Riperton's backing vocals as for the fenced-in harmonic sense.

Sonically Stevie's albums were growing stronger each time. Cecil and Margouleff triumph again here with the synth work on 'They Won't Go...'. Clavinets-as-guitars are back, and large BV arrangements are in, with The Persuasions adding effectively to the Wonderlove vocalists.

But the album is not without its niggles – like some of the bass, for instance. Although Reggie

McBride from Wonderlove plays bass on several tunes, there are moments where Stevie's use of the bass synth isn't quite in keeping with the mood – for instance on 'Please Don't Go'. On tunes other than the funk grooves, a bass synth sound with too many top frequencies and a heavy attack stands out like a sore thumb.

Also, with Stevie's vocabulary of musical influences growing all the time, could it be that the cohesion suffers here? There's not the same effort to link tracks as there was on *Innervisions*, and despite the lyrical connections, the variety of musical languages works against a unified feel. Of course another way of looking at this is to say it's just a great collection of songs by a songwriter absolutely at the dizzying height of his powers.

The rhythm tracks are still full of life, the care taken on BV arrangements and execution is staggering, and the musicians Stevie has brought into the project have added enormously to the end result. Mike Sembello, the Wonderlove guitarist at the time, who was equally at home in the classical and jazz world (though strangely a newcomer to soul music) contributes to several tunes: on 'Smile Please', for instance, he plays some graceful soloistic lines, and is a sympathetic partner to the Rhodes keyboard. Having established his mature writing and performing styles, Stevie clearly felt he could let go of the controlling reins and appreciate other musicians for what they brought to a track.

FFF achieved even more commercial success than *Innervisions*, scoring Number One in both R&B and pop charts. It was Stevie's first mainstream Number One album since 1963. By September 1974 Stevie's health had recovered sufficiently for him to contemplate touring again. A quick spin around the States and Japan ensued, before winter set in and it was back to the studio to begin work on yet another album.

Songs In The Key Of Life

The three-year Motown contract signed when he was 21 was now up for renewal, so Stevie again sent in Johanan Vigoda with a list of demands to new Motown president Ewart Abner (Gordy was now company chairman). The resulting contract awarded Stevie an unheard-of $13million spread over seven years. Berry Gordy's mouth still twitches at the corners when he thinks about it: "That's a lot of money".[41] As *Time* magazine reported in its news story, Stevie's deal was worth more than the record contracts of Elton John and Neil Diamond added together.

Stevie also won the right to vet any prospective Motown purchaser, should the situation ever arise, plus a generous 20 per cent record royalty. In return Motown required one album per year, or at least seven in total (double albums would count double – thankfully for Stevie, as three of his next four LPs would be double-length, the final one largely a compilation of old tracks.) Both parties felt the deal was workable, and Stevie was happy he could continue a relationship with Motown.

At the contract-signing he said: "I'm staying at Motown, because it is the only viable surviving black-owned company in the record industry. Motown represents hopes and opportunity for new as well as established black performers and producers. If it were not for Motown, many of us just wouldn't have had the shot we've had at success and fulfillment. It is vital that people in our business – particularly the black creative community, including artists, writers and producers – make sure that Motown stays emotionally stable, spiritually strong, and economically healthy." (Did you say *$13 million…?*)

At least he'd be able to afford some diapers when his new partner Yolanda Simmons gave birth to

Next page: Stevie with Motown bosses Berry Gordy and Ewart Abner – he's seen here presenting his contract-fulfilling *Original Musiquarium* album master tapes in 1982

Aisha Zakiya, a healthy (and evidently "lovely") baby girl, on April 7th 1975. Stevie had by now bought two houses, one in Manhattan, one in California, to act as bases while he was in the studio working on the first couple of projects from that seven-album deal.

In the meantime rumours were flapping around the press that Stevie was going to live in Ghana (the African country from which he believed his ancestors could be traced) in order to work with handicapped children there. Motown quashed that one pretty smartly, though Stevie did in fact set up a home there in later years. Stevie also visited South Africa with a view to moving there – which seems extraordinary, given the local politics, but he really did. (He would become very involved in the anti-apartheid cause – he was even arrested in the early 1980s for taking part in protests outside the South African embassy in Washington DC, which helped lead to the US imposing economic sanctions on the South African regime.)

The list of charities, deserving causes, and political campaigns that Stevie supported (and still supports) is extensive; he was recognised for his "humanitarian efforts and artistic brilliance" on Washington DC's *Human Kindness Day* in May 1975, which preceded a gig in front of 200,000 people in the Washington monument grounds.

A trip to Jamaica, jamming with Bob Marley, made a lasting impression too. Stevie donated $40,000 to a local school for the blind, and took part in a benefit concert there with Marley in November 1975 – the last time the original Wailers played together.

As we've seen, there had been intimations that Stevie's business affairs were at times dangerously disorganised, and there were corporate forces pulling him in different directions. It was a stressful time for him, as those close to him were well aware. As early as 1974, Margouleff and Cecil gave an interview to *Newsweek* that contained some alarm-raising comments.

Margouleff started by saying: "The Beatles changed the Sixties and Stevie has the power to change the Seventies, but you have to understand the pressure he's under. Unless he's prepared not to worry so much about his allegiance to the drones, they are going to pull him down and isolate him from the very things that made him good."

Cecil was even more frank on the subject: "Stevie's area of genius is music, and in other areas, although he's very competent, he's still only 24. He has to deal with many levels of his reality through the eyes and trust of many other people. I wouldn't put up with the crap his organisation puts me through if I didn't believe Stevie has the power to be a very, very important figure, and not just musically. His product does more than sell millions of records. It reaches people and breaks down ethnic barriers. All of a sudden there's money going from the white people to the black people, even if it's only for their bloody music."[42]

The 'drones' and the 'organisation' that Margouleff and Cecil felt were dragging Stevie astray, and putting them through 'crap', obviously became an insurmountable barrier for the production pair, and matters came to a head after the *Fulfillingness* album. The musical team that had so effectively launched Stevie on his album career – coaching him with synthesisers, coaxing his vocal performances, advising him on material – was disbanded (an appropriate term, as it must have felt like a band at times).

So Stevie was left on his own to produce the next album, which was being labelled alternately as *FFF2*, *We Are Seeing A Lot*, *Let's See Life The Way It Is*, but ended up as *Songs In The Key Of Life*.

The delay in releasing *Songs In The Key Of Life* (let's call it *SITKOL*) was due to Stevie's need to perfect every mix. He had picked up Gordy's habit of remixing again and again, which didn't sit well with delivering a record for release. This was the longest he had ever spent working on an album.

One deadline was missed, which Motown attempted to cash in on by producing a 'We're Almost Finished' T-shirt. From the middle of 1975, there was a 60'x270' hoarding up in New York spectacularly advertising the album – over a year prematurely, as it turned out. The public anticipation created huge advance orders – 1,300,000 in the States alone. Word also got around that Stevie couldn't squeeze all the songs onto a normal double album, and the package would instead consist of two LPs plus a four-track EP.

The official Motown release date was October 8th 1976 (though other sources put it back at the end of September). The bizarre launch in the rustic setting of Longview Farm, Massachusetts, featured Stevie in a cowboy suit and ten-gallon hat, with a couple of albums hanging from his gun belt.

His statement to the press was equally enigmatic: "An idea is to me a farmed thought in the subconscious, the unknown and sometimes sought-for impossibilities, but when believed strong enough, can become a reality … So let it be that I shall live the idea of the song and use its words as my sight into the unknown."

There's more of the same on the sleeve notes: "It is important that you do note permanently in your mind that I do not take a second for granted. For I do believe it is that Stevie Wonder is the necessary vehicle on which Stevland Morris must be carried on his mission to spread love mentalism … [*SITKOL*] is only a conglomerate of thoughts in my subconscious that my Maker decided to give me strength, the love+love-hate=love energy making it possible for me to bring to my conscious an idea…" – and so it goes on.

The massive contrapuntal arrangements are gone, but there is still synthesiser everywhere on the *SITKOL* album

If that sort of language has not weathered well, unfortunately the same can be said for parts of the album itself. Those verbal meanderings are reflected in the weaknesses of much of the lyrical content of the records, and even in a way some of the music too.

The first question, of course, is what's happened to the overall sound now that Cecil and Margouleff aren't around? The departure of Tonto was bound to usher in a new era in the synth section. The massive contrapuntal arrangements are gone, but there is still synthesiser everywhere on the *SITKOL* album.

The main addition is Yamaha's new synthesiser model, the GX-1, their first polyphonic synth (meaning it could play more than one note at a time), which cost a staggering $40,000 in 1976. (The Yamaha website history adds tersely: "Yamaha sold very few models.")

Laid out like an organ, with three 'manuals' (separate keyboards), two of which were full-sized and polyphonic and the top one a smaller monophonic keyboard, the GX-1 (also mysteriously listed as a GX10) was an all-singing, all-dancing, bells-and-whistles synthesiser, the upper-class version of the aspiring middle-class CS80. It came with presets, but everything could be changed and reprogrammed; it sported a pedal board, a knee expression lever, all manner of portamento controllers, an auto rhythm box, and enough levers and knobs to keep the most demanding synthesist quiet. It was, without doubt, state-of-the-art (Keith Emerson had one as well, so it must have been).

Stevie referred to the GX-1 as his "dream machine", and if you want to hear it in full string emulation mode go no further than 'Village Ghetto Land' for a demonstration – it's the only instrument on the track, so he must have thought it sounded good. And so it does, if a little flat and lifeless when the ear is accustomed to the Tonto soundscape. (Could it be that what was quirky, and probably annoying, about the practicalities of the Tonto set-up also gave it added colour?)

The involvement of so many musicians contributes to the large-scale feel of the album

The older synths are used for basslines and lead single line contributions, but the change of production direction heralds a larger degree of involvement from the Wonderlove members and other sessioneers. Nathan Watts is on bass, Mike Sembello and Ben Bridges on guitars, and there are even a couple of drummers, Raymond Pounds and Greg Brown. There was also percussion, horn players, BVs, and then the keyboards of Greg Phillinganes – the Detroit-born musician who relocated to LA to become everybody's first call (including Michael Jackson's). The involvement of so many musicians contributes to the large-scale all-encompassing feel of the *SITKOL* album.

Stevie had grand visions for the concept – like a Mahler symphony, he wanted all life to be there: "To me that was a challenge, to do an album relating to life…" – though he also realised the obvious pitfalls of such an ambition: "It's impossible to cover all of what life is about."[43]

With 21 tracks it's pretty comprehensive, but inevitably falls short of the initial vision. There are songs ("to make you smile") about childhood nostalgia, spiritual/religious need, black pride, musical/jazz figureheads, lost love, found love, endless love, the need for more love, planetary travel… the list goes on. The whole project is peppered with catchy tunes, chords that are generally more obvious than before (and therefore more immediate), funky horn lines, and impeccable vocal arrangements.

I have to come clean and admit here that side four of *SITKOL* was my Sunday morning tonic for a few years – the sense of positivity and ease was restorative after a complicated Saturday night. Gone are the introverted chord movements of *Innervisions*, instead it's 'play those major chords, and if they're working, why make it more complex?' I wouldn't want to give the impression that subtlety has gone out of the window – there's plenty of musical artistry to admire – but the lighter and more varied mood is refreshing after the relative seriousness of *FFF*, and the stripped-down approach works a treat on a couple of tracks.

It's an important album to many people. In 2004 Elton John told *Rolling Stone*, "Wherever I go in the world, I always take a copy of *Songs In The Key Of Life*. For me, it's the best album ever made, and I'm always left in awe after I listen to it."

So, if it's so good, are the contributions of Cecil and Margouleff missed at all?

Well for one thing they might have kept the project at a more manageable length by knowing when to stop. The songs sprawl over six sides of vinyl (four large, two small) partly to give them room to breathe, but more often because the faders have simply not been pulled down in time. For instance on 'Isn't She Lovely' (more of which in the 'pop' section, Chapter 9), is the harmonica solo a tad over-indulgent? Is the repetition at the end of 'Ordinary Pain' rather painful? Haven't we got the message of 'Black Man' way before the end? Does 'Love's In Need Of Love Today' outstay its welcome?

And yet, you have to say, in the majority of cases the groove carries the feel-good factor well after logic has said 'enough'. Basically, the songs do feel good. But we've become so accustomed to the three-minute pop song – largely thanks to labels like Motown (although the song time-limit idea most likely originated from the maximum playing time you could squeeze onto a 78rpm disc). Maybe there's a west-east cultural issue here too. Western music is mostly harmony/chord-based, constantly shifting towards a goal – and hanging around is not usually an option. The eastern approach is often melody-led, and any time spent in deliberation – or, in modern parlance, chilling – is not wasted but valued. It's also the reason some music works incredibly well on-stage but doesn't translate to record. Would 'Another Star' have felt so long in a live version?

There's clearly no attempt at a single 'direction' on *SITKOL* – with 21 songs spread over such a diverse range of styles, you wouldn't expect there to be. Instead you get the feeling you're walking through a gallery of paintings gathered from various periods of an artist's work, displaying a huge range of influences, employing the whole spectrum of colours – but each recognisably the work of the same artist. The viewer doesn't mind that the individual paintings don't make up a sum total, you're just happy they've been gathered in one place to enjoy.

One thing that I find does grate after a gap of almost 30 years is the occasional evangelising tendency of the lyrics. The poetic distance-through-imagery is too often replaced by an over-literal directness – so in 'Have A Talk With God' you get lines like: "He's the only free psychiatrist that's known throughout the world/For solving the problems of all men, women, little boys and girls."

I also feel that most people have an aversion to being told how to behave – even by someone they admire (in 'Love's In Need Of Love Today' we're entreated: "Don't delay/Send yours in right away/ … Stop it please/Before it's gone too far." These are noble sentiments and strong beliefs, to be sure, but I don't think I'm being too harsh in saying that Stevie had begun putting himself on the pedestal of world improvement, and was beginning to feel drunk with evangelical power – his own sense of stature inflated by success, and by those around him.

Stevie was beginning to feel drunk with evangelical power – his own sense of stature inflated by success, and by those around him

Perhaps this is a tendency that Margouleff and Cecil had to some extent helped keep a lid on. They generally encouraged and fostered a more matter-of-fact, down-to-earth approach to the work, unimpressed and unhindered by any notions of pop icon status or overblown egos.

I guess for those of us who have never been in the position of a star at the top of the tree, we can't imagine how tempting it might be to preach a little. But it's certainly the case that self-righteousness is not a predictable path to continued success.

There's a very strange angle at the end of the sleeve notes as well: "And finally to those who are unknown and who for various reasons, including devotion to duty and love for this project, lost their loves in the long and hard journey to completion of this album – may they live to love better!" Sounds more like a memorial to an unknown fallen soldier, or as if he's saying: 'Well done to all of you for sacrificing your love lives, I'm sure you feel it was worth it for the sake of a few songs...'

Enough negativity: let's look at some of the more positive aspects on display – and there are plenty. The final out-chorus of 'Love's In Need...' features a scat/improvised solo (or almost-solo) that's an impressive display of expressive vocal technique; the bare, classical/George Martinesque string synth arrangement coupled with stark lyrics like "Families buying dog food now..." (words from DJ Gary Bird) is effective as a contrast. Meanwhile 'Contusion' helps define the funky side of the 'jazz-rock' genre through Sembello's guitar, and the 'Sir Duke' vocal/horn arrangements brim with energy to the point of overflowing.

'I Wish' offers a tribute to James Jamerson in its wonderfully flowing and shaped bass/Rhodes line. Notice the pattern: down six steps and back up via small steps (E♭, C♭, A♭, B♭, A♭, C, D♭, D etc) – classic Nathan Watts, classic swung-funk feel.

'I Wish' offers a tribute to James Jamerson in its wonderfully flowing and shaped bassline

The pastoral piano-based colours of 'Knocks Me Off My Feet' and 'Summer Soft' sandwich the stringy 'Pastime Paradise', which challenges us to reject the past and look to "the peace of the world", with the aid of various denominations of choir (see Chapter 10).

'Ordinary Pain' is another song with dual sections, this time presenting both male and female sides of the argument: Shirley Brewer excels on the female lead vocal 'reply', but I still feel there's not sufficient development to merit the length. No, let's keep positive...

'Isn't She Lovely' showcases a joyous harmonica in a celebration of the birth of daughter Aisha, which sounds so much better than you remember it. (Speaking of tricks of memory, UK readers in particular may be under the impression that Stevie released this as a single at the time, but no, it was only issued in cover version form by singer David Parton, who had a Top Five hit with it in 1977.)

The unusual and memorable melody of 'Joy Inside My Tears' sits beautifully syncopated over the funk/ballad rhythm track. If you must have a two-bar riff that revolves for eight-and-a-half minutes, then it has to be well constructed – fortunately 'Black Man' is. With lyrics again by Gary Bird, it sports a symmetrical top and bottom line that's almost visual in its breathing architecture (like a chest rising and falling). Plus the bassline is a killer, again.

'Ngiculela – Es Una Historia – I Am Singing' (a Zulu/Spanish multicultural love song) may be on the oversweetened counter, but when Stevie says "I am singing", he really is singing. And it's such an innocent tune.

The second of the 'stripped-down tracks, 'If It's Magic' features the harp (that's the string-type, not harmonica) of Dorothy Ashby, a Detroit jazz player who lends the right delicacy of touch – the original version with piano (heard in earlier out-takes) sounds heavy-handed by comparison, though it points up the inner chromatic descending line on the bridge.

The insistence of 'As' is compelling, thanks to the jazz interest in keys and voice (see Chapter 10 for more). 'Another Star' takes a Latin sequence and piles on the texture: horns, percussion, guitar and flute all hooked to the groove wagon (more in the Latin quarter, see Chapter 8.)

The accompanying EP opens with 'Saturn' – originally called 'Saginaw', but it seems Sembello, in a Chinese whispers sort of a way, took it somewhere else. This track highlights some brassy GX-1 sounds (Emerson used similar ones in ELP's 'Fanfare For The Common Man') and some earthy synth bass slides (mirrored elsewhere by Nathan Watts on bass guitar).

Diana Ross seems to be the subject of 'Ebony Eyes' ("Miss beautiful supreme"), while the music has shades of 'Dock Of The Bay'/gospel/music hall piano, with some vocoded/'bagged' voices and an un-flattering sax sound. (Sorry, I *will* be more positive…)

'All Day Sucker' welcomes back the clavinet and starts well intentioned, as does 'Easy Goin' Evening (My Mama's Call)', a harmonica multi-tracked instrumental that recalls a lazy 'on the porch' feel, and uses the jazz language of 'Too High' to good effect (triads over an unrelated root), bringing the album to a conclusion with the 'popping' of stopped harmonica notes.

The horns deserve a special mention on this album: with Lawrence and Madaio still on board, the addition of Hank Redd (alto sax) and Raymond Maldonado (trumpet) provides a fuller sound without having to resort to overdubs. The phrasing is impeccable throughout, as are the backing vocalists. As a player Mike Sembello makes a memorable contribution with his guitar work (he's also credited as co-writer on 'Saturn').

All in all, two-and-a-half records of top tunes, not always best produced (the mixes are not as clear as they might be), but staggering in the width of the vision and the achievement. As the lyric of 'Sir Duke' has it: "Just because a record has a groove don't make it in the groove" – but there's no doubting this one was as embedded in the groove as it became in the public consciousness.

In 1977, to imagine that Stevie Wonder could have run out steam as a writer would have been considered anathema

On the *Billboard* chart *SITKOL* entered at Number One (in the UK its top position was Number Two – Stevie's highest-charting album ever in Britain), and the singles 'I Wish' and 'Sir Duke' were both US Number Ones (pretty close in the UK). Edited versions of 'Another Star' and 'As' made less impact on the charts, just breaking the Top 40 – although 'As' would provide a UK Top Five hit in 1999 for George Michael and Mary J. Blige.

Paul Simon, in his acceptance speech at the Grammy Awards ceremony in 1976, had thanked Stevie for not issuing an album in 1975, "to give the rest of us a chance". But in 1977 it was business as usual at the Grammys: *Songs In The Key Of Life* was Best Album Of The Year, and Stevie was voted Best Producer and Best Male R&B Vocal (for 'I Wish'), and Best Male Pop Vocal. This brought his grand total for the last four years to 17 Grammys – and that's including a year off.

The journey from Michigan ghetto to leafy Los Angeles, busker to superstar, harmonica and bongo player to complete multi-instrumentalist musician, from confident and showy teenager to writer of several of the best albums of popular music, was a tortuous and remarkable one. In 1977, to imagine that Stevie Wonder could have run out of steam as a writer would have been considered anathema. But the fact is that, whether you think his later work is of higher or lower quality, Stevie would never write and perform material that sounded like, or had the impact on society of, those five early Seventies albums: *Music Of My Mind, Talking Book, Innervisions, Fulfillingness' First Finale,* and *Songs In The Key Of Life.*

I've already noted some of the songs on these albums as candidates for closer examination, and that's what I'll be doing over the next several chapters. I've grouped the tracks in themed categories – even though some of the songs would easily fit into several of the categories – just to make it simpler to trace stylistic developments. The categories I've opted for are: funk, ballads, social comment, Latin, pop statements, and jazz (incorporating miscellaneous, hard-to-classify styles).

The categorisation criteria are based more on the music than the lyrics – a 'love' category would probably contain most of Stevie's songs. The scrutiny of individual tracks is also mostly musical in approach, though the lyrics and historical background are looked at where appropriate, and the technical language is hopefully kept within manageable limits (there's a short glossary at the back of the book that'll help the less musical readers with the odd explanation).

As an introduction to Stevie's work, the four-CD box set *At The Close Of A Century* contains many of the tracks covered in the following chapters, but I would recommend having the relevant original album handy while reading about it – hopefully it will all make more sense that way.

Just after the release of *Songs In The Key Of Life*, Stevie told *Rock Around The World*: "If you listen to the songs I've written, or to the songs of others I record, you will hear how I feel. I guess it's the deepest me. Sometimes I feel that the people who listen to my music, or the fans that I have, are closer to me than some of the people who are my close acquaintances or friends."

The idea behind the next few chapters is that close-listening will shed more light on an amazing musician, skillful songwriter, and a remarkable personality.

CHAPTER 5
FUNK

'**Keep On Running**'
(from *Music Of My Mind*)
'**Superstition**' (from *Talking Book*)
'**Boogie On Reggae Woman**'
(from *Fulfillingness' First Finale*)

O K, we'll start by trying a definition of funk. How about this: "Music of an African-American blues origin with at least one syncopated element, a weighty bass part, and drums with a heavy accent on beats one and three, backbeat on or somewhere near beats two and four." Not a very snappy description, but it's as close as mere words can get – it's certainly no substitute for listening and *feeling* a funk groove. Obvious examples? James Brown's 'Get up (I Feel Like Being A Sex Machine)'; The Meters' 'Cissy Strut'; almost anything by Prince; and Stevie Wonder's 'Superstition'.

There are many claims on the title 'inventor of funk', and as with most historical matters, the origins and development of the style and the people responsible for its creation are not inscribed in black and white (as it were). But the first port of call has to be "the hardest working man in showbiz" himself, James Brown.

James Brown's is an archetypal story of black music business experience in the mid 20th century: from a poor background, growing up in his aunt's brothel, he was convicted of armed robbery and car theft at age 16. After dabbling in sports (including boxing, naturally) he started working in bars and drew the attention of Little Richard's manager. Playing organ and drums with various gospel/R&B line-ups, he ended up with a black touring revue called The Famous Flames, in which he not only played several instruments but danced as well (any of this sound familiar?).

Despite the R&B chart success of singles like 'Please, Please, Please' and 'Try Me', major record company backing was hard to come by, so in 1963 Brown paid almost $6,000 out of his own pocket to record his *Live At The Apollo* album – which became the most successful in-concert recording in its day, and the first pop album to sell more than a million copies. The rhythm section is still pre-funk, but some elements are starting to fit into the puzzle, such as the horn arrangement on 'Think' with its 16th-note syncopated lines.

The year 1965 is widely seen as the official birthdate of funk, with the release of Brown's single 'Papa's Got A Brand New Bag'. The bass is now notably heavier – though it still lacks a bit of sideways pull, falling straight on the beat. There's a rule of thumb in funk music that says short sounds are better than long: thus the drier the guitar hit, the tighter the horn stab, the slappier the bass, the more clipped the clavinet etc, the better. It's the bits of silence in-between these short events that builds the anticipation for the next one – the tension/release principle in rhythmic form.

Through the 1960s and early 1970s Brown and his various line-ups defined what funk would mean for generations to come: among the great musicians he hired were Maceo Parker, Fred Wesley, Pee Wee Ellis, and bassist Bootsy Collins.

Another bass player essential to funk development, Larry Graham, was working at the time with Sly Stone. Sly (Texas-born Sylvester Stewart) was another multi-instrumentalist, who had started his music career as a producer then an eclectic DJ. From the idea that various musical elements could co-exist on a radio show came the logical expansion (logical with hindsight, of course) to a band context, where facets of rock, soul, pop and the new-fangled funk could be mixed and performed on-stage. He called his band Sly & The Family Stone.

Right from their first album, *A Whole New Thing*, the funk was present. The single 'Underdog', with its offbeat horn line, and bass drum (16th-note) anticipation, set the pattern for a string of albums. *Dance To The Music* was their mainstream breakthrough, and by 1969 the formula was largely based on funk habits: the guitar high up the neck, sliding down a fret and up again, bass slapping, using the thumb to strike the string instead of fingers plucking, and drums anticipating the third beat in the bar, thereby creating a hole of tension/anticipation.

George Clinton was another fascinating and influential figure in funk history – a former staff writer for Motown, he had a hit with a vocal group called The Parliaments before 'borrowing' a large chunk of James Brown's band in the early 1970s and launching Funkadelic. Featuring psychedelic guitar, and weird stuff from the synths of Bernie Worrell, as well as the heavy funk bass of Bootsy Collins, Clinton was at that time to funk what Sun Ra was to jazz – musically adventurous, and a consummate showman, as well as responsible for one of the world's best song titles: 'Tear The Roof Off The Sucker (Give Up The Funk)'.

Thanks to Brown, Stone and Clinton, the funk was well-and-truly established. Its more cerebral offshoot, jazz-funk (pioneered by Herbie Hancock, the Brecker Brothers etc), took the basics of funk syncopation, but this became exploited over the years to the point of cliché. Then in the era of hip-hop, samplers of Seventies funk had a field day with the likes of Clinton and Brown – JB's drummer Clyde Stubblefield even acquired iconic status as the source of the 'funky drummer' rhythm sample.

Whereas Prince would take James Brown and completely recycle some of his musical tricks (as in 'Kiss', to take one of many examples), Stevie Wonder took more of a cross section of funk influences and sewed them seamlessly into the funk fabric.

Certainly Stevie could scream and holler in a Brown/Stone style, but on a musical arrangement level he was more often too concerned with song structure and harmonic movement to include the kind of one-chord, bass-riffing passages beloved of funksters. With Stevie, the song is the thing. Probably the reason that the three songs I'm going to look at in this chapter are all relatively early tracks is because Stevie's work became less stylistically funky from 1974 onwards. That doesn't mean it was no longer danceable, or it made you feel like moving about any less, but there came to be more variation in the style of grooves – above all on *Songs In The Key Of Life*.

The three songs under the microscope here represent various gradations of funk: 'Keep On Running' (not to be confused with the Spencer Davis/Steve Winwood track of the same name) is a fast-tempo, clavinet-driven, one-person jam; the same could be said for 'Superstition', except it's tighter and slower and more obviously funky; while in terms of bass and drums, 'Boogie On Reggae Woman', despite the reggae intimations, is as funky as it gets. The really extraordinary thing about these three tracks is how much energy and forward drive they still have when you listen after some 30 years or so.

'Keep On Running'

To judge the effect of a song best, it's often worth rewinding to the preceding track on the relevant album. The track before 'Keep On Running' on *Music Of My Mind*, 'Seems So Long', benefits from probably the heaviest use of atmospheric keyboards and synthesised textures on any Stevie track thus far: swirling 'Leslie' organ pads, the statement of the vocal melody at the top on lead synth, modulated rising pitch effects, rather nasal string-like parts building to the climax. All this bears out the sleeve note claim: "The man is his own instrument. The instrument is an orchestra."

But the orchestral approach and calm, settled mood are shoved brutally aside for the subsequent track. 'Keep On Running' hits the ground not so much running as stalking around, over an intro that's as stark as the somewhat sinister "someone's gonna jump out of the bushes and grab ya" lyric.

The first two bars consist of repeated notes (eighth-note A♭s) played on low bass synth and piano, which build an air of menace; the tension is increased by the clavinet riff (G♭ to A♭), again repeated notes but this time twice as fast, which requires a fair degree of technique to maintain. Tambourine rolls and oddly-spaced drum hits increase the sense of anticipation before finally it comes to a halt, after a good 24 bars. Then the piano, playing in suitably disco-esque octaves (and notes: E♭, G♭ and G leading to the A♭ tonic) points up the main groove, and they're off and running.

When I say 'they', obviously it's just Stevie playing everything here, but the overall effect is so tight and 'in the pocket' that the resultant groove has a real band feel to it. Jogging along at 136bpm, it's the clavinets that provide the energetic centre. In terms of overdubbing parts to form a greater whole, it's a triumph. Not one clav part, not even two, but three, honking along beside each other in a perfect wired mesh. Add to that a fairly unobtrusive bass synth part, a slightly roguish piano (more of that later) and skippy but driving drums, and you have the funkiest groove on *Music Of My Mind* – all executed by one person, in a very intense jam. One instrument, indeed.

As ever it's the things you can't quite tie down that are the most interesting features in a song, and this one is full of them. The most obvious is the key. Is this in a major or a minor key? The thing that defines major or minor is the 3rd note of the scale, and that occurs here in the first line of the first verse on the '-in' of 'runnin''. It's definitely a minor 3rd (C♭), as is the top note of the just-right-of-centre wah-clav part. And yet, on the inside of one of the clavinet parts (it really does get impossible to tell which) is a major 3rd (C natural), which is reinforced on the second vocal phrase by the voice scooping up almost to the major.

Why is this important? Mainly because it shows Stevie's debt to the blues tradition, where there's an ambivalence of major/minor compared to the more strait-laced European approach to classical (and pop) harmony.

It's just Stevie playing everything here, but the overall effect is so tight and 'in the pocket', the resultant groove has a real band feel to it

The bridge that follows the short (eight-bar) verse doesn't provide too many clues either, although vocally it's more weighted towards a minor. Halfway through the bridge there's a crunch chord (E♭7♯9) that contains both 3rds, serving as the archetypal blues/jazz tensioner. There's not much resolution either, as we're led back to another verse via that rogue piano break mentioned earlier.

The rhythm track halts for a second while voice and piano, in somewhat rough unison, execute (almost literally) a just-south-of-pentatonic 16th-note run that seems to land over the edge of the piano somewhere in time to be rescued by the restarting rhythm section. Whether Stevie knew what he was trying to play or not doesn't really matter; the end effect is one of helter-skelter pursuit and stumble. Next time around it's even clumsier, and as for the third time... it's a scramble down and up the piano in an anarchic starburst of pent-up energy.

It's the second break that leads finally to the chorus, where there's a couple more surprises. Firstly the lead vocal doesn't sing the chorus tag, and secondly the chorus melody line is angled more to the major – some sort of resolution at last. Stevie gives the chorus vocal to a 'choir' made up of (it sounds like) himself and some female voices, possibly Syreeta and/or Yvonne Wright, who both have co-writing credits on *MOMM*, though there are no mentions for extra vocalists on the album. The other explanation is that it's his own voice 'sped-up' to heighten the pitch and double-tracked for the BVs – a studio trick he wouldn't be beyond considering. Once the chorus is in, it's going to run and run, and with the exception of a bridge, a couple of instrumental breakdowns and a few 'hey hey heys', it's there for the duration.

It's quite a duration too: the first chorus is at 1:53 and the track ends at 6:35. Reminiscent of the extended fade in The Beatles' 'Hey Jude', both in the chorus repetition and the freedom Stevie has to improvise over the chorus vocals, it's a fade-out-and-a-half.

Is the chorus line strong enough to take it? Well, the melody line is certainly pretty intriguing: it swoops downwards and loops around again in an obsessive way that mirrors the persistence in the lyrics ("I know I'm gonna get you in the end"). The chord harmony underneath is also fairly static and repetitive ($A\flat$ for two bars, $D\flat9$ for two), and if it wasn't for the exuberance and shifting improvised patterns of the backing track, and the invention of Stevie's ad lib main vocal, there wouldn't be much to hang on to in terms of interest.

There's not a moment where you feel like saying, 'Stop the tape and go back, the timing's not quite right there'

To come off the fence, yes, it probably does outstay its welcome – despite the fine performances and differences in texture provided in the breakdowns. The second of these, at around four minutes in, provides an opportunity for the synth bass to come out from under the shadow of the clavinets' incessant chattering with a funkier line (even incorporating gaps) that harks back to classic Motown/Jamerson days. Yes it's that shape again, with the offbeat chromatic stepping. It also looks forward to the busier but transcendentally funky bass part of 'Boogie On Reggae Woman'.

The way the three clavinet parts combine contributes to the overall funk level. While one of them sticks to the repeated note idea, another (over on the right of the stereo field) has a heavy hit on beat two and a very short one on beat 'four-and'. The third clav seems to hover between the two main parts, more of a floating voter, unwilling or unable to commit, just keeping an eye on the balance of power and shifting accordingly.

Two of the parts run through an 'auto-wah' pedal, which also increases the funk quotient. The original 'Cry Baby' wah-wah pedal, as used by guitarists since the mid-to-late 1960s, works by varying the tone as you step through the range of a footpedal. As you move your foot up and down it cuts out high frequencies (and/or low ones), resulting in the sobbing sound that gives the unit its name. Jimi Hendrix's 'Voodoo Chile', most Frank Zappa solos, and many early late-Sixties/early Seventies Motown records used the fashionable psychedelic sound. Norman Whitfield (who produced The Temptations' 'Cloud Nine') was responsible for getting in Dennis Coffey and 'Wah-Wah' Watson on Motown sessions as wah-wah specialists.

An auto-wah either moves in its own time, sweeping the frequencies automatically, or else responds to what is being fed into it, triggering a filter, with the sound itself dependent on volume and pitch. Guitar pedals were used by keyboardists in the early days to enhance the sound of Rhodes, clavs, anything they had. Phased, chorused, distorted or flanged effects were up for grabs too. These days an auto-wah is included as a built-in effect in most synths. (Engineer/programmer Paul Wiffen, who also worked on the sound for live shows, revealed that, by the 1980s at least, Stevie wasn't too fussed about what keyboard he used in order to get a clavinet sound – a Yamaha DX7 synth would do – as long as it went through the auto-wah pedal.)

To return to 'Keep On Running': I wonder how long it would take the average player to record those three inter-weaving clavinet tracks, at least without the aid of modern computer quantisation which pulls stray notes into time. There's not a moment where you feel like saying, 'Stop the tape and go back, the timing's not quite right there'.

The drum part is strangely funky – it lies underneath the tambourine/clavinet/piano texture, beavering away without much weight, adding more than occasional inventive fills (lots of 16th-note snares), and with a busy bass drum pattern. Not only does it hit every beat, but others in-between (8th and 16th-note anticipations), emphasising the skipping/stumbling nature of the track.

The freedom and fluidity of the hi-hat is noteworthy too. It typifies a Stevie Wonder drum track: start with a pattern, keep it going only until boredom threatens, then add a bit extra, before returning to something like you were doing before. (Judging by the amount of change and invention that goes into his recordings, I'd imagine Stevie has a fairly low boredom threshold.) That's probably the reason his early Seventies rhythm tracks generally sound un-mechanical in their execution – the performance is not a dry exercise in keeping a part going, more a celebration of energy, movement and invention. It's an instinctive skill.

A quick word about jamming. It's normally a band exercise, though obviously not in this case. Jamming can be all sorts of things to different people, but broadly it involves establishing an idea – it could be a riff/chord sequence/drum groove/whatever – then playing with the material, developing it, but normally keeping the groove while vocal ad libs/solos/ improvisations are added on top. It's a risky business on-stage – if there are dull moments they can be very dull – but as a rehearsal routine, jamming is a great way to come up with new ideas. Stevie's studio jams with himself work pretty well 90 per cent of the time, with enough going on to keep the listener interested. This is especially crucial when, as is the case this time, the track has come to the end in songwriting terms, and is hanging around waiting for the axe to fall.

Eventually 'Keep On Running' does come to an end, slowing to a final chorus tag and a flurry of studio applause. Again the drama of album compilation comes into its own as 'Evil' juxtaposes its dark mood – straight from the heat of the chase to the disturbing, portentous synths that close the *MOMM* album.

'Superstition'

There's no doubt that 'Superstition' had a difficult pregnancy and birth. It's all tied up with Cecil and Margouleff producing Jeff Beck, the ex-Yardbirds guitarist, at Electric Lady studios. The story goes that Stevie had met Beck in London and the two had agreed Jeff could do a version of Stevie's 'Maybe Your Baby' for his own album. They met again in New York by which time Stevie had changed his mind, he wanted to keep the song for himself, but instead he offered Beck 'Superstition' to record. (The way Beck tells it, it was he who originally inspired the groove for 'Superstition' anyway, when messing about on Stevie's drum kit in the studio, and that's why Stevie donated it to him.)

But it seems when Stevie heard Beck's version of 'Superstition,' he revised his opinion and tried to hang on to the song again, realising its potential. Beck's record label, Columbia, were naturally hacked off at this, and it seemingly soured Margouleff & Cecil's relations with Beck. By this time Motown had sussed that a huge single was possible here, and despite Stevie's attempts at a conciliatory move, suggesting they release 'Big Brother' as the first single off *Talking Book*, or even 'You Are The Sunshine Of My Life', Motown were adamant that 'Superstition' be issued right away.

Stevie later explained: "I told Motown it was going to cause a lot of static, but they said, 'No, man.' They had control of releasing the singles."[44] And so, on October 24th 1972, Stevie's 'Superstition' was finally let loose – a forceps delivery, but a very healthy baby.

A shall-we-say disappointed Jeff Beck released his own version on the album *Beck, Bogart & Appice* in 1973. Despite this episode, Stevie and Jeff worked together again, and Beck recorded two Wonder tunes on his 1975 classic *Blow By Blow*. Beck of course appears elsewhere on *Talking Book*, lending his sliding and bendy-note style to 'Looking For Another Pure Love'.

There's no mystery to the main notes of the riff – a pentatonic run of steady eighth-notes … it's the 'ghost-notes' in-between where the funk resides

When 'Superstition' first hit the shops, it wasn't an immediate success – it took over three months to climb to the top of the charts. But by January 27th 1973 it had reached Number One in both the pop and R&B charts – the first time Stevie had done so since 'Fingertips' back in 1963.

If a hit single has to push as many positive buttons as possible, this one never misses. Cool but very funky drum intro, aggressive clavinet arrangement, direct lyric, strongly delivered, hooky horn arrangement, James Brown-ish song climax… are we there yet?

Stevie wanted to showcase his clavinet (Hohner model C) as being "a funky, dirty, stinky, nasty instrument."[45] I guess having just come off a Rolling Stones tour you would naturally be wanting to emulate some of the dirt found in Keith Richard's raw and rancid repository of rock'n'roll riffs. In a way comparison is unfair, as the 'nastiness' of a clavinet can never quite match the rawness of a hard-driven electric guitar and the way that makes you feel. The clavinet maybe doesn't touch the same raw nerve, but you can't deny it's more than a bit funky.

After the drum intro (more of which in a minute) the clav riff starts, and you hear it once in its entirety before a second clav comes winging its way in from the right side of the mix. This gives you just two bars to figure out how it's done, what exactly he's playing. The task isn't made any easier by the fact that the first clav part has a short delay on it, which is brought back behind and central in the overall mix.

There's no mystery to the main notes of the riff: a pentatonic (black-note) run of steady eighth-notes that works from the bottom (E♭) up and down again (roughly E♭-D♭-E♭-F♯-E♭-D♭/A♭-B♭-D♭-E♭-F♯-E♭-D♭). But it's the 'ghost' notes in-between where the funk resides. If vocalised it would sound like 'ker-chah-ka' — a choked collection of notes around beat four. It's the clavinet at its best, sounding like a damped guitar stroke, and yes, like a more than suitable definition of funk.

Funk is all about timing. The first thing you notice about the hi-hats on the intro is that they're not straight notes but swung: 'duk duk-ka/duk duk-ka/duk duk-ka/duk-ka duk'. Not swung as in jazz at its strictest, but a lazier swing. Drum programmers nowadays are accustomed to adjusting the percentage of 'swing' of a track – 'maximum swing' of the two parts of the 'duk-ka' would mean the 'duk' being twice as long as the 'ka', whereas no swing at all would make them the same length, and of course there's all stations in-between. (Time for a drink, I feel…)

The 'only-just swung' is probably the hardest to play, as you have to keep it evenly subtle, but in terms of groove it provides exactly the right mix of laid-back and swung. (And let's make it quite clear, I'm not talking here about Dixieland/trad-jazz type of swing, as played by men in beards and stripey straw hats.)

The advantage of being the only rhythm player on a song is of course you can more easily match the same feel from track to track – check how well the clav line and the snare fill line up in bar eight. The drum sound itself serves the funk groove too: as dry as the Sahara at noon, bass drum punchy and round, snare crisp but not thin.

Come to think of it, how many times is that snare being hit? All the backbeat snare hits seem to be flammed – hit twice in quick succession, just slightly out of time so you hear two attacks. This carries on throughout the song, and is a clear attempt to beef up the drum sound. In comparison to the Motown drummers, Stevie isn't generally a hard player. John Lennon once observed, "the Motown drummer hit a snare with so much force it sounded like he hit it with a bloody tree". That's the effect being pursued here.

The synth bass part is mostly simple and to the point – there's nothing quite like a repeated note for tying a track to its moorings (as Larry Graham and Trevor Horn are well aware). The tone of the bass synth is very finely adjusted, just the right degree of cut to allow it to sit below the sharp-as-a-razor clavinets, slotting in at the true bass end of the mix. Things do heat up in the bass part, but I'll come back to that later. The key contributes to the depth of the bass part too; we're used to hearing the bottom note of an electric bass (E1), but this is in a typically black-note key, pitched a half-step lower (E♭1).

So far, then, it's drums, clavinets and bass providing the backbone of the groove. Actually, that's all there is. No superfluous parts here, no spare ribs. Lean as a marathon-running cow.

We get eight bars of everything playing and then the vocals chime in – good enough vocals to earn a Grammy in 1974 for 'Best R&B Performance, Male' (pipped to the 'Best Pop Vocal Performance, Male' by his own 'You Are The Sunshine Of My Life'). It's a snappy series of lyrics that provides the perfect foil to the majority of the album's concern with love and relationships ('Big Brother' aside). 'Superstition' runs with the idea that lack of knowledge and understanding, allied to an unquestioning trust in supernatural notions, is a dangerous combination. An unlikely stance, you might think, for someone with a firm set of religious beliefs, but superstition here is equated with anti-faith, the devil's work. The biblical references ("writing on the wall", "wash your face and hands" and "the devil's on his way") re-inforce the Christian viewpoint.

The bridge section and hook-line (look, no chorus), all crammed economically into four bars (see, no flab), provide the kernel of the lyric:

"When you believe in things that you don't understand,
Then you suffer,
Superstition ain't the way."

The verses cite various superstitious habits that us frail humans find hard to eradicate from our common or cultural background:

"Very superstitious, writing's on the wall,
Very superstitious, ladders 'bout to fall,
Thirteen-month-old baby, broke the lookin' glass
Seven years of bad luck, the good things in your past."

The second verse seems to veer towards a more personal experience, but it's a murky depth to fathom:

"Rid me of the problem, do all that you can,
Keep me in a daydream, keep me goin' strong,
You don't wanna save me, sad is my song."

Stevie said near the time of release: "The worst thing is, the more you believe in it, the more bad things really happen to you. You're so afraid that something terrible is going to come up, that you are much more vulnerable."

If individual sections are hard to follow, the main thrust of the lyric is clear enough, and very effective. Ideal syllables for syncopation too: in the hook-line, only the first and third syllables fall on beat, while some of the verse lines hardly touch ground at all.

The vocal seems conservatively placed in the range to begin with, but soon reaches the upper limits as the tune progresses. Vocal highlights include a fabulous falsetto "aah" (an incredible $E\flat4$ to $G\flat4$) at the end of the instrumental bridge, around two-and-a-half minutes in, and the second time he sings "13-month-old baby". Mere mortals need not apply to sing that one.

It might well be its economy that helps 'Superstition' remain so immediate ... in this case less is very definitely more

No BVs, no vocal overdubs – one straight vocal track and no fuss. It might well be this kind of economy that helps 'Superstition' remain so immediate. All the sounds are very up-front, with space to inhabit, and in this case less is very definitely more.

The one feature of this tune not covered so far is the horn arrangement. Trevor Laurence plays saxophone and Steve Madaio trumpet in a kind of patchwork-quilt arrangement. The approach, particularly at the end, where various snippets of the arrangement loop around over other sections,

Stevie in the studio with guitarist Jeff Beck during the *Talking Book* sessions, 1972 –
as well as his 'Superstition' connections, Jeff played the teasingly delicate guitar parts on
'Looking For Another Pure Love'

is more reminiscent of today's hard disk cut-and-paste techniques: record something then shove it around and see if it fits. The two players obviously worked hard by overdubbing themselves (unless it's all done with mirrors – or rather delays) to make a large section sound. The two parts are basically unison, trumpet up an octave above the sax to give extra bite where necessary.

For me the gem in the brass chart is the point during the verse where the riff is starting to become familiar, so Stevie obviously felt something else was needed to keep momentum running high. At that juncture brass and bass join in riff number two, giving the bass a chance to shine (I told you it would) and the brass a chance to show off some very fine phrasing. The brass timing on the stabs before the word "superstition" is rather strange, and I think provides more evidence of the use of delays – it's a very fast triplet figure (triplet semiquavers), made more complex by the sound treatment.

Needless to say, most people who bought the 'Superstition' single and sent it to Number One would have been largely unconcerned with brass triplets and more worried about *having a good time*. Which it's pretty hard not to do listening to this, unless your legs and hips have become completely divorced from your ears.

'Boogie On Reggae Woman'

The presence of 'Boogie On' on *Fulfillingness' First Finale* – an album that was intended to reflect Stevie's increased spiritual and personal awareness after his accident – is a reminder of far more earthy matters such as lust, and even frustration. (It was originally worked on at the same time as 'Jesus Children Of America, but didn't make *Innervisions*, unsurprisingly, given its mood.)

Sex and love get bound together into a longing for a woman who is driving the singer mad with a dancing display guaranteed to excite the more basic urges. Again it's interesting how many times imagined sight is mentioned:

"I'd like to see both of us
Fall deeply in love – yeah
I'd like to see you in the raw
Under the stars above."

If it's hard for Stevie to imagine what a woman looks like 'in the raw', it's equally hard for us to imagine what he sees when he imagines a woman 'in the raw'... Anyway, moving swiftly onwards, there's a fine tradition of 'boogie' and 'reggae' connections to explore.

"Boogie on reggae woman
What is wrong with me
Boogie on reggae woman
Baby can't you see."

Although in this context 'boogie' presumably means dance, there are all sorts of other fruitier resonances for the word. Let's dispense with one of them quickly and efficiently – it's a synonym for sex. The early history of blues, jazz and boogie-woogie is all tied up with brothels, liquor, and dance – embodied by those dubious places of gentlemen's entertainment known as 'honky-tonks'. (The

Rolling Stones were certainly aware of the history – just think of 'Honky-Tonk Women' with its tale of a Memphis "gin-soaked, bar-room queen" and attendant sexual innuendo.)

Boogie-woogie in particular emerged from shacks in the south called barrelhouses, where the blues was sung, with singers accompanying themselves on piano. Unlike ragtime, the basic form of boogie-woogie was always the blues, and the instrumental style was shaped by playing fast blues, designed for dancing to.

The first recording using the term is Clarence 'Pinetop' Smith's 'Pinetop's Boogie-Woogie' in 1928, just a year before he was hit by a stray bullet in a spot of trouble at a Chicago dance-hall. Chicago was the centre of the scene, again fuelled by the migration patterns of the 1920s and 1930s. Other notable names of that era include Jimmy Yancey, Albert Ammons and Meade Lux Lewis, who recorded 'Honky-Tonk Train' in 1927. Kansas had a strong scene too, due to the fact that you could get a drink there during prohibition, and that's where Pete Johnson worked with blues singer Joe Turner. Ammons, Lewis and Johnson went on to form the highly commercially successful Boogie-Woogie Trio, capitalising on the craze for boogie-woogie that engulfed the States before the end of World War II. Some of the elements of boogie-woogie were later imported into rock'n'roll – Little Richard and Jerry Lee Lewis spring to mind. (Joe Turner once said: "We was doin' rock'n'roll before anyone had ever heard of it.")

So is there anything of the boogie-woogie piano style in Stevie's 'Boogie On Reggae Woman'? Not the left-hand part, certainly, which was stylistically the driving force of the genre – the pounding eighth-note repeated pattern is replaced here by a pounding bass synth. But the right hand has echoes of barrelhouse, as we'll see in a moment.

What about the reggae part of the title – is there anything of reggae rhythm in the track? Well, not strictly. The speed (106bpm) is a touch fast for reggae, and the backbeat snare pretty straight, no trace of a sidestick or rimshot. There is at least an accented off-beat in the hi-hat, and a hard-to-identify metallic clicky guitar-hit noise that continues scratching itself for the duration. But the spirit

It's Stevie's first flirtation with reggae, and as with all the styles he visits, there's hardly ever a conscious aping, more an infiltration

is there: it's Stevie's first flirtation with reggae, and as with all the styles he visits, there's hardly ever a conscious aping, more an infiltration. He would go on to meet and learn with Bob Marley in Jamaica, as well as perform live with him, and reggae would appear again, in an only slightly more fully-fledged form, on *Hotter Than July* (see 'Master Blaster (Jammin')' in Chapter 9).

It seems to me that reggae's immediate predecessor, ska, left more of a mark on Stevie's work. For a taste of ska's history and sound, look no further than producer/artist/visionary Lee 'Scratch' Perry, who started out working at Studio One (Jamaica's equivalent of Hitsville) in the early 1960s – they even had their own house band, The Skatalites. Perry further developed the original bright ska tunes – themselves partly based on American soul – by slowing down the rhythm tracks. The first result was the characteristic reggae sound (Perry even worked with Marley & The Wailers for a while), before Lee headed to the outer limits of studio creativity and helped to create 'dub'. Perry's own Black Ark studio, kitted out with a Teac quarter-inch four-track tape machine and a Roland Space Echo, and little else, became one of the most infamous and remarkable reggae settings. The inimitable Lee once claimed, abstrusely: "It was only four tracks on the machine, but I was picking up 20 from the extra-terrestrial squad."

Whether you follow Perry's thought processes or not (few people do), the basic point is that, to me, there's a direct connection with Lee's early ska work in a Stevie tune like 'Boogie On Reggae Woman'. Take 'Roast Duck' from Perry's mid-1960s collection *Chicken Scratch*: though the tempo is faster, it has the typical offbeat brass 'skanking', the open hi-hat on the offbeat, snare on a backbeat, and a bassline that steps through a three-note chord. Which is all, to a greater or lesser extent, what we find in 'Boogie On'.

Basic instrumentation on 'Boogie On' is drum kit, congas (courtesy of Rocky Dzidzornu), synth bass, piano and wah-wah'd Rhodes. Add some harmonica, the clicky thing previously mentioned, stir and leave to marinade for a fuller flavour.

It's hard to believe, but there is a review of this track somewhere that incorporates the word 'fluffy'. In fact it's as taut as a tightrope-walker's wire, though not in a machine-like/quantised/stiff way – it's still as supple as a tightrope walker's body. (No, all right, I don't know any tightrope-walkers that well.)

The first four bars set up this liquid groove: a deliciously ringy snare, hi-hat 'chik chi-ka' (one eighth and two 16th-notes), and Stevie's synth bass fooling around gloriously, as if sliding up and down a fretless bass neck in-between static 16th-note pulsings. Congas join in, and eight bars of full groove introduce the other instrumental ingredients.

Stevie's piano part is all loose, bluesy right-hand fills – structural in that they repeat and wait their turn to provide interest, but also decorative and lazily dysfunctional. There's a conversational relationship between the Rhodes and the piano: piano has its say first with a descending blues-

There isn't really a precedent for this bass part – plenty of synth basslines, but none as relentlessly groovy and busy as this

shaped riff (7th and 5th of A♭ coming down through 6th and 4th to 5th and 3rd at the top of the next bar). Rhodes replies with almost the same phrase but in reverse, and so they bat it back and forth every bar during the verse.

The harmony/chord structure is non-eventful, aside from the trademark chromatic bass descent in bar four, stepping outside of the close circle before coming back round again. There's a lot of the same type of chord – it's as if a guitarist fingered one shape (a dominant 7th chord) and just moved it up and down the neck of a guitar. There are no minor chords in the whole track. Plenty of minor 3rd blues inflections in the vocal track, of course, and also plenty of bending minor-through-major notes in the bassline.

And it's the bassline, and its sound, that's the most startling thing about this track. The reason the

other keyboard parts have to be so disciplined and un-busy in the lower-mid area is the busy-ness of the synth bass part. It lands on a root and stays there maybe for a half-second (one beat), then it's off again, as restless as a fly on heat. There isn't really a precedent for this – plenty of synth basslines, but none as relentlessly groovy and busy as this. It's a stunning bit of playing.

There is a Jamaican influence in the shape of the line, working its way up the chordal notes (in an arpeggio), before reaching the top and worming back down again. All the detail is in that worming – the between-action fills that leap up to the high end of the bass range and crash down to the roots again in time for the next chord change, and never a slip between the cracks.

The bass synth sound demands attention in the mix – there's a scary amount of punch to it. My money is on it being a Moog, simply because of its superior attack times. Everything opens up faster on a Moog, and you can almost hear the filter working hard to keep up with the open crunch at the head of each note before it snaps shut, which happens when a large amount of envelope is applied to the filter. It sounds a bit like 'diaaioww'. Another reason it inhabits space in the mix is down to the two oscillators being tuned to the same note in a different pitch range – an octave apart.

It's impossible to write about a bass track as interesting as this without mentioning James Jamerson (again), who clearly influenced Stevie in the early Motown days with his intuitive knack for

It's quite a skill to create completely different characters and feels for each instrument ... but it does make the eventual groove wider

providing a bass hook for a song. Jamerson actually appears on 'Fulfillingness' First Finale', playing double bass on 'Too Shy To Say', where he disappointingly does little more than re-inforce the root notes already present in the piano part.

But back to 'Boogie On…', and what it is that makes it funky. You keep coming back to the fact that it's just a great feel. Whereas bass and drums are dead on the beat, the main keyboard parts sit in a relaxed or even lazy way over the top.

It's quite a skill to create completely different characters and feels for each instrument as they're layered in separate takes, but it does make the eventual groove wider. The right-hand piano part is almost a solo in itself, though the featured solo is of course taken by Stevie's by-now famous, almost legendary harmonica. (When Stevie asks, rhetorically, "Can I play?", is he being the young kid asking Clarence Paul whether he can do a harmonica solo tonight…?)

And how about that barrelhouse piano? Check the first chorus and you'll see that, yes, this track does have a bona fide eight-bar blues-style chorus. And indeed some of the playing is blues-soaked – the tremolo in bar one (on the 7th), and the squashed-note fills in bars three and five. Those phrases do sound worked-out, though, unlike the Herbie Hancock fills in 'As', where you feel he could come up with fresh stuff all day. Here the same sequence of notes repeats in each chorus with a modicum of variation.

It makes you wonder what Stevie could have done with a piano in a jazz context. When asked once why he doesn't solo more often, the modest reply came back: "I'm always practising to be better.''[46] Aren't we all... but unfortunately you have to make a few mistakes in public to get better – which is something artists with high profiles can't afford to risk.

Just a final footnote to this song: apparently Stevie was not too happy with the way 'Boogie On' turned out – so much so that Margouleff and Cecil had to persuade him to include it on the album at all. Gulp...

The list of Stevie tracks touched by the funk is a long one – I've just looked at three of many – and his use of funk patterns and sounds is never formulaic. Funk instrumentation is unsurprisingly often employed when the subject of the song concerns social or black issues – like 'You Haven't Done Nothin'', 'Black Man', and so on. Some of his slower tunes too, such as 'Have A Talk With God', 'Maybe Your Baby', even 'Pastime Paradise', have a strut about them, a displaced beat here or there, that kicks in the funk feel.

Again, Stevie had the knack of being in the right place at the right time, able to pick up and adapt an emerging energy for his own use – and often using it in a subtler way than most. It's no surprise that his tracks were still turning up on funk compilations 30 years after they were recorded – and will doubtless be around for as long as music with a groove is enjoyed.

CHAPTER 6
BALLADS

Pop ballads are the ultimate weapon of the songwriter – a bit like slow movements for a classical composer. The emotional core of many a symphony lies within the confessional revelations of the second movement, hinting at the tortuous psychological journeys to which the (particularly 19th century) composer was prey. In pop, the ballad is where you will often find writers at their most raw, and Stevie Wonder is no exception.

Although in later years his ballads would become less complex and almost formulaic, the three songs I've chosen here, plus others like 'Never Dreamed You'd Leave In Summer' and 'Lately', are the personification of the aching heart.

You have to live the life to know the life, as they say, and Stevie has certainly known love and loss, as is evident in these songs – but just as importantly he possesses the writing and performing skills to communicate personal feelings and project them onto a wider stage.

'You And I'

'You And I (We Can Conquer The World)', the third track on *Talking Book*, is a totally self-penned 'big' ballad – bigger in scale and scope than most of the other tracks on the album. Following the soft-edged but groovy (oh, all right, let's call it middle-of-the-road) 'You Are The Sunshine Of My Life' and the downright nasty disillusion of 'Maybe Your Baby', 'You And I' is how it might have been, and might still be – a hymn to ideal, past, and above all lasting love.

Rolling Stone reviewer Vince Aletti summed up the rather subdued feel of the host album like this: "*Talking Book* is more relaxed, dreamy at times, the laidback funk of the vocals resting on a deliciously liquid instrumental track like a body on a waterbed ... Yet there's never a lack of energy; even at its dreamiest, the music has a glowing vibrancy."[47] That's certainly true of 'You And I'.

Aside from the synth work the song is basically piano and voice; no drums, no bass, no drive from underneath, even with the synths in. The river-like forward-motion is in the piano track, there's ornament and orchestral vision in the synthesisers, but it's the voice that carries the song. And that's about all you need.

Several writers and reviewers have dismissed this song as being below average in the tune department, to which I would say, what are you listening to? Apart from being one of the most haunting textures of his career so far, the tune and harmonic language are superb – and it contains one of the best climax moments in the history of anything. The way the final bars build and then resolve is a songwriter absolutely on top of his game.

Maybe it's a big chorus that some people miss. But quite honestly, the presence of a flag-waving, cigarette-lighter-burning refrain would make the whole thing too obvious and unsubtle, quelling the constantly shifting sands of harmony. And how they shift: a nine-bar 'A' section travels halfway around the globe and back, taking the extra bar to make the final leg of the journey.

I'll come back to the musical detail in a moment, but if you're someone who listens primarily to the lyrics when hearing a song for the first time, how will you fare here? Well, unfortunately the news is not so good. And if you're an atheist the news is even worse, because the couple depicted have not just fallen in love on a strictly human level, there's divine intervention involved: "God has made us fall in love, it's true."

Whereas 'You Are The Sunshine Of My Life' lyrically basks in the freshness of a new love, 'You And I' seems to portray an imagined state of loving, looking simultaneously backwards and forwards, aware of past experience but able to imagine a future, imagined romantic perfection. Or perhaps it's just confusion – after all the blinkered optimism of the first section, the second verse looks back over its shoulder:

> "I am glad at least in my life I found someone
> That may not be here forever to see me through,
> But I found strength in you,
> I only pray that I have shown you a brighter day,
> Because that's all that I am living for, you see,
> Don't worry what happens to me."

If there's an element of resentfulness in the self-denying last line, the rest is genuinely heartfelt post-relationship analysis. Which places the inspiration for the song ultimately at the feet of Syreeta Wright. The path from secretary/employee to artist at Motown was fairly well trodden. Martha Reeves first left her desk and made it into the studio when deputising for Mary Wells; similarly Syreeta was in the office when Stevie walked through with a large pile of songs to be recorded. Syreeta worked on some of them and, trying out his talents as a producer, 18-year-old Stevie and Syreeta recorded a single, 'I Can't Give Back The Love I Feel For You'.

A couple of years later, Syreeta was invited over to Stevie's mother Lula's, along with Stevie's friend Lee Garrett, and the four of them came up with 'Signed, Sealed, Delivered, I'm Yours'. A writing, performing as well as amorous relationship between Stevie and Syreeta was soon in the making. It took a while though: Syreeta was initially wary of Stevie, as word had got around the office he had a certain reputation with the opposite sex.

(He's quoted in an interview in the *Afro-American* paper around the time saying: "A black man is not complete without a woman. He needs a woman, not as a crutch or a substitute for his mother, but as a woman. She should be intelligent, warm, black-oriented, and cookin' at both ends." Not entirely a 'new man', then – but it was the 1970s after all…)

As well as being lyrically strong, Syreeta was responsible for opening Stevie up to the possibilities of eastern thought and self-awareness

Stevie and Syreeta got engaged during a visit to London in July, and four months later were married at the Burnette Baptist Church in Detroit, on September 14th 1970. After a reception at Motown, they honeymooned in Bermuda and then returned to work together on Stevie's album *Where I'm Coming From*, which would take the couple almost a year.

As well as being lyrically strong, Syreeta was responsible for opening Stevie up to the possibilities of eastern thought and self-awareness (she was a devotee of transcendental meditation). But their relationship ran into icebergs and was sinking by the time Stevie toured with the Rolling Stones in 1972, after the release of *Music Of My Mind*. It's likely that 'Superwoman' from *MOMM* tracks the differing attitudes in the relationship, and the regret at parting, but it doesn't run as deep as the emotions laid out in 'You And I'.

The hand is certainly on the heart here (and the heart on the sleeve), and even though it might look clumsy on paper, the lyric sings very well:

"Will it stay, the love you feel for me, will it say,
That you will be by my side
To see me through,
Until my life is through."

If that's a question being asked of the longevity of love, the answer is given in the next verse, the "may not be here forever to see me through" section. But even though the love has gone, the writer doesn't regret what has passed and, wishing her well, enters the realm of the imagination – in his head it's possible for her to "stay here always".

"In my mind we can conquer the world
In love, you and I, you and I, you and I."

Again, it doesn't look that big a deal on paper, but the lines are given at least 110 per cent conviction in the recording. There's absolutely no way the writer/singer doesn't wholeheartedly believe what he's singing (either that or he would have made an extraordinary used car salesman). The performance is utterly convincing, and the listener is left with a mixed message: it hurts when affairs end, but no regrets – and besides, we live on in each other's heads.

Syreeta and Stevie do seem to have been philosophical about their own break-up, and they were to stay friends and work with each other again, producing two more albums together: *Syreeta* and *Stevie Wonder Presents Syreeta* in 1972 and 1974 respectively.

Margouleff and Cecil had used a semi-orchestral approach to the synthesiser programming on 'Evil' on *MOMM*, but whereas the result verges towards the overblown and melodramatic there, on 'You And I' the greater restraint works to the song's advantage. Unlike the orchestral synth sounds on 'Evil', the palette here is more restricted and the disembodied, unearthly tones have their own identity, unrelated to any acoustic imitations.

'You And I' may not sound like anything you've ever heard, but the musical approach utilises the string arrangement as a starting point. The contrapuntal independence of individual lines, as against the block chord approach of string sounds on many later pop records, reveals educated arrangers used to dealing with the relative complexity of interweaving musical lines – in a linear or 'horizontal' fashion, moving through the song – rather than static one-note-per-bar parts stacked one on top of another (in a 'vertical' fashion). Of course a good string arrangement has elements of both approaches, mainly because single lines can draw too much attention to themselves, which is liable to detract from the vocal.

There's another obvious technical reason for the process of sequencing single lines on top of each other: the synths at the time were monophonic – they could only produce one note at a time – so any attempt at plonking down chords would result in little more than a messy flurry of one-note burblings.

Notice the pitch register of the synth lines over the intro as well – one is in tenor range (centred around E♭2) and appears just left of centre in the mix; the next, on the far left, is in soprano range, (centred around G♭4); and the one on the right is in 'ether' range (about a 5th up from that, D♭). You can also just make out a synth bass part, blended in the mix, which follows the left-hand piano through the song.

Each 'voice' has its territory and distinct line (apart from the bass) and they're joined by another voice in alto range in the last bar. At that point the texture seems satisfyingly full. It's no coincidence that classical vocal music (church or secular) and string music rely mainly on four elements for a rich, full blend – soprano, alto, tenor and bass for vocals; and for strings it's violins violas, cellos, and double basses.

Stevie studied classical music at school, where lessons ranged from piano, voice, double bass and violin to orchestral arrangement, composition and harmony. (Sometimes I find pop and rock musicians play down their formal training to appear more 'street' and intuitive, but that fact is Stevie appears to have had a pretty rounded musical education.) And it shows here – a finely balanced piece of arranging, whether it's improvised parts recorded straight to tape, or a more formal worked out 'written' synth part.

It's the sound that makes the difference, though. At the time the reaction of most listeners would have been, "What's that strange noise?" It certainly is eerie and other-worldly – the synth tone is flat in upper harmonics, and though the waveform is too rich to be a plain sine wave, it's largely uncoloured and pastel. This contributes to the 'siren' effect (as in luring seafarers to their deaths, not the police car type), as does the variation of pitch within a sustained note (vibrato) and the scooping from one note to the next (portamento), which was one of the most strangely exciting features of early analog synths. Here the effect is extreme, which somehow helps to place the sound in internal imagination rather than physical reality.

The piano carries the main weight of the backing track. For the first four bars of the verse all you hear is piano and voice (because the bass synth is subliminal). The voice is, by today's standards,

Stevie studied classical music at school, where lessons ranged from piano, double bass and violin to orchestral arrangement and harmony

rather crudely doubled using ADT, or automatic double tracking – meaning the vocal track is sent to a delay line, held up there for a few hundred milliseconds and then returned to the mix, where it's normally placed off-centre (this time on the right). The crude bit here is the rather long delay and feedback on it, which catches consonants and turns them into a short-lived spinning top (listen to "it's true"). The advantage of doubling is the increased presence of the vocal tracks, which undeniably dominate the mix.

Time to get to the musical core of this song. There's no blues chord vocabulary here: the song's basic harmony is on the level of sophistication of a jazz standard from the 1940s, or perhaps more appropriately an Antonio Carlos Jobim song. Jobim, the great Brazilian composer, has the reputation of being able to twist and turn his way through all the keys in a very short time, a bit like an ice skater including all the fancy prescribed moves in one elongated jump. Stevie has the same skill with chords (I don't know about his ice skating abilities, though there is a picture of him on the ice) – he's able to make a surprising twist that takes you out of the usual realm of comfortable chords and places you on a sunny bench facing the sea. To me that's what happens at bar six ("it's true" again).

There's a fondness for turning major into minor, and vice versa; the second chord of the verse is major (lots of flats coming up again, I'm afraid – the song is of course in G♭: second chord C♭/G♭), and the third a minor (C♭m6/G♭). But the startling change of harmony is at bar six where the ear expects a minor chord (E♭m7 maybe?) but instead you get a bright, positive major (E♭major 7th).

The resulting distance from 'home' means there's a lot of work to be done to return for the next verse – work which takes place in the ninth bar of the verse sequence (one bar later than you'd expect). It's skilfully done: the pivot chord that turns the wheel (Fminor7♭5/C♭) and the last chord of the verse, the mechanics of return, are made to seem smooth and easy – you only feel a slight bump before you've landed back at the start of a repeat of the nine bars.

For the next section (the refrain), the major/minor surprise re-occurs in the second bar, but the complexity is in the fourth bar where two tension notes at the front of the bar (F♭ and C♭ over an E♭7 aug ♭9), supplied by the top two synth lines, resolve in a small way before the main movement of harmony also resolves and revolves back to the top for the three "you and I" repeats. That (♭9) suspension resolving down is more typical of music from the late 17th century than 1970s rock – more Bach than Bachman-Turner, you might say.

Apart from the nine-bar verse, the structure of the song is plain enough: a repeat of the verse leads to another refrain, which in turn leads to a 12-bar coda. It's there that we're assailed with the affirmation of love conquering all. There are a few musical tricks at work here: instead of the voice following down at the end of the refrain, instead it rises, then rises again, and suddenly from being in a comfortable, relaxed area of vocal range – which has been emphasising the intimate feel – the refrain is now a dramatic octave higher. The result, as I've said before and will probably say again, is completely uplifting – there's no choice but to be carried along on the wave of conviction, vocal control and melismatic expression.

There's no choice but to be carried along on the wave of conviction, vocal control and expression

The vocal embellishment of a melody has always been common in gospel and soul music, but in the 1990s it would rise to such a level of ornament that a ceasefire had to be declared to halt the devaluation of the vocabulary. The level of decoration here is just enough. Two phrases stand out: the bar before the refrain comes round again on "I…", and the most striking example on the penultimate "I", where the range of the voice is really stretched, then it falls in a succession of pentatonic steps that has since become a stock phrase (listen to Whitney Houston et al), down to the last held note. With that note holding steady (G♭3), the backing shifts through a series of chords that harmonise with the top note (Dmaj7, Amaj7, E, D♭11) before resolving to the home base. By which time you feel as if you've been put through the wash cycle and left out to drip-dry and regain your shape.

With Sixties ballad-meister Burt Bacharach on the TV show *Opus 3* in February 1973

A few more arrangement observations: the piano part has a gospel-influence here – the right-hand voicing spans a handstretch (an octave with two or three chord notes in the middle), and the left hand is firmly on root notes and lower double (an octave down). The octave in both hands is typical of gospel style, even though the chord progressions here are a cut above the average. Another point worth making is how effective it is when the two top synths – which have been circling each other like two boxers in a ring – join up for the instrumental refrain hook. Very satisfying.

The piano part does teeter on the edge of being over-dramatic during the closing refrain, with its downward (chromatic) triplet – but given the intensity of the action elsewhere some reflection of that angst is to be expected.

All in all then, an engrossing and musically elevating track, thanks to Stevie's almost operatic vocal control (thankfully not with an operatic tone, though), a fine set of chord changes and a haunting synth chart. It's interesting that not a great number of Stevie's songs from this era are covered by other artists. Generally the reason some songs get covered more than others is simply down to how easy or difficult they are to sing. Most people would listen to a song like 'You And I' and think, "Absolutely no way am I going to try to go there" – which is a shame, because I regard this not only as a great recording, but also a fine song.

'All In Love Is Fair'

If 'Visions' is the obligatory slow tune on the first side of *Innervisions*, 'All In Love Is Fair' is the filling in the double sandwich of the second side. (For the CD-only generation, I'm obviously referring to the original vinyl 12" album.) The clavinet-driven funk of 'Higher Ground' and the softer but ecstatically groovy 'Jesus Children Of America' open the side, and the Latin/funk tracks 'Don't You Worry 'Bout A Thing' and 'He's Misstra Know-It-All' close the album. Set in the middle of these, 'All In Love Is Fair' provides the personal, intimate, soul-searching, dare-one-say Kleenex-grabbing moment of reflection.

It's another piano ballad, but unlike the intense weirdness of 'You And I', the instrumentation here is softened by some light drums, bass and Rhodes. None of which detracts from the conviction of delivery: Stevie offers another fiercely committed vocal, rivalling if not exceeding previous tracks in its level of singing prowess.

Just as the extra instruments distance the emotional intimacy of the music, there's also a distancing of attitude in the lyric towards affairs of the heart. It's generally agreed that the song is another lament on the loss of Syreeta: the lyric starts with a more objective look at the way such things are liable to develop and crumble, only coming around to Stevie's own real voice for the heartfelt, "I should have never left your side", before returning to the apparent detachment of the song title.

It's the voice of experience, looking back over a failed affair with a degree of resignation, but at the same time not blaming either party for the way things change within a relationship:

"All is fair in love
Love's a crazy game
Two people vow to stay
In love as one they say

But all is changed with time
The future none can see
The road you leave behind
Ahead lies mystery."

These are among the most assured, mature, observational lyrics that Stevie has produced. They also scan well, and have a rhyme scheme that sounds good without being too obvious (see 'Livin' For The City' in this regard too).

In the final three lines an image is constructed of a writer (is it Stevie or an imaginary narrator – a letter or a story?) experiencing another loss and coming again to the same resigned conclusion. It's certainly one way of dealing with loss to say it was nobody's fault, and fate is to blame, but it does imply a lack of personal will and a handover of power to outside forces:

"A writer takes his pen
To write the words again
That all in love is fair."
The second verse descends further towards self-pity:
"But all in war is so cold
You either win or lose
When all is put away
The losing side I'll play."

By this point in the song the temperature is raised, and there's no doubting the hurt involved in the whole process. But in fact the track ends up in a positive, major key, in almost a triumphal mood (complete with a fanfare-ish section), before it drops back to the minor key piano touches that linger over the pause between this track and the next. The mood is then severed abruptly (as if to say, "but that's all behind me now") by the percussive Latin piano and cheeky vocal "Eee-eee!" exclamation of 'Don't You Worry 'Bout A Thing'.

One question that has to be faced when tackling a full musical inspection of 'All In Love Is Fair' is the similarity in the second bar of the verse to the 1967 Procol Harum hit 'A Whiter Shade Of Pale'. Procol Harum were a British band who suddenly found themselves selling 380,000 records in three weeks, topping the UK charts and reaching the US Top Five, with a track that might be described as baroque-meets-the-blues-meets-psychedelia. Featuring a bassline derived from Bach's 'Air On A G-String', and eight bars of classically influenced organ melody (played on a Hammond), 'A Whiter Shade Of Pale' starts in a major and descends faster than Stevie's track, but it's the shape of the melody in the latter half of the second bar which is of concern here. There's a string of notes there (G#, F#, E, D#, E, F#, G#, E then up to C#) that is pretty close to the shape in 'All In Love Is Fair' (G#F#, G#, E, E then up to C#).

Having said that, there's no suggestion that the bassline or melody have been appropriated by Stevie: for one thing, the descending bass – a favourite device of the baroque period, from Purcell to Bach – is a common enough occurrence, while the similar shape of the vocal line is only troublesome for half-a-bar out of eight. Another factor that throws you well off the 'plagiarism' scent is the

harmony on bar three – a surprising half-step down as against the full step of the Procol Harum tune. It's perfectly possible that Stevie heard the older song, but just as possible to put it down to subconscious assimilation. No case to answer, your honour…

Much of Stevie's output is written and played in a *nasty* key for your average keyboardist (not to mention guitar/bass players), and 'All In Love Is Fair' is no exception. I mention this because at least two published transcriptions go so far as to change the key (up a semitone) from the original C#m for ease of playing. At least in the *Stevie Wonder Written Musiquarium* book (a collection of 41 tunes) there is an acknowledgement of this fact, and they give the same treatment to 'Living For The City'. By the end of the book, though, they're less conscientious: 'You And I' is not only a half-step down on the original (G♭ to F) – with no accompanying explanation – the song also stops before the thrilling outro. The *Real Book*, a collection of jazz standards, has 'All In Love Is Fair' in the easier key (Dm), and it also leaves out some awkward time changes. But the question is, why did Stevie choose these keys in the first place?

The obvious answer is that it was the best key for the vocals in that song. Singing is a lot easier than playing in most of the keys Stevie writes in. (As Stevie said, rather formally, at the time of *Songs In The Key Of Life*: "Give me a key in which I am to sing, and if it is a key that you too feel, may you join and sing with me.")

For a keyboard player, the classical hand position is with curved fingers poised over the white notes, able to extend over the black keys when required. Looking at Stevie's fingers when he plays, they are more flat than rounded, and that takes them up into the black key area as a default position (this is a position favoured by many 'flat-fingered' jazz players). The quirkiest thing is that his thumbs are often well outside the playing area, seemingly acting more as stabilisers and direction finders than useful note contributors. Which makes perfect sense – as a non-sighted player you would have to keep your bearings somehow, but it does mean that finding your way initially to the keys involves first feeling out the black notes. So maybe that's where you feel most comfortable, and if you're writing at a piano or a Rhodes, those are the keys in which the songs are often going to end up.

The other way of looking at the key question is that it gives Stevie's output a particular sound. The way the vocals lie in the range, and the way in which the black-note keys resonate, are distinctive trade marks. For someone with perfect pitch as Stevie has (the ability to pitch an exact note out of their head, from memory, without the aid of an instrument), the sound of individual keys would be of huge importance, as each key possesses its own personality or colour.

It's an example of a process known as synaesthesia. Without going into it too deeply, it's where one kind of stimulus, say a sound, can be experienced in an alternative form sense, say a colour. Things are obviously made more complicated in Stevie's case by the fact that he hasn't really experienced colours in the way sighted people have, but it helps us comprehend that he might hear the world slightly differently, perhaps with more clarity than sighted folks – separating and defining sounds in ways and to degrees that most of either wouldn't or couldn't perceive.

There's a good quote from 17th century philosopher John Locke that seems remarkably apt in this context, about a "studious blind man" who for a long time struggled to "understand those names of light and colours which often came his way". The man's breakthrough came when he determined his own definition of the colour scarlet, deciding it was, "like the sound of a trumpet."

Whatever's going on in Stevie's head, there can be no doubt that right from the first piano chords of 'All In Love Is Fair', not only do you know it's in a traditionally 'sad' (minor) key, but a finely-tuned ear might guess it's in a complex key too (D♭/C♯ minor).

It's an unusual intro: the top melody line hovers around the emotive addition to the straight chord (a 9th), and the bassline falls in whole steps up to the fourth bar, where it settles and then pauses again ready to launch into the song. In the third bar the right hand on the piano plays one of the rare examples of a scale passage (an A lydian mode, starting again on the 9th). The pause before the verse adds another two beats to the fourth bar, a re-grouping moment that nicely sets up the vocal entry.

The 'band' texture is straight-down-the-line piano, bass, drums with a stereo Rhodes track vibrato'd to the hilt for extra warmth/colour. The Rhodes enters two bars before the first verse repeats, and it's well worth a try joining in for the satisfaction of playing a 'Chico Marx' back-of-the-hand black note slide (upwards glissando over F♯9), which sounds exactly like the record.

There's not a great deal to the drums here. In 'beatbox' language the predominant pattern is 'dom-chi-ka-dom-dom-chi-ka-chi' – 'dom' being the bass drum, 'chi' being hi-hat, and 'ka' a sidestick snare, hitting the rim of the snare drum rather than the skin, a sound beloved of hip-hop artists and producers. (Of course if the human beatbox was polyphonic there would be several things happening at once, but such are the limitations of the human condition.)

Scott Edwards supplies the bass, and I wish I could say it contributes enormously to the tune but actually it just 'goes along', as it were, raising its head above the parapet only for a couple of half-step skips.

To recreate the piano part would be a harder task. It's full of additions to the basic chordal shapes, borrowing language from jazz harmony – which Stevie learnt at the feet of the many jazz-influenced musicians at Motown.

Joe Hunter, the keyboard player and bandleader on a myriad of Motown sessions before the arrival of Earl Van Dyke, recalls Stevie in the Hitsville snakepit: "Stevie came here with Mr Paul, Clarence Paul, they were standing on the steps as you go into the studio. When we got through doin' the little ditty, the first thing he walked over to was the piano, where I was. He says, 'Oh I like the way you play the piano.' Then I showed him a few chords. He said, 'What's that?' I says, 'That's E♭ major, I'm throwing a colour tone in there, which is the flatted 5th,' and so forth and so on. He said, 'Yeah yeah', he'd shake his head you know. Finally I found out, about a year later, he didn't need me. He'd learned more than I'd learned."[48]

Bars three-five of the chorus are a case in point: the first three bars are a repeat of the verse, with the 'surprise' flatted 5th chord (A♯min7♭5), but there's a further twist in bar four where the minor chord replaces major (Am6/9), then sidesteps to a near relation (D7/13) before shimmying back to home ground (E/B). The chordal knowledge and ease of use is apparent (if only from the amount of numbers used to describe them), and that chordal interest is the reason the song has found its way into a book of standard jazz tunes, where the harmonic changes supply the materials and motivation for a soloist.

The structural importance of a strong bassline is also made plain here. With the piano left-hand doubling the bass for added cohesion, the bassline is really like the foundation of a house, providing support for the upper storeys. That solidity is achieved by using the kind of movement exemplified in bars five-eight of the verse, with the roots stamping firmly on a series of modulating 7th chords, in a succession of jazz-influenced turnarounds.

Even though the musical language is jazz influenced, the keyboard style is more rock/gospel ballad; those pillar-like octaves in the left hand and the full voicings of the right hand are both rooted on the downbeat – another reason the song sounds so centred. All this instrumental weight, of course, is there essentially to underpin the raison d'etre of the whole piece – the voice. To most casual listeners, this song is all about the vocal.

And in the singing there is no hiding place and no apology. The vocal track is refreshingly clean, with some reverb but no delay this time. From the outset the vocal intensity is right back on the level of 'You And I', with the mid-range fullness in the vocal sound, the melismatic decoration of the melody, and the sustained notes at the end of phrases. And how well Stevie sustains those notes.

Throughout the song the basic plan is: sing the lyric for a bar, syncopated if possible, then hold the note over all of the next bar, and beyond if possible, keeping up the interest by introducing the mildest of vibratos on the long notes. So the words "love", "game" etc are at least as long as a bar, and it's only on the refrain ("A writer takes his pen…") that this pattern changes. This means there is an insistent and cumulative effect. And what's more, by the chorus the voice is at the top of the range, Stevie pulling back from the microphone to avoid overloading (good mike technique) while singing very loudly. If you were in the same room as him at the time you'd certainly know about it.

Stevie had a wonderful way of taking his life experiences and putting them to music and making them real, raw, and yet very commercial

It's interesting how Stevie abandons the open "a" vowel sound on words like "stay", "say", "play", "away", replacing it with a more bottled-up "y" sound – you can almost feel the tension in the clenched jaw.

I know it's standard gospel practice, but the vocal ornamentation – hitting the note then slipping up and down around it – is very baroque in character (and something that will become even more evident on 'They Won't Go When I Go'). The finale is a vocal tour de force: there's another of those strategic pauses at the end of the second time through, in advance of the final "love".

By the end of the song we seem to be firmly in the major key (E), but don't worry because during the next four bars the pulse startlingly changes (to a 3/4 time signature), and the bassline drags the tonality inexorably back to the minor. Throughout this the voice is holding the word "fair" (at E3), fading as the last chord is reached. That's 11 seconds or so, with no breath control glitches, no tuning problems, just what singing teachers call a perfectly supported note.

It's an impressive climax, but for me the high point in the song, the moment that makes the most searing impression (and delivers the real goosebump effect) is the line, "I should have never left your side" – a phrase that reaches out over the top of the range (C♯4), struggling to contain a personal cry of bitter experience.

To quote Berry Gordy (and you can't help wondering if his use of the past tense is deliberate here): "Stevie had a wonderful way of taking his life experiences and putting them to music and making them real, raw, and yet very commercial … That's very hard to do."

'They Won't Go When I Go'

There is a clear path from gospel song repertoire to 'They Won't Go When I Go'. The lyric is based on the conviction that there is a 'heaven' (although it's not mentioned by name) for those who merit it, and presumably a somewhere-down-below where the others go – again the word 'hell' isn't used, but the implication is clear.

The language borrows from the church at times ("with him I'll bide"), and of course the sound of piano and voices is the basic formula for a gospel track. There is also a huge sense of drama: having arrived at the day of judgement, the sinners shall be rejected, but the innocent shall find their "resting place". The discomfort and pain of human life, and the relief to be found in the next, is classic gospel material.

The church and the secular were always bound together in the development of African-American gospel music. The blues, European hymn tunes, boogie-woogie jazz piano, spirituals, have all been used as material for cross-fertilisation.

Thomas A. Dorsey, the gospel composer and performer, typifies the crossover from secular to sacred (Stevie of course – like Ray Charles and Aretha Franklin – started singing in church and moved across to a wider pop audience). Having worked with Bessie Smith and Ma Rainey in the 1920s (nothing but the best), Dorsey heard some tunes of Charles A. Tindley, another writer of blues/gospel songs. Inspired, he started to write blues/jazz tunes for use in church, but came up against the powers-that-be who discouraged secular contemporary music in church. Dorsey was not to be dissuaded: "When I realised how hard some folks were fighting the gospel idea, I was determined to carry the banner."[49]

A whole generation of performers followed in his footsteps: Clara Ward, James Cleveland and probably the best known, Mahalia Jackson, of whom musical historian Wilfred Mellers said: "The magnificent voice and the fervent faith are almost inseparable; a voice of such vibrancy, over so wide a range, creates a sound that is all-embracing, as secure as the womb, from which singer and listener may be reborn."[50] Having grown up in New Orleans, the cradle of jazz, Mahalia Jackson had gone north to Chicago in the late 1920s, where she joined the Greater Salem Baptist Church choir, as well as enrolling as a member of the Johnson Gospel Singers. Her talents drew the attention of none other than Louis Armstrong, who tried to persuade her into the music business to sing the blues, but Mahalia couldn't be enticed out of church at the time.

After hooking up with musical director Thomas Dorsey in 1937, Jackson did in fact go on to sell millions of copies of songs such as 'I Can Put My Trust In Jesus' and 'Move On Up A Little Higher'. But despite landing a massive deal with Columbia Records in 1954, she never wavered from singing religious tunes. World success and touring followed and several notable appearances sealed her reputation as the finest gospel singer – not least at the Washington rally in 1963 where Martin Luther King delivered the "I have a dream" speech, and Mahalia sang 'How I Got Over'.

But to me Mahalia's most stunning work was with jazz composer Duke Ellington in 1943, when she recorded his suite 'Black, Brown And Beige'. It was, in Ellington's words, "a tone parallel to the history of the American Negro", and featured a moving a cappella version of 'Come Sunday' – a song that has interesting tie-ups with Stevie's 'They Won't Go When I Go'.

Musically, the tempos of the two pieces are achingly slow, and lyrically they are both concerned with 'delivery' from the human condition. The closing line of 'Come Sunday' is, "Please look down and see my people through", while another verse talks of the next world: "He'll give peace and comfort to every troubled mind/Come Sunday, oh, come Sunday, that's the day." Compare it with the crunch line of 'They Won't Go When I Go':

"And they won't go when I go
And I'll go where I've longed
To go so long
Away from tears."

Both songs speak of leaving behind "trouble" and "tears", but there is a difference in the perspective of the writer/singer. The first, the Ellington/Jackson song, talks more charitably and inclusively of 'a whole people', whereas the tone of Stevie's track seems more exclusive – is the singer condemning a large proportion of humanity to suffer in hell by suggesting they're not going where he's going. Or is that unfair?

It has been suggested that the lyric here was written by Yvonne Wright – the song is credited to Stevie and Yvonne, but sometimes it's hard to tell who wrote what when it comes to lyrics. One of their earlier co-written ballads, 'Evil' from *Music Of My Mind*, examined how evil has corrupted the human race, looking on it as an external force, whereas 'They Won't Go When I Go' ('TWGWIG') views evil as part of human existence, with each person responsible for controlling it, or otherwise. The next world is seen as a haven, safe from the "lying friends" and "bleeding hearts" that will not be taking the upwards trip, but will instead "fall" to whichever alternative world it is they end up in. There is definitely an element of 'I'm all right, Jack' about these lyrics.

The choice of the phrase "*when* I go" rather than "where I go" is intriguing too – the implication being that 'they', the others, *might* still go at some point, but just not as soon as the good and the 'innocent'. Could this be a reference to the traditional Catholic concept of purgatory, a post-death waiting room where 'slightly-soiled' souls go to sweat for a while if they don't quite qualify for immediate admission to paradise?

Whatever their fate, the declamatory bridge section intensifies the disdain felt towards 'sinners':

"Unclean minds mislead the pure
The innocent will leave for sure
For them there is a resting place
People sinning just for fun
They will never see the sun
For they can never show their faces."

There's a closer lyric tie-in with Curtis Mayfield's 'People Get Ready (There's A Train Coming)'. In fact the first of these lines from Mayfield's song is directly quoted in 'TWGWIG':

"There ain't no room for the hopeless sinner
Who would hurt all mankind
Just to save his own."

Originally a hit for The Impressions (and later, among many others, for Jeff Beck and Rod Stewart), the soul-inflected musical style bears little relation to 'They Won't Go…' but lyrically it sits somewhere between that and 'Come Sunday': the basic premise is a guaranteed "ticket" to heaven for everyone except the "sinners", for whom there's no hiding place, or even 'resting place'.

Whether he wrote all the words or not, Stevie is clearly comfortable enough to sing them with some conviction. Can all this 'afterlife' talk be a direct consequence of his traumatic accident and subsequent coma? It certainly fits very neatly with an increased awareness of mortality, coupled with a fear of 'judgement day', following a brush with the Grim Reaper. The subject is serious, the lines are emotive, and the music is some of the most haunting to be found in Stevie's whole body of work.

From the piano intro onwards, 'They Won't Go When I Go' pitches the listener into a personal and intimate soundscape. No drum kits or groove material here, instead the plan is to settle into a calm, delicate, sense of security. Solo piano is probably the most confessional instrument for a songwriter, with an emotional range that, in my opinion, is wider than it's possible to extract from a guitar. The way the piano is recorded here emphasises the intimacy: not only are you in the same room, you're sat at the same piano stool as Stevie.

I say piano, singular, but when you listen to the track with headphone volume cranked up, it sounds suspiciously like it's two individual takes, skilfully blended together. The possible giveaways

Solo piano is probably the most confessional instrument for a songwriter

are the occasional blurrings, and some points where the playing sounds impossible with only ten fingers, even for a virtuoso like Mr Wonder. The answer could be that Stevie in fact has 20 fingers at his disposal – the two takes just make it possible to bring out the separate lines that make up the whole picture.

The most powerful thing that strikes you about this song is the desperation of the minor key. The next thing you notice is that, contrary to normal ballad expectations, there are three beats in every bar instead of four. The third aspect to observe is the speed with which things unfold – the song is very slow indeed (58bpm).

Dealing first with the key, it will be no surprise to learn that the hand is firmly positioned over black notes (the song is in F#m), although the actual sound of the key isn't that dark. Since the home key is the relative minor of a bright, sharp key (A major, three sharps), there is a lightness to the sound that perfectly suits the subject matter of the song.

Although the three beats in a bar never even hints at a Viennese waltz here, the way the intro moves does immerse the listener in a previous period of musical history. Whether it's a Mendelssohn 'song without words' or a Bach 'French suite', the atmosphere recalls musical ghosts, as well as lyrically dealing with spirits in transition.

With chord changes happening after two beats, then one, and so on for each bar, there's more action harmonically than you'd expect from a one-chord-per-bar rock ballad. The outer lines (the top-line melody and the bass) start by co-operating then diverge towards the end of the four-bar phrase – in contrary motion, in accordance with the best classical practice. Further proof (if any were needed by now) that Stevie was aware of the guidelines of classical theory, either consciously or as a result of absorption from listening.

This time, unlike in 'All In Love Is Fair', the bassline is ascending in direction (there's a similar movement in the chorus of 'As', which we'll look at in Chapter 10). After ten bars – a four-bar phrase repeated then two more bars to calm things down – the texture has become even more fragile. The right hand plays a decorated line, this time lifted straight from 18th century ornamentation. There's a frailty about the playing and the way the accompaniment climbs through the register (an octave higher than the previous six bars).

In the fourth bar of that section there is what's commonly called a 'smudge', right at the end of the melody. It's really the equivalent of a guitar or wind instrument sliding or bending up to a note – except you can't bend notes on a piano (unless you were unfeasibly strong), so you have to play several fast half-steps (semitones) up to the note you want to end on. It's not often that you hear Stevie being so expressive on a piano melody, as opposed to chords.

Four bars of settling and dropping down the register over the home key prepare us for the arrival of the vocals – and after a 55-second intro we're reminded this really is a song, not an instrumental. One piano, one voice is the rule for the first stanza, a restatement of the higher piano tune, and sung straighter than the previous played version. Then the synths appear, in what is to be Cecil/Margouleff's programming swansong, and probably their finest hour. The album credits don't fail to acknowledge this: "Bob and Malcolm – your programming of the Moog on 'They Won't Go When I Go' is outa sight."

Two reedy, almost north-African pipes (a 6th apart) meander up and back down the scale, this time in a common direction – the timbre seems to reach even further back into the musical unconscious. Another stanza follows, and then we're presented with one of the most extraordinary passages in popular music (in music generally, perhaps). Stevie's overdubbed voices (one to the left, one to the right) join the synths in their descent – like going down an underground spiral staircase crowded with spirits sinking into Hades. The effect of submerging, as if trying to walk through quicksand, is achieved musically by the constantly turning roots of the harmony. Up until that section (it's not a chorus, so let's call it a refrain), the song's harmony, though fluidly shifting, has stayed in closely related keys. But now, things change radically. It's a musical process that deserves some further exploration.

To get technical for a moment, the rule is that dominant (7th) chords always want to lead back to their parent, home chord, a 5th below. But what if the parent turns out to be another child, just another dominant chord wanting to be led to the next parent, who then turns out to be yet another child, and so on. If you were to do that through 12 moves, you'd have encompassed the whole girth of the harmonic universe, ending up where you left. That's exactly what Stevie does here.

In the space of six bars (two chords to a bar) he twists, turns, and drops through every 7th chord there is – starting on B7, E7, A7 etc, ending C#7 back to F#m. Which is astonishing enough in itself – Vivaldi was partial to that kind of movement, but he had nothing on Stevie. The thing that heightens the sense of falling is that two lines result from this modulating harmony, and by picking alternate notes in the chord (3rd and 7th) those two lines drop half-step by half-step through the 12 semitones of the chromatic scale.

This means that, as far as the western musical format is concerned, you've just about flown through the entire gamut in the space of six bars. It's a relief to find yourself back in your armchair after such a dizzying journey.

The top synth announces the arrival with a line that's straight out of Stevie's vocal phrasebook (and presages the last line of the whole song), and in that melody the synth has become a musical voice. And they said it couldn't be done...

After all the early Luddite controversy over synthesisers – about them being inhuman, machine-like, and not 'real' instruments – here is the perfect proof that they can be truly expressive, in the hands of the right player/programmer/writer.

The icing on the cake at the end of the refrain is the addition of a bass synth that doubles the final drop and floods the track with a warm bath of sweet-smelling foam. With voices moaning/wailing, the intro returns and we're ready for another verse/refrain before plunging into the middle section.

Here is the perfect proof that synths can be truly expressive in the hands of the right player

There's a splendid moment on the "from tears" part of the refrain where the three voices converge from opposite directions, using the same pentatonic scale for the flowery embellishment, and landing on a harmony. The dynamic builds, there's urgency, a lift in the register and a need to get a point over in the lead vocal track, and the chords now hit one-per-bar in a strengthening, underpinning way. When we come to "hopeless sinner", though, the energy is dissipating, the piano is lighter, and the synths are left to do their version of wailing. There's plenty of sliding around (portamento), and the top line, based around C#5, E5, B4, A4, guards the bass roots down to the home key.

There seem to be four synth parts: one up very high, with a whistley sine-wave sound; one mid-soprano register with a slightly more nasal timbre; the reedy tenor; and the full, round, but upper-partials-free bass. These all come in for the last verse, and the interest alternates between backing voices (now higher up the register) and synths.

The lead voice emotes deliciously on "destiny" at the top before cascading downwards. Then there's a bit of an overdub nightmare as the piano comes in before everything else is ready, but it eventually drifts together for the final "They won't go when I go", as the synths brighten up for the closing statement.

It's an extraordinary piece of music. And before you've got time to absorb it all, the next track on the album, 'Bird Of Beauty', kicks in, and suddenly you're wondering what's making the noise that sounds like an asthmatic horse enjoying a joke? (All is revealed in Chapter 8.) Breaking up the mood in any set of songs is very hard to do, so you might as well be ruthless, and 'Bird Of Beauty' is an excellent dispeller of the inward-looking gospel ballad atmosphere.

Stevie's ballads are so intense that an antidote is often needed in the form of some light relief, but for me he remains the ballad singer/writer par excellence. For sheer sincerity of expression and honesty of performance, he knocks the competition out of the park.

CHAPTER 7
SOCIAL/POLITICAL COMMENT

From the time of 'Blowin' In The Wind' onwards, Stevie has constantly fed a need to change society for the better. More often than not he finds a way of expressing that need without alienating others who might not necessarily be in concurrence – more often than not the cause he is embracing is common to all. Occasionally he's over-obvious (as in 'Don't Drive Drunk' from *The Woman In Red*), at other times too preachy ('Cash In Your Face' on *Hotter Than July*). In the three tracks I've chosen for this chapter, the balance between the message and the medium varies, but when it's at its most poised and crafted, the songs can deliver a venomous attack.

Given the surfeit of problems facing the Afro-American communities in the States (and minorities elsewhere, come to that), Stevie's songs were and are still seen as an outlet for frustration, highlighting problems, and providing a blueprint for change. He was very much part of a movement – much of his involvement originally stemmed from the 1960s civil rights/Martin Luther King campaigns, and he would subsequently become a potent campaigning voice himself, for instance working for the King National Holiday, as well as many other charitable and fund-raising activities.

Two of these three songs are hard-hitting and targeted straight at the government: 'Living For The City', arguably the most subtle of the three in its storytelling, uses words and music and drama to describe life in the ghetto. In the end it all stems from imagination – the power to imagine a better way of ordering human society, and then the bravery to stand up and articulate your views in the face of disagreement.

'Big Brother'

Following after the funk of 'Superstition' on *Talking Book*, the first few bars of 'Big Brother' are initially calming, but what follows is the most direct attack on politicians, and governments in general, that Stevie had written up to that point – and probably ever since.

In 1948 George Orwell completed a book that would leave a profound mark on generations to come. His influential and disturbing novel *1984* introduced ominous phrases such as 'newspeak', 'thought police', 'doublethink' and 'Big Brother' into everyday usage – long before the 'Big Brother' label was heisted by the reality TV series. Stevie apparently had a fascination with the book, so it's worth looking briefly at Orwell's particular vision of an intensely bleak future for mankind.

The main target of *1984* is the unchecked power of the state. Orwell outlines a totalitarian society in which the government, referred to as the Party, has almost complete control over the people:

"On each landing, opposite the lift shaft, the poster with the enormous face gazed from the wall. It was one of those pictures which are so contrived that the eyes follow you about when you move. BIG BROTHER IS WATCHING YOU, the caption beneath it ran."

Big Brother is the supreme ruler of the Party, and is constantly "watching you" via telescreens that you can't switch off – instead they bombard the population endlessly with brainwashing propaganda promoting the latest government campaigns and slogans ("War is peace. Freedom is slavery. Ignorance is strength."). Even just thinking non-Party thoughts is a crime, and the Thought Police doggedly root out 'deviants' from society.

Newspeak was Orwell's name for the Party language, twisted and corrupted for political purposes – the forerunner of 20th/21st century 'spin'. The use and abuse of language was something Orwell had experienced for himself during the Spanish Civil War: "I saw history being written not in terms of what happened but of what ought to have happened, according to the party; this kind of thing is frightening to me. If a leader says of such-and-such an event that it never happened – well, it never happened. If he says that two and two are five – well, two and two are five." Orwell says he wrote *1984*, "to alter other people's idea of the kind of society they should strive after."

Stevie takes the idea of Big Brother and projects it directly at the president. Although the lyric doesn't quite have the surveillance angle of the book, the song starts pretty much in Orwellian mode:

"Your name is big brother / You say that you're watching me on the tele."

There are references to protest, and dying children, until the whole thing turns more personal:

"Your name is 'I'll see ya',
I'll change if you vote me in as the pres,
President of your soul
I live in the ghetto,
You just come to visit me 'round election time."

In the middle of all this there is one sentence of optimism: "Someday I will move on my feet to the other side." But then the mood reverts to the grimmest of images:

"My name is secluded,
We live in a house the size of a matchbox
Roaches live with us wall to wall."

The directness of the vitriol is surprising, especially from someone who had already been introduced to the president (Stevie was presented with the Distinguished Service Award by President Nixon's Committee on Employment of Handicapped People back in 1969.) It's quite something to remain solid with your ghetto roots when you're rubbing shoulders with presidents, but then Stevie seems to understand the temporal nature of politics – presidents come and go, opposition leaders are assassinated, and all great civilisations eventually tear themselves apart. Hence the return to pessimism in the last section:

"You've killed all our leaders,
I don't even have to do nothin' to you,
You'll cause your own country to fall."

You have to go back to the exploratory tracks on *Where I'm Coming From* to find songs that tackle the racial/political spectrum as head-on as this. That album's opener, 'Look Around', takes a similar apocalyptic stance:

"Look around and you'll see
Ruins of human history."

There's a clear line back through Orwell to the death of idealism manifested by the devastation of both the Spanish Civil War and WWII. In 1972, with what many considered another futile war in Vietnam still under way (over a million lives lost in all, with precious little to show), Stevie took the Orwellian vision to a new generation of anti-war of protesters.

The musical atmosphere of 'Big Brother' bears little hint of the menace contained in the lyric. The backing track serves as a perfect example of how, in Stevie's hands, the clavinet could become a guitar substitute – not in its all-out funky strut form, but in subtle plucked string/acoustic guitar emulation mode. The playing is finger-style guitar arpeggiation, surely a conscious imitation of stepping across guitar strings.

There's one thing you would be hard-pushed to get a guitarist to do, though, and that's play in a key with so many flats (D♭ – a typical Stevie black-note choice of key). Sure enough, the key doesn't sound right for a guitar – the first two chords (D♭-E♭m) sound dull and uninviting compared to the way they'd resonate a half-step higher on the real thing. (Not to suggest the clavinet isn't a real thing, of course.)

Arpeggiation – where you pick through the notes of a chord individually, one after the other – has roots not only in lute/guitar instrumentation but also in classical keyboard styles. The Bach C major prelude from book 1 of the *Well-Tempered Klavier* and Beethoven's *Moonlight Sonata* (first movement) are just two of the most obvious models.

In the case of 'Big Brother' the mood is more of a folk-influenced picking style, more Dylan than Beethoven. The harmonica also hints at the spirit of Bob Dylan, even though the phrases are more sophisticated than the 'suck and blow' basics Dylan pursued. In fact, with the harmonica on top of the 'guitar' sound, and the protest theme, there's an obvious Dylan theme here – but of course, as usual with Stevie, nothing emerges as imitation, merely inventive reworking. The harmonica actually provides the only real cutting edge to the track – it's rough and packed full of blues history, a poor man's instrument to express the viewpoint of the underdog.

The song is simple in form and soundly constructed, with a 16-bar verse that leads to an eight-bar refrain section, making the whole a repeating 24-bar form. If you have the sort of brain that says half of 24 is 12 and that reminds you of the (12-bar) blues, then you wouldn't be far off the mark. The harmonic areas involved in the structure of 'Big Brother' are blues derived: from the home chord (D♭) via a couple of trips to the neighbours (G♭ at Number Four and A♭ across the way at Number Five), then back home, it more or less does what a standard 12-bar blues does, in a more condensed fashion.

There's not much evidence of the blues in the rhythm track – no swung or shuffle beats. Instead there's an African/Latin-flavoured conga-dominated groove (with enough weight and drive that you don't miss a drum kit), allied to the clavinets and an understated sit-in-the-mix synth bass. The use of congas on Marvin Gaye's *What's Going On* sessions could have influenced the choice here: again it's a sound reminiscent of more ancient black history, and still quite unusual and exotic for the listener at large, in the days before the world music boom. For Stevie the sound of skin-on-skin was probably more representative of the sound of the street/voice of the people compared to the relative sophistication of the drum kit.

Motown always had easy access to this kind of percussion in the shape and form of Eddie 'Bongo' Brown, Marvin Gaye's former valet and the snakepit's favourite comedian, who played on the track 'What's Going On', among many others. But there's no indication as to who plays congas on 'Big

Brother'; Daniel Ben Zebulon is credited on two other tracks on *Talking Book* ('You Are The Sunshine Of My Life' and 'You've Got It Bad Girl'), and may have been working down the corridor with Richie Havens at Electric Lady studios. But a process of elimination implies that Stevie plays percussion here himself (which he'd been doing as far back as 'Fingertips', of course). And quite a mixture of percussion there is: there's also something lower-pitched than the congas, perhaps toms hit with sticks, though it's hard to separate all the elements from the corporate groove.

Speaking of several things contributing to a whole, the clav parts are, as per usual, intertwined like stems on a vine. It could be two parts, with one voiced slightly higher (a min3rd?) than the other, but at other times it seems as if it's made of fewer elements that are being bounced around the stereo image by an auto-panning device, to give the impression of more complexity. However it's done, the overall effect is that of a double-tracked guitar part.

That just leaves the vocals and the roving harmonica, freewheeling around each other. Stevie's vocal is pitched lower than usual (the reason becomes apparent with the octave jump in the third and fourth verses), and this also contributes to the relatively relaxed air of the tune compared to the subject matter. It's not helped by the fact that the second verse vocal seems to lack the power of the previous verse – maybe it was done in a different take. But no matter, because soon an echoing/doubling voice appears and, as mentioned, the temperature of the track increases as the new voice doubles the original an octave higher.

Most voices would be struggling in falsetto, but Stevie manages to make top notes (like D♭3s) easily accessible, and from "My name is secluded" onwards the vocal intent matches the anger in the lyric. The harmonica is growling by now too, and its insistence on the blues third (minor 3rd of D♭, E) clashing with the second chord (E♭m) means that at least the track goes out on a high.

'Big Brother' is a curiosity in that the vocal scores low on the aggression-ometer, considering how scathing the lyrics are. Maybe Stevie figured that an understated track conveys the message more insidiously than a raucous attack would. Or maybe he was just biding his time before coming up with the most lyrically appropriate and musically fitting 'protest' song he would ever write...

Most voices would struggle in falsetto, but Stevie manages to make top notes easily accessible

'Living For The City'

Innervisions is arguably Stevie's most consistent album in terms of marrying lyrical subject matter and maturity of musical writing. It's also hard to imagine its tracks in any other order: the first side just has to be 'Too High', 'Visions' followed by 'Living For The City' and finishing up with 'Golden Lady' – it's a logical development of the particular and global social messages with which Stevie had been concerned on the previous two or three albums.

'Too High', with its description of drugs gone wrong; 'Visions', with its Utopian glimpse of a paradise that's neither mental nor physical but elusive to both; then 'Living For The City' with its graphic adventure and urban warning. Each track with a strong lyric mood, concise and direct expression. It all seems to stem from a confidence in the writing, less experimenting and more consolidation. The rhyme schemes are more regulated and the scanning less forced. Take this from 'Too High':

"She's a girl in a dream
She sees a four-eyed cartoon monster on the TV screen
She takes another puff and says, 'It's a crazy scene'
That red is green
And she's a tangerine."

With its echoes of The Beatles' supposedly drug-influenced 'Lucy In The Sky With Diamonds' (dreams and tangerines figure there too… and what about the synth band Tangerine Dream?), it's already a snappy enough set of lines even before it's set to such bouncily off-beat and syncopated music. 'Visions', with its almost confessional honesty, gives the feeling that there's not a line wasted:

"People hand in hand
Have I lived to see the milk and honey land?
Where hate's a dream and love forever stands
Or is this a vision in my mind?"

But the album seems to step up a gear with 'Living For The City'. There's no preamble as in 'Big Brother': the voice and the lyric are hard-edged from the start, and the story evolves naturally through the description of a family background to misadventures in New York City to a desperate back-of-the-throat warning about inner-city troubles.

The first four verses set up the characters, and from the outset it's clear that Stevie identifies with the family being described, even though the actual details don't match his own upbringing. Some probably come close, such as: "Surrounded by four walls that ain't so pretty"; and "His mother goes to scrub the floors for many/And you'd best believe she hardly gets a penny."

There's no mere 'suggestion' here – he's telling us, no-holds-barred, that this is the way it was, and is. For a lot of black America, this is the reality (Lula's experience certainly tallies). It's almost as if, as an artist born in ghettoland, he feels a responsibility to portray and warn of the dangers inherent in that repressive way of ordering society.

There's pride, though, in elements of daily life – for instance the sister's clothes: "Her clothes are old but never are they dirty."

Once the brother is introduced he becomes the main protagonist of the drama about to unfold. Smart, jobless and patient he heads for the city. At which point in the song, a very surprising thing happens (on the album version at least – on the single this part is edited out). Over a static musical backdrop a script is acted out in dialogue, a kind of docu-song, cinema verité enactment of a scene.

The sounds come from a variety of sources: Margouleff and Cecil used a recording they had made in the streets of New York and added the voices of Stevie's brother Calvin, who plays the innocent stepping off a bus: "New York – just like I pictured it, skyscrapers and everything." From there on it goes horribly wrong: to the accompaniment of wailing police sirens he somehow gets himself involved in a wrongful arrest for a drugs offence, which results in him being sent to prison for ten years:

The words, "Come on, come on, get in that cell, nigger…" are chillingly delivered by a white cleaner who happened to be working at the studio, acting the role of a prison guard. Ira Tucker, Stevie's road manager, gets roped in to play a drug pusher, and lawyer Johanan Vigoda appropriately enough voices the judge.

What's interesting is that an audio soundtrack is all that Stevie would get from a cinema movie, and that's exactly what is presented here. To push home the point, when *Innervisions* was released a bunch of press and media people were bundled blindfold into a coach in Times Square and driven around New York, then to the studio, still 'blind'. Stevie's idea was to enable them to really listen to the sounds of the city. (Would you refuse? Certainly not.) *Rolling Stone* said of the track's playlet: "Though that cut's audio montage would crumble in the hands of a lesser artist, he makes it work through the force of his personality."[51]

The track kicks in again and we're off on the last two verses – firstly more description of how tough city life is (pollution and no representation), and then the final raspy if slightly message-laden summing up. It's a message that's probably more relevant today even than it was in 1973:

"This place is cruel, nowhere could be much colder
If we don't change, the world will soon be over
Living just enough, (stop giving) just enough for the city."

The best song titles are enigmatic to a degree, and this is no exception: the song might easily have been about just scraping by *in* the city, but it's even harsher if you're living *for* the city – implying that the city only takes, never gives, like some kind of evil entity feeding its polluting, greed-motivated habits. The opposite, the ideal, would be a city of co-operative inhabitants, where the infrastructure works *for* you.

The track is a grand design, incorporating a strong social lyric, deeply felt personal fears for the future, a 'reality' re-enactment… oh yes and some stunning musical ideas. The first of these is a two-bar stereo-panning Rhodes riff that, as with the best of ideas, seems to have always been there. That's probably because it has, in varying guises, been around for a good couple of hundred years. In blues-derived music a simplified version of this riff is standard fare, from boogie-woogie to rhythm & blues – it's an inner movement (affecting the mid-toned instruments) that gives variation to the blues pattern, often chugging along on guitar while the bass holds the root note.

Just to get technical again for a moment: the 3rd and 5th of the chord move up on the second beat to 4th and 6th, up again on beat three to 5th and 7th, and down again on beat four (in the key of G it's: G/B/D; G/C/E; G/D/F; G/C/E). Stevie takes the movement of this and instead of the shuffling of the blues (in a 12/8 rhythm), he lays it over a straight 4/4, a plodding world-weary footstep, while adding more top voices to the chord, which in the end gives it its distinctive individuality.

The top note reaches the blues/minor 3rd, lending a definite 'al dente' bite to the harmony. Michael Jackson was to plunder the same cupboard – actually the same tin in the cupboard – for 'Billie Jean' on *Thriller*, the only difference being the minor first chord.

(Incidentally, I stumbled upon that same supposedly 'blues' phrase in a piece by William Byrd called 'Jhon Come Kisse Me Now' from a collection of 16th century keyboard music – so I guess there really is nothing new under the sun.)

A *Rolling Stone* review at the time said, "'Living For The City' has the most compelling, pounding, throbbing, unyielding beat to be heard anywhere at all."[51] And who could have disagreed back then? It would be harder to make that statement nowadays because, let's face it, the last 20 years in pop music has been about defining and refining the beat. But the great thing about the best of Stevie's grooves is that, as a listener, you instantly need to get involved – and no more so than here. There's an air of foreboding and darkness about the scowling keyboard textures, but it does draw you in. Perhaps it's because the drums don't join in straight away – so while you're enjoying the fullness of the groove, you suspect at the back of your mind there's more intensity to come.

The repeated note bassline is insistent and unforgiving – and in another parallel reality matches the line of 'Billie Jean' in its last two-note turnaround (D♭ and E). There's no hanging about in this tune: as soon as the riff has been around twice, it's cut-to-the-chase with bass drum pumping and urgent vocal verse.

Notice the phrasing of something like "a boy is born", by the way. That could easily have been sung as four equal notes, but instead the last two are pushed forward in syncopation, so they end up snapped and angrily crunchy. And, using a different device, the fact that the syllables of "in hard-time Mississippi" are all straight on the beat helps to emphasise the downtrodden feel through repetition. The song's vocal line is pitched exactly at the top of Stevie's range, rising highest at "four walls *that* (D♭4) ain't so pretty". The harmony (by which I mean the chord progression) is static over the verse then rises to the two other blues chords in this key (B and D♭) for the hook-line. (Strangely, or perhaps not so strangely, there isn't really a chorus.)

Full drums arrive (in perfect time for the party) at the start of verse two; straight backbeat snare, and things proceed pretty much as you'd expect until the end of that verse, when a sharp left-hand corner takes you to a very unconventional-looking bridge.

I can still just about remember what it was like hearing that bridge for the very first time. The lead synth, a doubled, open, bright, sawtooth wave kind of a thing, fanfares over a really bizarre set of chords (given the simple harmonic context of the song so far). The voice doubles the top line in what could be seen as a too-comfortable BV chant – "da-da-da daa…", were it not for the fact that the line is *so* strong.

The harmonic movement in this bit belongs to another era: the bass descends, like a baroque 'ground bass', starting from the 7th of the home chord (E under a G♭ chord) and sinking through a series of semitones and tones through an octave. There are strange, twisted half-diminished chords before a series of major triad stepping stones returns us to the main plaza. So, not yer average rock'n'roll progression then. More like something from Pachelbel via Wagner via the Beach Boys.

As for the synth sound, well, I have to confess it's the one that first got me into synthesisers. Soon after the release of the *Innervisions* album I recall passing a music shop window and my eye caught a glimpse of an ARP 2600. I realised that this machine (or something like it), with its keyboard, knobs and sliders, was responsible for making that extraordinary sound on 'Living For The City'. I knew there and then that sooner or later I would have to get my hands on one. In fact, as it turns out, I've never owned an ARP, although plenty of other ancient synths have passed through my house since. But enough of this tissue-soaking nostalgia – back to the song.

The heat is turned up in verse four with the addition of a synth-riffing line, and then a swooping, glissando-like synth (with slow portamento) that heralds the return of the bridge. This is mirrored by

all manner of vocal 'oos' an 'ows', as if Stevie is showing young Michael Jackson the ropes. Somewhat lonely but upfront handclaps usher in the cycling of the song title over the home riff – a consolidation/chorus section, if you like. This repetition is saved from boredom by a soaring gospel vocal and various freewheeling synth lines that weave in and out and around the vocal.

Another bridge, and then at about four minutes into the song, you'd think, "That's probably it, isn't it?" Not so: the textures shrink to a ticking snare, ghostly held high synth notes and the revving of a bus engine announce the central spoken docu-drama.

Musically there's just enough happening under the dialogue to keep things ticking along. The synths become harmonically ambivalent, meandering around a tritone (three tones apart, D♭ and G) which unsettles the listener, and even paves the way for the police siren when it comes in – there's a sense of having heard the siren already in the synth orchestration. From here on the synth lines are higher, and there's at least two of them gliding like circling crows across the last two verses and three bridges.

The vocal is stripped straight off the back of the throat, delivering the message in no uncertain manner. According to Robert Margouleff, whenever he felt Stevie wasn't coming up with the right tone of angst he would stop the tape mid take, which was apparently guaranteed to wind Stevie up and start him shouting. Whatever you've got to do, I guess... It certainly suggests that the co-producers played their part in creating a performance to match the intensity of the material. They were also responsible for one of the most orchestrated, and by the end powerful, pieces of synth programming/arrangement achieved up to that time.

Two more things to be mentioned: the first is the alternative vocal line over the last three bridges, which is really a vocal harmony but in its direction and independence works as a counterpoint to the original line. Not only does it pitch the voice into a more expressive area, it also strengthens the structure with its contrary movement, again reminiscent of classical lines and structure.

The other point concerns the drumming after the end of the final verse: there's a hiatus before the closing bridges, where the song takes a dip as if to give the message a chance to sink in. Heard through 21st century ears, the tom-tom fills are a little bit self-important, but it does increase the sense of expectation. You can almost hear orchestral timpani over the end bridges, the apocalypse looming over the horizon. But for all the foreboding of the lyric, the song ends with a touch of triumphalism (firmly in the major), synth band/backing vocals fanfaring/testifying into a crossfade with the next track, 'Golden Lady'.

(Just one personal postscript: in 1973 I remember wanting to play 'Living For The City' so much – especially the synth line on my spanking new EMS Synthi AKS – that I even agreed to sing the vocal on it. Suffice to say the result was excruciating, and what's more I couldn't even manage the synth line reliably due to the fact that the EMS only had a touch-pad keyboard. Ah, the bravado of youth...)

'You Haven't Done Nothin''

The third in this group of social comment songs was released as a single in July 1974, with earlier track 'Big Brother' on the b-side (just to push the message home). On August 9th 1974, Richard Milhous Nixon – a fellow piano player, incidentally – resigned after presiding over one of the most shabby administrations the USA has ever experienced. The timing of the single release worked a treat, and radio stations soon picked up on the track. By November 'You Haven't Done Nothin'' had reached Number One in both the R&B and pop charts.

It could be argued that, as a force of change, the song missed its mark, since the president was gone by the time most people got to hear it. But that doesn't detract from its power as a polemic, attacking the government for its misdemeanours and mishandling of the truth. Stevie said at the time, "I don't vote for anybody until after they have really done something that I know about. I want to see them *do* something first." Which is of course a problem – if you're electing an opposition all you have to go on is promises, and how often do they disappear in a puff of smoke?

"We are amazed but not amused
By all the things you say that you'll do."

The song's demand for transparency was particularly resonant amid the Watergate fallout: "We want the truth and nothing else…" It's as if Stevie has become (in that dread phrase) 'the voice of the people'. If there's a touch of political naivety there's also the angry sincerity of an idealist disappointed by his elected government.

The year 1973 was a strange one for Richard Nixon. He'd just been re-elected by a landslide, taking 18 million more votes than democrat George McGovern in the largest majority ever. The war in Vietnam had come to an (official) end on January 27th, then Congress subsequently intervened to thwart Nixon and Kissinger's plans to bomb Cambodia. Meanwhile, domestically, the government was having trouble on a variety of fronts: inflation, food shortages, and a fuel crisis, for starters. But there was much worse was to come.

The break-in at the Watergate office of the Democratic party's national headquarters in June 1972 began a chain reaction of events that ultimately led to Nixon's resignation just over two years later. *Washington Post* reporters Woodward and Bernstein helped uncover evidence that, despite denials, White House staff had been involved in concealing evidence in the Watergate investigation, and the CIA and FBI were implicated in the cover-up. By April, Nixon was forced to argue his innocence in public, and launch an official investigation, stating there would be no "whitewash at the White House". The subsequent discovery of tapes of official conversations proved otherwise; several of the president's staff were indicted, and eventually Nixon himself resigned to avoid impeachment. All-in-all, a sorry tale of misuse of political power.

'You Haven't Done Nothin'' ('YHDN') includes some personal jibes directed at the president:

"It's not too cool to be ridiculed
But you brought this upon yourself."

But the song's main concern is the government's inability to deliver what it promised, coupled with a feeling of disenfranchisement, and awareness that the people are not being listened to. The main expression of dissatisfaction comes at the bridge/chorus section:

"But we are sick and tired of hearing your song
Telling how you are gonna change right from wrong
'Cause if you really want to hear our views
You haven't done nothin'."

This time Stevie is talking not just on behalf of the underprivileged parts of society – as signified by the 'street' grammar and spelling in the title – but of America as a whole.

Musically, the refrain part of the song recalls an earlier age of pop – the doo-wop singing groups, fashionable as far back as the 1940s but incorporated into rock'n'roll in the 1950s. Officially the phrase 'doo-wop' first appeared on wax in 1954, in a song by little-known Los Angeles group Carlyle Dundee & The Dundees (excellent name, don't you think), though the first to make the charts was The Turbans' 'When You Dance', where "doo-wops" crop up in the refrain. But arguably the earliest use of the musical style (if not the phrase) was back in the 1930s in Duke Ellington's 'It Don't Mean A Thing If It Ain't Got That Swing', where the horn section replies to the vocal with the instrumental equivalent of 'doo-wop'.

It must be said the refrain lyrics in 'YHDN' do look strange on the page:

"Doo doo wop – hey hey hey
Doo doo wop – wow wow wow
Doo doo wop – co co co
Doo doo wop – naw naw naw
Doo doo wop – bom bom bom..."

It sounds strange too – such seemingly throwaway playfulness in the context of a hard-hitting political statement – but the resonances are logical. The doo-wop sound was undeniably American, and started as an urban black music, emerging in New York and Chicago. Closely associated with a cappella (meaning literally 'in church', but coming to signify any voices unaccompanied by instruments), it grew out of the popular vocal groups of the 1940s like The Inkspots ('Whispering Grass' etc) and The Mills Brothers ('Lazy River'). The vein of close-harmony singing ran on via The Drifters ('Lucille'), The Platters ('Only You') and The Clovers ('Hey Miss Fannie') to Motown groups themselves. Smokey Robinson started out in a mid-1950s four-piece vocal group called The Matadors, who later became The Miracles.

Doo-wop also influenced a wide (and white) spectrum of rock'n'roll and pop acts, from The Everly Brothers to The Beach Boys, whose hit 'Barbara Ann' was originally recorded by doo-wop group The Regents. So it already had quite a wide cross-cultural appeal and resonance for most Americans by the time Stevie made 'YHDN', even if it wasn't familiar in a rock/funk context.

It's the hardness of the groove that saves it from cliché in this context – not to mention the novelty of having The Jackson 5 supplying the vocal expertise: "Jackson 5 join along with me..." And of course the Jackson 5 are musically exactly in line with the history of doo-wop. Plus they were Motown stablemates, just coming off the boil at the time. But they don't actually make a massive contribution to the track – Stevie's voice stacked up would have fulfilled the same function.

The last verse has a curious turn of phrase:

"We would not care to wake up to the nightmare
That's becomin' real life...
But when misled who knows a person's mind
Can turn as cold as ice... mmm hmm."

That first line probably has as much to do with scanning the right number of syllables as anything else, but it has an odd air of gentility given the 'voice on the street' slant. But it's mostly a straight, hard-hitting lyric that manages to convey the immediate anger and frustration of the time. As Stevie said, "You always hear the president or people say that they are doing all they can. And they feed you with hopes for years. But that is probably typical of most people in very important positions who have a lot of power. I'm sick and tired of listening to all their lies."

The instrumental elements also tap into that anger. You wouldn't think so at the start: the intro's muted beatbox (a very early example of drum machine use on a commercial recording, which I'll come back to in a moment) and harp-like clavinets, rippling down the black-note ebonies, sound comfortable enough – but it's when they settle that the action really starts. With a final tumble down the pentatonic staircase the bass-end-of-clavinet riff begins to grind. And grind it does, as inexorably as a millstone fuelled by floodwater – at least as hard as a Keith Richard guitar riff would under the same circumstances.

The clavinet tone harks back to the time of 'Superstition'. To be brutal, it's more than just the tone that sounds familiar: the clav riff and arrangement, the harmonic structure, the horn lines, the tempo, the drum-then-riff intro, the way the last line of bridge serves as a chorus… In fact, if I try and recall one or the other song now it's a bit tricky, as both tracks are in danger of melting down into one enormous E♭ minor riff…

It is a killer riff, though. Probably two clavinet parts, with mostly the same movement, but there's more shifting of the root notes (at the bottom of chords) than there is in 'Superstition'.

With a final tumble down the pentatonic staircase the bass-end-of clavinet riff begins to grind

The first half of each bar is based on the home chord (E♭) then the line shifts up to the 5th (B♭) and back home via the 4th (A♭) for the second half of the bar, a beat on each of the chords. This actually gives the groove more weight, as it's constantly hauling itself up and then dumping down again to the root note.

The *sound* of that root note is heavy too. We're used to hearing guitars riffing in E, a pretty bright key no matter how hard you try. Here it's a semitone down in about as dull a key as you'll ever stumble across on a dark night (just the six flats – unless of course you want to start dealing in sharps, but let's not go there…).

The style of clav playing is even more guitaristic here than on 'Superstition', with lots of notes that quickly slur to the ones next door, in a process guitarists call 'hammering on' – fingering one note on the neck then putting another finger on the fret above it, producing (as it might be called in doo-wop language) a kind of 'dow-wow' effect.

There's plenty of examples here, as well as a proliferation of syncopated 16th-notes, bouncing around the place like a tube-full of slightly-tamed quarks. The rhythmic emphasis of the chord changes is varied in a two-bar pattern; in the second bar the move to the 5th is pushed forward an eighth-note, upping the tension at that point. There's the customary uncertainty over major/minor, as there's no 3rd in the home chord. (The 5th is unusually minor, though, which adds to the feeling of

bleakness, while the major 4th is less of a surprise.) The vocal line supplies the answer to the nature of the enigmatic 3rd on the words "do" and "you" – it's official, the key is minor, albeit bluesy and liable to become more so.

The drum track deserves a bit more investigation, not least because of the beatbox – presumably one of those pre-programmed ballroom-dance-rhythm machines. It plays from the intro onwards all the way through, but mostly below the rest of the rhythm track. If you listen close you can hear the machine's open hi-hat/swept brush snare sound and bass drum that insistently kick off each bar. There's a rogue element in there as well, which sounds like single tom hit added to emphasise the beat, or perhaps a marching-band bass drum – it's clear enough over the intro but disappears in the overall mix once the clavinets are in.

There's a reason those clavs are loud: they're really bearing the weight of the structure, because in terms of drums there's only a hi-hat where you'd expect a backbeat snare, and the occasional signpost cymbal crashes.

I should mention the electric bass guitar part as well, which is played by Reggie McBride, but is generally such an indistinct sound against the rasping clavs you'd be forgiven for overlooking it. In a way it's a shame five-string basses, with their extra low notes, weren't around in those days, because a root note down the octave (a low E♭) would have been weightier.

The combination of musical punch and a lyric that was bang-on-target increased the feeling that Stevie was a spokesperson for the times

As usual there's an avoidance of chorus, just a bridge-like departure that 'returns to go', using the song title as hook. Structurally speaking, the harmonic movement away from home isn't by any means extreme – more of a day-trip than a week-long cruise. The line "Cause if you really want to hear our views" provides the trademark chords, moving down by small (chromatic) steps, ready to set up the return to home base. Actually you hear that descending line in the vocal at "hearing your song", even before it's shipped down to the bass department. Once there, though, it's full speed ahead for the major/minor blues chord (B♭7#9) that sets up the hook-line, and the arrival of the horn section.

It's a strange old sound, that horn section. Some people have even questioned its acoustic parentage and suggested it's a synth mock-up, but I reckon it's too good for that – both in terms of the sounds available at the time and the natural playing technique. What makes it sound synthetic could be the double-tracking of the brass players, who are sent over to augment the other side of the sax, which makes the whole timbre brighter. Here the unison low honking (especially on the second half of the bridge), even upfront in the mix, lends a muddier, though I guess less formulaic sound to the part. It's an unusual part – you might have said low-budget if you didn't know better – but again it does have an appealing directness.

It's an unusual mix too. As mentioned before, the clavinets rule above all else, except maybe the horns, running them a close second, while the vocals seem a pace back, and drums lodged even further behind that. The Jackson 5 are certainly nicely close-up when they get around to 'Doo-doo-wop'-ing, and their part is similarly simple but effective.

And that's about it really. There's not much growth to the arrangement, so it stomps on with a few classic Wonder vocal touches along the way – check "that's becoming real *life*" at the start of the third verse for an amazing almost-yodelling-but-better leap to a high note. Listen to the hook-line on the last bridge too. Up until that point the song is pitched to show off Stevie's top range (B♭3 top note), but suddenly a whole new area is opened up on the "*haven't*" as he shoots for the top root note (E♭4) and spirals down again to an area of relative safety.

The outro line, "Sing it loud for your people, say…", is a top-drawer Stevie vocal workout, after which the fade seems to come too soon. But in the end it's only a three-and-a-half-minute straight-to-the-point pop song, with no added pretensions.

It was a formula that certainly worked for the singles market – the combination of musical punch and a lyric that was bang-on-target increased the feeling that Stevie was becoming a spokesperson for the times. (As a writer it was his fourth hit of the year, including the recording of his 'Tell Me Something Good' by Chaka Khan's group Rufus.)

Watergate marked the end of an era when it was possible to feel hopeful about American politics. "Everybody promises you everything but in the end, nothing comes out of it," said Stevie in 1974. Not exactly an idealist viewpoint – in future Stevie would more often look inwards rather than outwards to seek personal satisfaction and fulfillment.

CHAPTER 8
LATIN INFLUENCES

S ay the phrase 'Latin feel' to a bunch of educated musicians these days and you're asking for trouble. They'd complain it was far too unspecific. That wasn't always the case – in the 1970s it would have been a perfectly acceptable description to give before playing a tune – yet in recent years most people's knowledge of world music has increased exponentially. The *Buena Vista Social Club* movie and the salsa dance wave have been responsible for opening many ears and minds.

A 'Latin feel' could in fact mean anything from a Cuban 'son' to a Brazilian 'samba' or the even more exotic Puerto Rican 'bomba' or 'plena'. I don't intend to describe every South American rhythm here, but some background on the roots of Latin music, and how that music would have travelled to New York or Detroit, would seem useful.

Stepping smartly aside from the debate that continues to rage over the origins of salsa music, Cuban son can be traced to the mountains of Cuba's Oriente province during the 19th century. It can be traced further back to its African roots, which lie in a form called the 'changui', but the son took the African elements and combined them with Hispanic influences. When African workers moved into Havana, son quickly became popular. By the 1920s, all levels of society had adopted the son as the Cuban dance music. Soon Havana nightlife was injected with the sound of 'conjuntos' (groups) of musicians playing anything from acoustic bass to maracas, bongos, claves, guitar, trumpets, and of course there would be at least two singers.

The instrument called the claves – two short lengths of wood which, when hit together, are guaranteed to cut through any mix (or large salsa band) – are not to be confused with the 'clave', a term used to describe a rhythm and the way the rhythm is formed. The clave is often played by the claves, if that's not too confusing, but it also governs the patterns of the rest of the rhythm section, and indeed the top lines, or melodies.

By the 1930s, Cuban composer Arsenio Rodriguez (who, in an odd parallel with Stevie, was known as "El Ciego Maravilloso" – the wonderful blind man) had refined the style by putting back some of the African elements that had been excised in order to sanitise the music for white audiences. The resulting sound became known as 'son montuno'; it added congas and cowbell to the band line-up and introduced an instrumental 'montuno' section for soloing over.

It was basically this form of Cuban music that found its way to Puerto Rico in the 1930s. From there the music moved up (through emigration again) to New York, where a group of mostly Puerto Rican musicians, such as Tito Puente, spread the style through the clubs. There was a jazz link-up as well in the late 1940s/early 1950s, when the likes of trumpeter Dizzy Gillespie ('Night In Tunisia'), George Russell ('Cubano-be Cubano-bop'), Duke Ellington ('Caravan'), and pianist Bud Powell were all influenced by the Cuban/Puerto Rican sound. George Russell (the pioneer of modal jazz) still uses a recording of Luciano 'Chano' Pozo Gonzalez at his concerts – Chano pretty much single-handedly set up the Latin/jazz crossover in New York before being killed in a bar fight in Harlem in 1948.

But back to Puerto Rico. The bomba, purely African in source, was being sung in the sugar plantations of the 1600s; the plena, drawing from more local influences, is shorter on history but is said to use rhythms from the Taino tribes, as well as flavours from Spain. It's possible that the Taino invented the guiro, a gourd with cut grooves that's played with a stick (same principle as the washboard beloved of skiffle bands). Under the name 'Latin gourd', this instrument features on 'Don't You Worry 'Bout A Thing' – as do the bongos, another instrument crucial to a salsa rhythm section.

It's not clear how Stevie first got his bongos, but we do know that in his busking days with John Glover the harmonica would be in the pocket and the bongos slung around the hips. Of course at the Motown studio there would be a significant Latin influence, and not just the percussion of Eddie 'Bongo' Brown. The studio musicians often worked on gigs that borrowed from Latin styles. Drummer Uriel Jones, who played on Motown hits like 'Ain't No Mountain High Enough', recalls working with an 'exotic' dancer named Lottie 'The Body' Claiborne: "A lot of the rhythms we did in the studio were rhythms that came from working with Lottie ... So Marvin Gaye's 'Grapevine', and Gladys [Knight], all that's Latin stuff. We did all that stuff with Lottie."[52]

After the trade embargo was imposed on Cuba in 1962, Cuban musicians found themselves isolated, deprived of the two-way exchange from New York to Havana. That made room for the Puerto Rican labels to clean up and define a mass market for salsa music, which left some Cubans with a sense of grievance – and it still simmers today. As Mario Bauza – probably first on the New York Cuban jazz scene – put it: "They try to play my music, Afro-Cuban jazz, and they call it 'Latin-jazz'."

There's certainly a strong sense of pride at work in the traditions of the various styles of Afro-Cuban music. Who came up with what first, and where, is serious business. One thing is for sure, the majority of development of the New York Latin-jazz style took place at the hands of Cuban musicians, whichever city they happened to be in; the Puerto Ricans added their influences, their skill in performance, and their ability to judge a market.

What eventually became the staple diet of New York salsa was a blend called 'son-montuno-mambo', combining big-band jazz and Afro-Cuban grooves. It starts out with a 'coro', or sung improvisation, followed by a mambo section, instrumental solo (often trumpet), and a call-and-response section between soloist and horn section.

'Don't You Worry 'Bout A Thing'

Though it's in no way a strict copy, the first four bars of 'Don't You Worry 'Bout A Thing' ('DYWBAT') are completely based on the Cuban rhythmic style of the mambo. Having said that, in fact it's more complicated – the piano part is similar to a 'son montuno', but given what the other instruments do, and despite the bass end rhythm being completely mambo-less, it's a good enough place to kick off.

So, what does a mambo sound like? It sounds like salsa music – or to be more exact it sounds like the Tito Puente track 'Ran Kan Kan'. Sure enough 'DYWBAT' has the same rhythm in the piano track as 'Ran Kan Kan', with a guiro scratching away, and a cowbell somewhere in there, but that's where the comparisons end. In 'DYWBAT' the bassline lands squarely on the first beat of the bar (as opposed to always slightly off-beat), and there are obviously no big-band punches. As usual, Stevie is concerned with getting the flavour of a style and then making it his own. The result is a kind of funky mambo with a unique swing, and a distinct taste of Havana.

After the piano and the joyous "Eee-Eee!" at the end of the phrase, the various percussion elements fall into place. Cowbell and shaker are the first to appear (quarter-note and eighth-note respectively), followed by the guiro next time around. Yusuf Roahman plays shaker, and Sheila Wilkerson takes care of guiro and bongos. You'd think Stevie might have played bongos himself – something of a trip down memory lane for him – but perhaps there was a stylistic problem. In any case he already plays piano, synth bass and drums, sings backing vocals, and provides an entertaining rap over the extended introduction.

It's quite difficult to pick up all of the spoken intro because he's in full mimicry flow (another strange parallel with Paul McCartney, who's also an excellent mimic). Basically Stevie's character is sat in a bar/club, chatting up/trying to impress a woman with his citizen-of-the-world experience… "Paris, Beirut, Iraq, Iran, Eurasia…", and his multi-linguality, helping translate the track's raucous opening phrases for her:

"You understand that?"

"No."

"I speak very, very, um, fluent Spanish … 'Todo está bien chevere' … You understand what that means? 'Chevere'…"

And so on. 'Chevere' translates as cool, groovy, fab; 'Todo está bien chevere', which will reappear as a choice backing vocal line later in the song, literally means 'Everything's well cool'.

The song lyric sounds lightweight when sung, with the carefree delivery of a Latin 'Don't Worry Be Happy', but on closer examination there's a sensitive man on hand (despite the swagger of the intro). It's a mature, caring stance – if I've read it right – coming from someone experienced enough to know that the only constant is change. The song is a re-assurance to a female friend, letting her know that whether she resists exploring the outside world and its tempting offers, or goes out there to 'check it out', he will support her every inch of the way. At least, that's one interpretation:

"Everybody's got a thing
But some don't know how to handle it
Always reachin' out in vain
Just taking the things not worth having…" (The sleeve lyric sheet says "accepting the things".)

Could it be that the subject of the song is trying out various lifestyles/substances with little thought – visiting 'other places', taking 'things not worth having' – and the message is not to feel guilty, and it's OK:

"Cause I'll be standing on the side
When you check it out…
When you get off… your trip."

A drug innuendo there, perhaps. Maybe the frenzied Hispanic babble at the top of the song is so speedy in order to mimic 'altered' behaviour; maybe the 'chevere' is an expression of drug 'chilling'; or maybe I should stop there before I flog that horse to death with the wrong end of a stick.

It's certainly another well thought-out lyric, socially aware, and undoubtedly intriguing, as is generally the case on *Innervisions*. The music track is equally confident in its execution, the input of the other musicians just enough to flavour and contribute without taking charge altogether. The piano, bass and drums dictate the overall feel – which is pure Stevie. The drums are mixed curiously far back, only dominating on tom fills, while the bass – a shy, retiring sort of synth character – links uncannily with the left hand of the piano. The intro is the only time the mambo montuno (the rolling piano figures) gets played in its pure form; once the song has found its stride, the part reverts to a more familiar chordal 'comping' (short for accompaniment).

Those chords deserve a closer look. Once into the verse the harmony travels further than the static intro: from the home key – which is minor and, unsurprisingly in a flat key (E♭m, even though the books often write Em) – the roots stride around the lower reaches in steps of four at a time (E♭m7, A♭7, D♭m7, G♭7sus etc), while the top line of the chord, the leading voice, uses other notes of those chords and wanders down one step at a time, through six different chord changes.

This sort of movement reaches its apotheosis with the scary 'They Won't Go When I Go' on the next album, *Fulfillingness' First Finale*, but there's a lot of it about on *Innervisions*. 'Golden Lady' also has a downwards curving inner line (unison, maj7, 7th, 6th), as has 'He's Misstra Know-It-All (unison, 7th, 6th, min 6th). It's something I'm sure contributes to the organic sound of the album.

Another new feature of the period is Stevie's interest in half-step consecutive movement, or chromaticism, whether it's in the top or bottom end of the track (or both). For example, once the chorus has been around the park almost twice on 'DYWBAT' (it's in the relative major key now), it's interrupted by a kind of chorus extension that lengthens the "check it out" by eight bars.

The arrangement at this point gives the dynamic a kick too: the snare drum is now audible, BVs come in, and the hi-hat has an off-beat eighth-note open splash on every beat – the kind of disco-type hi-hat that was starting to appear (take Harold Melvin & The Blue Notes' 'The Love I Lost'), but didn't become ubiquitous till a couple of years later.

But that half-step downward movement remains the dominant feature; the bass, still on the major, falls in semitones through the four bars and then lands back. The vocal line follows at an interval that's out-of-step then in-step (suspended 4th to a 3rd), all in a downward direction. In classical terms it's a fairly crude device, and that's probably why it sounds refreshing here – something no one's quite tried before.

We need to go back to 'Too High', the opening track on *Innervisions*, for the most extreme half-step, semitonal business: after the opening riffs, the BVs and Rhodes navigate a tricky, not-to-say perilous, rollercoaster through the ups and downs of chromatic motion, guaranteed to induce sea-sickness in less acclimatised travellers. (Hats off to the singers on that track: Lani Groves, Tasha Thomas and Jim Gilstrap – how long did that take to learn?) While we're at it, how about the chorus of 'Too High', coming down (appropriately) through five stages of whole-steps, then touching ground.

A new feature of the period is Stevie's interest in half-step consecutive movement, or chromaticism

Signatures from previous tracks crop up on 'Don't You Worry...': the short half-step transitions (triplet eighth-notes) seen before in the closing stages of 'You And I' are repeated on the fourth bar of the chorus, "'Cause I'll be". That same harmonic move makes a return appearance in 'Boogie On Reggae Woman' (D♭ chromatic down to B♭), but it has a long lineage, all the way back to 'Signed, Sealed, Delivered' at least. It's a personal trademark, that's for sure, and what it boils down to is an interest in melodic and harmonic ideas far outside the ordinary soul/funk (and certainly pop) domain.

Innervisions is widely considered to be Stevie's best album (except by the people who prefer *Songs*

In The Key Of Life). It perhaps has the most satisfactory overall feel to it – music and lyric working in tandem to produce a cohesiveness brought about by (probably subconscious) musical connections. The lyrics on the album are certainly more inward-looking (and better crafted), with an emphasis on the spiritual – it's believed Stevie had a premonition before his accident in August 1973, and this may have coloured the album's feel. "Something must have been telling me something was going to happen to make me aware of a lot of things and get myself together".[53] Stevie matches this with a new musical vocabulary, full of idiosyncratic ideas that would never show up in such concentration again.

Where Marvin Gaye's *What's Going On* made use of thematic repetition to link tunes, Stevie uses more subtle devices (perhaps 'inner' line similarity for inner visions?) coupled with a restricted range of instrumental colour that provides continuity from track to track. And yet there's still an abundant diversity and contrast between tracks – it's a long way in mood from 'Visions' to 'Don't You Worry…'.

From a vocal point of view, 'DYWBAT' is a fine example of the way Stevie builds an arrangement from small beginnings. It was almost established practice by this time: start soft and work your way up. The tone of the first verse is intimate, almost confessional, definitely supportive compared to the exuberance of the opening sequence. He's pitched well down the range (with a touch of ADT on the voice?) and it stays that way right through the chorus, chorus extension to refrain, where the chords settle down slightly but the vocal shoots up the range (to hit the top B♭3), like a ferret up a trouserleg.

The melody in the refrain part is pentatonic, all black notes till the last – amazing what you can do with five notes. After that the song goes back to the verse, but the vocal doesn't want to leave the higher energy area, preferring to have some fun with yet another line. This time it's an adaptation of the verse, but split between two voices – almost a canon, at a beat's distance apart. (A canon is an identical repetition of a phrase by another part: 'Frère Jacques' is the obvious popular model, Bach is the master – try some of his *Goldberg Variations*.) The strict canon doesn't last long here, but it's an ear-catching moment – the one-beat distance between the two entries gives a real piling-up effect. Another two choruses and then the verse hits in again with extra energy because, yes, the vocal part has shifted sharply to the upper range (an octave up) and there's a harmony on top (a 3rd above) – which signifies big trouble for anyone trying to cover this tune, with the top note now at D♭.

At this point the 'Todo está bien chevere' BVs are back, stretching out and syncopating the words, as the track steams with Afro-American/Cuban/Puerto Rican vibrancy, and the toms are filling like crazy behind the percussion groove – like Ginger Baker having a particularly good day.

The groove really does hit the spot. It's not organised as rigidly as a mambo, but the combination of the upfront/downbeat shakers (have you ever considered what an onomatopoeic word 'shakers' is) and occasionally double-speed guiro on the chorus (16th-note 'chic-chicka'), working against the predominantly offbeat bass drum, bassline and vocal, all forms a perfect hybrid.

'Bird Of Beauty'

The earliest example of a defined South American influence in one of Stevie's rhythm tracks was back on *Talking Book*. 'You Are The Sunshine Of My Life', a song beloved of lounge-goers the world over, reached Number One in the pop charts in the States, and was covered by Frank Sinatra – which is about as much of a garland as you can wear.

Again it's the overall *sound* that's Latin-influenced, rather than the instrumental parts – with the exception of the bass drum and bass (beatbox-style transcript of which would go something like

'boom-chick-bom-boom-chick', the second bom half as long as the other two). That rhythm identifies the bottom end as a Brazilian style, which could be either bossa nova or samba. As the former is a slowed down version of the latter, it's hard to place a mid-tempo version in either category.

The next time a Brazilian influence is apparent from Stevie's music is on the *FFF* album, in 'Bird Of Beauty' – the track that breaks up the sombre mood of 'They Won't Go When I Go' (with the help of that strange wheezing whinny noise at the start).

Brazilian music swept the world in the early 1960s, largely thanks to the contributions of home-grown talent like Antônio Carlos Jobim, João Gilberto (and wife Astrud), and interested outsiders like Charlie Byrd and Stan Getz. But the story of Brazilian music goes way further back than bossa nova. The roots of the faster parent form, samba, can be traced all the way to the 19th century 'carnaval' celebrations (the great Brazilian composer/songwriter Dorival Caymmi once famously remarked: "If you don't like samba, you're either sick in the head, or sick in your feet.") Similar to the New Orleans

"If you don't like samba, you're either sick in the head, or sick in your feet"

Mardi Gras end-of-Lent celebrations, Brazilian carnival processions featured (and still do) unfeasibly large percussion ensembles, firmly rooted in the African tradition. It seems that the new musics of the Americas relied on input from African and European traditions – which is probably why they're so genealogically healthy. Samba is no exception.

The Brazilian cultural melting pot contained several ingredients: not only were there indigenous 'Indians', who had been there all along, there were also white colonialists, and inevitably the black slaves they brought from Africa. As these cultures inter-related over the decades, new 'mulatto' generations followed, matched by a musical fusion. The convergence of choro and samba resulted in a new kind of samba, which found its feet with the compositions of Sinhô, otherwise known as José Barbosa da Silva. His namesake, Ismael Silva, the renowned 'professor of samba', established a samba school in 1929, and was first to create a template for carnival bands.

The arrival of radio and records stimulated demand for new compositions and performers, and it was on the wave of 1930s samba popularity that singers such as Carmen Miranda and Mário Reis landed on the beaches of Rio. Carmen was associated with the most successful writer of that period, Ary Barroso, whose song 'Aquarela Do Brasil' ('Brazilian Watercolour' – better known as simply 'Brazil'), is not only one of the most famous sambas, it's the most recorded Brazilian song ever. It became Brazil's international calling card – at least until the arrival of a particular girl from Ipanema. (It was revived in the 1980s thanks to Terry Gilliam's use of it in his movie *Brazil*.)

There are a couple of musical characteristics in the song 'Brazil' that have become Brazilian fingerprints. The first is the movement of the leading line in the accompaniment, which (unlike 'Don't You Worry') goes up a half-step, twice (5th to #5th to 6th). If it sounds familiar it's because it's famously used in Monty Norman's 'James Bond Theme', as arranged by John Barry, but in that case over a minor chord.

Secondly, just as the choro featured a complicated chromatic melody, something of the same lingers here in the use of the lazily drifting half-step tune – an element that Jobim then Wonder would develop.

'Baião' was an older, folkloric dance music from the north east of Brazil that enjoyed a revival in the mid 20th century (thanks largely to Luis Gonzaga and Humberto Teixeira), its infectious rhythms catching on in a big way in the cities. At this point the samba was slowing down and acquiring a more orchestral approach, metamorphosing into 'samba-canção', and already preparing the ground for bossa nova (the 'new idea') in the late 1950s

João Gilberto was the premier musical inspiration. By slowing the samba still further, and allying that to a gentle guitar sound, he defined the bossa nova style from the start. Teaming up with the poet Vinícius de Moraes, and Antônio Carlos Jobim, who provided much of the musical interest and concept, they recorded an album in 1958 called *The Song Of Too Much Love*.

At first the new style received nothing but abuse from critics, who labelled it monotonous (Jobim's riposte would come in the track 'One-Note Samba'), but by the early 1960s the music had reached the States and beyond to universal success. The *Getz/Gilberto* album recorded in New York in 1963 – featuring Jobim backing fellow countryman Gilberto and jazz saxophonist Stan Getz – is one of many that cemented the mix of ultra-cool sax and sultry (some would say naive) vocals fronting a guitar-led rhythm section, with piano interjecting rather than comping, and a cool, even unexcitable drum/bass partnership.

The percussive parts were fairly well set in stone. The sidestick on the snare (see 'All In Love Is Fair') ticks out a version of what's known as the 3:2 clave – that's three notes (two dotted quarter-notes plus a quarter-note) in the first bar, two notes in the second bar (a quarter-note rest, then two dotted quarter-notes to complete the bar). In the meantime the bass drum plays the 'You Are The Sunshine Of My Life' pattern, with an extra 'bom' for luck (boom-chick-bom-boom-chick-bom).

The songs written/performed by Jobim and Gilberto – including 'Garota de Ipanema' ('The Girl From Ipanema'), 'Desafinado', 'Insensatez', and 'Corcovado' – helped create a movement back in Brazil, binding artists from every genre and funnelling them into the cafes and universities of Rio. The next generation, musicians such as João Donato, Edison Machado, and later Sergio Mendes, were devotees. In Jobim's compositions they were witnessing a musical/poetic partnership that has rarely been equalled in popular music.

By the end of the 1960s the Brazilian sound was extremely well travelled, many Grammies had been won, and many musicians had picked up on the freshness those songs carried. Brazilian musicians were travelling too – Airto Moreira and Nana Vasconcelos were both establishing

The instrument behind the enigmatic animal noises on 'Bird Of Beauty' is the quica

reputations as percussionists in the States, capable of adding new sounds to new fusions of styles. Miles Davis was first on the scene (wasn't he always?) with Brazilian percussion, hiring Airto to play on the fusion album that split the jazz world into warring factions, *Bitches Brew*. A completely revolutionary soundscape, where you could almost hear the sound of bullfrogs discussing Aristotle... Or was it a laughing horse?

The instrument behind the enigmatic 'animal noises' you hear in Brazilian music (and of course on Stevie's 'Bird Of Beauty') is the quica, or cuica. It's a strange device – a kind of drum, with the usual skin stretched over the top, but with a thin stick attached to the inside of the skin. The player moistens a chamois leather, then proceeds to rub the stick up and down briskly with the cloth. In the process of sticking/letting go (using the same principle as a rosined violin bow) the stick vibrates, the sound is amplified by the drum skin, and suddenly everyone wonders where those whinnying, barking, roaring noises are coming from. (Apparently its African heritage relates to lion-hunting.)

The instrument only plays two tones, so it's what you can do with it rhythmically that matters. Percussionist Bobbye Hall manages to extract a very satisfactory (as well as entertaining) groove from it here, and cruising alongside some more-funk-than-samba drums, 'Bird Of Beauty' is off to a flying start.

Apart from the quica, other external input on this track is supplied by the Wonderlove backing vocal team extraordinaire of Shirley Brewer, Lani Groves and Deniece Williams. They make their presence felt strongly over the intro, firstly with four bars of sustained notes, then what is essentially a samba percussion pattern sung to "doot-doo" etc. In a samba you would expect this rhythm to be provided instrumentally, whether by percussion or guitar or piano, but the use of it vocally adds an unusual texture.

It works because nothing else on the rhythm track has very much to do with samba: the bass drum is straight down the beat, with a curiously ambient sound to it, and the synth bass, deliciously ambiguous in tone, has a fast-moving (eighth-note) repeated figure that takes its cue more from the quica than anything else. No sign of a sidestick snare either – it seems as if the snare is going to be on the backbeat, but the second hit in the pattern is pushed forward (by an eighth-note) to tie in with the second half of the BV pattern.

The song is an invitation to everyone (especially himself?) to relax more

That sort of displacement is a funk tool. Herbie Hancock had just released his album *Headhunters* in 1973: an all-funk workout, which was one of the first gold-selling jazz albums, it included a track called 'Chameleon', featuring the rhythm section of bassist Paul Jackson and drummer Harvey Mason. The same displacement occurs there, not in the second half of the phrase but, more surprisingly, in the first; the second hit comes straight on beat four. It's there to tie in with the stronger-than-cement bass riff and its persuasive kick on 'one-and'. The Headhunters would take this technique to the limit on the next album, *Thrust*, where an accent could be placed anywhere in the bar. (Sometimes at the cost of the groove, but mostly not.) The groove is definitely enhanced by an open hi-hat that points up the strong beat in the first bar – another early fusion device that loosens up the groove.

This pretty much plants the 'Bird Of Beauty' backing track firmly in the area of 'samba funk', another in the great fusing traditions of samba (there's also a 'samba reggae'). Strip out the quica, BVs and lead vocals and the track would be funky with no obvious pointers in the direction of Rio.

So is there a reason for the reference to Brazilian music? Well, the song is certainly an invitation to everyone (especially himself?) to relax more, in the stereotypical Brazilian tradition: "Your mind deserves a vacation". It's important I think, given my earlier suggestions, to dispel the idea that this song is concerned with recreational drug-taking, despite the mention of multi-hued medication:

"There is so much in life for you to feel
Unfound in white, red, or yellow pills."

Stevie is clearly saying you *don't* need drugs, and instead extolling the virtues of taking time off. He said in an interview: "I meditate, but it's a different kind of thing ... Observation of your surroundings as well as yourself is the greatest way of having peace within. For instance when I did the song 'Bird Of Beauty' I felt God was telling me to take a vacation."[54]

And what's the physical equivalent of a mind vacation? Probably a break in Rio, where people know how to relax – just collect your ticket at the "please have a good time station", as the song says.

There are some odd phrases buried in there – this is from the second verse:

"Simon says that your mind is requesting furlough,
Let it find the answers to things
That you've always wanted to know."

Furlough is apparently a military expression for leave or time off. The use of "Simon says" reinforces the idea of gameplaying/recreation – and given Stevie's working regime in the first three years of the 1970s, a little vacation would seem to have been in order. As for the "bird of beauty" itself, it can mean all sorts of things to different people: a mental image of flight from the mundane, or space for the imagination to fly freely...

Sergio Mendes, the Brazilian composer and 'cultural ambassador', translated the third verse, as Stevie says in his sleeve credits, "to enable me to speak to my people of Mozambique and the beautiful people of Brazil." Translating it back to English is a tall order, but it starts something like this:

"All right
You must rest your mind.
It doesn't matter what's going to happen,
From now on…"

There are a couple of lines not transcribed on the sleeve – the Brazilian Portuguese version is: "Vai cantar, alegria que chegou/ Tao de repente." Which translates as: "Go and sing the happiness/ That has arrived so suddenly." This seems to give a more personal angle to the lyric, perhaps hinting at a relationship Stevie was forming, post-accident, with Yolanda Simmons.

Yolanda had rung up Stevie's publishing company asking for a job as a secretary. During his convalescence Stevie was in the habit of answering the phone in the office himself – he liked the sound of her, and one thing, as they say, led to another. Before long they were engaged, but it seems marriage had lost its attraction for Stevie, who felt personal commitment was enough without the need for what he considered a possessive formal agreement.

So could the "happiness that has arrived so suddenly" be down to a new romance (which would blossom further with the arrival of children later on). Could it even be that Yolanda is the "bird of beauty"? Or could the bird be singer Minnie Riperton? She and Stevie were also close around this time, and besides contributing memorably to *FFF* on the track 'Creeping', Minnie had been persuaded to join Wonderlove in 1973. The following year she signed a deal with Epic for a solo album, with Stevie producing. The album, *Perfect Angel*, contained the single 'Lovin' You', one of the most haunting vocal performances ever to top the charts in the States. Throughout her subsequent unsuccessful battle with cancer, Minnie remained close to Stevie, disclosing at one point: "Aside from my family, only Stevie knew what was happening to me in terms of the operations. He's always been real close to me and really sensitive."[55]

Some lines in 'Bird Of Beauty' might refuse to be marshalled into sense, but you have to take it for what it is – a mixture of high-sounding and fun-sounding escapism. If the words look strange on paper ("free to join in fun and plenty recreation"?), the sung phrasing makes it worthwhile. Perhaps not so strangely, the Brazilian words scan much more comfortably over the track than the English.

The chorus in particular moves in very groovy ways, and for Stevie is in an unusual melodic and rhythmic setting. Not unusual in its syncopation, we're well used to that, but in the laziness of the timing over the groove, which is itself a loping, backward-leaning creature.

Despite a few quibbles, and flawed as it is in the lyric department, the song remains a highly enjoyable experience, thanks to the good-time groove. Although the feel is straight rather than swung, there is a tiny percentage of swingage, which is a natural result of the accenting supplied by quica and anticipated snare. The bassline swings slightly too – check the "there a-*waits…*" at bar 17 of the verse, which digs into the swing groove fiercely. The shape of the bassline harks back to 'Too High' in places in its use of 'in-between' notes a step away from the root and the 5th note of the

The chorus in particular moves in very groovy ways, and for Stevie is in an unusual melodic and rhythmic setting

scale. These two notes are the ones you would expect to find underpinning samba and bossa patterns (and a lot of Afro-Cuban ones for that matter); what Stevie does is to lead up to each from a whole-note step away (4th to 5th, 7th to root), which provides more interest and character to the line – the second half of the 'Superstition' riff is exactly that sequence too.

Of course adding 'more interest and character' also means it's more difficult to play. In the keyboard lines there are many repeated notes that are hard to articulate cleanly – but that's something Stevie is clearly very good at, probably because he does it a lot. 'Boogie On Reggae Woman' comes to mind, as does all the picky clavinet work, which is also highly demanding of repeated-note dexterity.

You might notice I've not said anything about black-note, flat keys yet in this track. Well, for once there's nothing to say. The song's in a bright, uncomplicated, hand-over-the-white-notes sort of a key (G major). There are no gloomy edges to the chords, though there are a few slick half-step moves at the beginning of the verse, as well as a few 'substitute' chords (a substitute is a more complex chord that fulfils the same steering role as the one it's replacing). These run into and end the chorus section – for instance D$\flat$9$\sharp$11 replaces G7 and E$\flat$m7/A$\flat$ replaces D7 for a while, both tritone substitutions.

There is a definite Brazilian flavour in the use of some additions to the chords. Instead of the

straight major chord, or the bluesy 7th addition that pervades a significant number of the early tracks, here we have a much lighter, even happier palette. The extra notes to the basic chord are supplied here by the 'doot-doo' BVs (G major with a 6th and a 9th added).

The chorus also kicks off with a similar sound, starting major then veering minor in a move reminiscent of the 'You And I' chorus (C6 to Cm6). But context is everything, and while in 'You And I' the minor chord was all searing intensity, here it's a comfortable easing down through the gears to prepare to turn a corner. On the harmonic front too, the coda of this song uses the same chord progression as the standard outro to Jobim's 'Girl From Ipanema' (G6/9 to A♭13, though the whole thing is a tone lower in Jobim's song).

The contribution the BVs make to 'Bird Of Beauty' is enormous. Pitched above the lead vocal (top voice an octave higher), with the second voice interestingly in the middle (a 4th down from top voice), the two parts again lend a bright, open sound to the texture, which has an air of carefree, innocent naivety about it. They're also present for an uncommonly large part of the arrangement, and because the BVs take the melody on the choruses, it leaves space for Stevie to turn up the heat the last time around.

The line going into that chorus is pretty liberated too, but then the improvising starts in earnest: for the first half of the chorus Stevie's toying with the melody, tossing it around like a dog with a rabbit. Then he just can't resist the urge to pitch up higher, up with the BVs, and he's soaring alongside and around them on the last few lines, the "bird of beauty of the sky" part. Unusually the fade is really quick on this track – I don't know if there were problems fitting it all onto the second side of the LP – but it makes a refreshingly un-milked outro.

'Another Star'

You couldn't exactly say anything happens succinctly in the last of this Latin group, 'Another Star'. Whereas 'Bird Of Beauty' runs for 3:46, 'Another Star' manages to top the eight-minute mark at 8:22 – which makes it the longest track under the microscope in the book, beating 'Superwoman' (which is in two parts anyway) into second place.

Like several other tracks on *Songs In The Key Of Life*, this one loiters in the hallway for a while before finally going out and getting in the cab – but that was just the style and mood of the time. You get the feeling that *SITKOL* had to be bigger and better, partly because of the tremendous sense of expectation (even hype?), and in this case that meant *longer*.

There's quite a roster of musicians involved here, from George Benson on guitar (and BVs) to Bobbi Humphrey on flute and Nathan Watts on bass, and then there's percussion and brass, but we'll come to those later. It *sounds* like a large ensemble for sure – horn stabs and congas and timbales rushing headlong in a semi-Latin, semi-disco, constantly-driving groove. The rhythm track appears to have flown in from the Caribbean, the piano on the intro hammering the riff in octaves while percussion and drums emphatically sow the seed for the groove.

The Latin roots of this song are fairly mixed up: the baby has a Brazilian nose, Cuban ears, and its father's mouth. The Brazilian influences are particularly strong – not only the hint of samba but more importantly the north-eastern rhythm, the baião (principal feel of which is: dotted quarter-note, dotted quarter-note, quarter-note.) The Afro-Cuban flavour is more centred on the way the track sounds than the musical ideas. The left-hand doubling of the bass end, the machine-gun horn rattles, and the clatter of timbales are more likely salsa than Brazilian attributes.

Then of course there's Stevie's drum track, which is its own master. It employs a four-on-the-floor bass drum (one on every quarter-note), and another interesting open hi-hat part that balances the weight of the bass figure in the first half of the bar with an accent on the offbeat of beats three and four (three-and-four-and). If a disco feel comes to mind, or the later dance music scene, well that's not Stevie's fault (then again, on the other hand, maybe it is...).

With the snare on a two and a four backbeat, but lurking low in the mix (congas and timbales are way up front), that's the basic drum groove – but the main energy and push in the rhythm track is supplied by the piano and percussion.

If a disco feel comes to mind, or the later dance music scene, well that's not Stevie's fault (then again, on the other hand, maybe it is...)

Just to break down who's playing what in that percussion arrangement: Carmello Hungria Garcia plays timbales (a pair of metal drums that look like snareless snares), and Nathan Alford Jr is credited with 'percussion', so the presumption is that he played shaker and congas. Not that you can hear the shaker after the intro... In fact for me one of the problems with this track is that the arrangement is so huge that hearing (and maximising) the impact of each individual element is not easy.

Take the piano, for instance – or should that be pianos? The piano riff sounds so percussively heavy on the intro, and in so many registers, that it's hard to believe it comes from the one instrument. Sure enough, closer listening reveals the presence of two separate piano takes, occasionally playing very similar things, but with one more responsible for the bass region and the other more of a chordal comper. The first is panned mid-left and the second just right of centre, which makes sense in a combined piano picture (bass strings to the left).

The giveaway moment is the last bar of the intro, where the forceful lower octaves take a break and the right hand plays a figure leading into the refrain. Suddenly it sounds weaker, further away than before, and it's only filling one side of the sound picture. The line itself is interesting though – there are two parts starting an octave apart then converging (in contrary motion) towards the same note (C♯3/4 to C♯3), which in itself gives a clue to the shape of things to come.

Stevie's partiality for descending basslines hasn't diminished at all. This one goes down like this: F♯, E, D, C♯, B, C♯, F♯. That's the line that underpins probably 85 per cent of the song, including the refrain and the verse, with a couple of brief respites for the bridge.

The top line of the refrain, with true diverging baroque grace, goes up the minor scale five steps, then back down a slightly winding staircase. It's intriguing how the choice of key seems to trigger similar lines in Stevie's mind. The key here is the same as 'They Won't Go When I Go' (F♯m), and if you look at the instrumental line that follows the first verse in that tune, the shape is broadly similar. The emotional context is obviously a million miles away: no other-worldly spirits here, just the chorus of BVs (Josie James and George Benson, no less) with Stevie joining in – a refrain of la-la-las that appears happy and carefree... But there's more to the story.

The minor key setting provides the clue to the intent of the song, which concerns the aftermath

of an affair in which the woman has left the relationship to look for another "brighter star", leaving the man to bemoan the fact that he still only has eyes for her, so to speak. The imagery is certainly visual:

"For you there might be a brighter star
But through my eyes the light of you is all I see."

For the second two lines, further senses are called upon:

"For you there might be another song
But all my heart can hear is your melody."

So far, so good. But the track soon falls prey to what a *Rolling Stone* reviewer at the time scathingly called, "uncomfortable, twisted phrasing ... convoluted, awkward, atrociously rhymed and so tangled in their pretensions to 'poetic' style that they become almost comical."[56] And I'm afraid that critic had a point. The bridge is a perfect illustration of these traits:

"So long ago my heart without demanding
Informed me that no other love could do
But listen did I not though understanding
I fell in love with one
Who would break my heart in two."

It's one thing recycling musical devices from previous centuries, but lyrical borrowing is off the menu – this kind of pseudo-antiquated language just doesn't ring true.

The second verse calls on the sense of taste:

"Love might bring a toast of wine
But with each sparkle know the best for you I pray."

The third verse does nothing more than reiterate the first, with a rephrasing of the last line. *Rolling Stone* reviewer Vince Aletti summed up: "Even the most preposterous lyrics are salvaged by Wonder's melodies and sure, sharp, production sense ... What he can't say in words he can say more fluidly, subtly and powerfully in his music."[57]

I agree totally with the last part of this, but I'm not so sure about the "sure, sharp, production sense" in relation to this track. If one of the definitions of a producer's role is to shape the track so the overall form feels satisfying, and if another is to make sure everything on the track is crucial to the whole, then there's something lacking in the production here.

For instance, to return to the two piano thing, although it works as a strengthening ploy in places, at other points the two of them comping side-by-side in a similar sort of range ends up sounding sloppy, most of all in the bridge section. To make matters more muddy, I suspect there's a Rhodes track in there as well, which even though it lends some mid-range warmth, just adds to the general mêlée.

The devil's advocate reply would be that the presence of so many parts/colours actually re-creates the excitement of a live band 'going for it', to which my response would be, surely if you could hear fewer parts more clearly, you would generate the same, if not more, excitement. Comparison is never precise, but 'Don't You Worry 'Bout A Thing' has a far more focused overall sound, with the keyboard parts restricted to one piano.

To re-enforce the point that the more things you put on a track the harder it is to make each element audible, the contributions of the guest soloists might be looked at – a bit like tasting the individual ingredients and spices that make up a recipe.

Since the recording of *SITKOL* was split between New York and California, Stevie presumably had an enlarged circle of musicians to draw from. Guitarist George Benson – a jazz player by instinct, like Herbie Hancock – was at the height of his powers, and just on the verge of massive commercial success as a singer with his 1976 album *Breezin'* (the first jazz album to go platinum.) His session here starts midway through the second bridge with some jazz guitar lines that slot between vocal phrases. Very nice they are too, but the effort required to hear them, due to their lack of bite in the mix, means they can easily be overlooked.

The guitar line over the refrain isn't as much of a problem: its register lies above most of the action (apart from the brass) so it rings clearer, even if the space is as crowded as a department store at Christmas. It's a strange line, though – an attempt to find an instrumental hook, which almost works, but not quite. It's reminiscent of a chime, consisting of two-note phrases, consistently falling further from the same height in the second half of each bar (G#4 to E4, F#4 to C#4, F#4 to B3 etc).

Vocally the song has another impressive performance, though the voice sound is thinner than under Cecil & Margouleff's regime

But even the clarity of that sound gets masked by the horn line when it's active at the same time.

Another guest on the track, also a jazzer making a name for herself at the time, is flautist Bobbi Humphrey. Her album *Satin Doll*, released in 1974, has an interesting line-up: Larry Mizell producing and playing ARP, Don Preston (from Zappa's Mothers Of Invention) on Moog, and Headhunter Harvey Mason on drums – a West Coast selection of personnel, I would hazard. And the last track on her album is a version of none other than 'You Are The Sunshine Of My Life'.

Bobbi's contribution is significant on 'Another Star', as she manages to grab one of the few solo spaces that crop up in Stevie's work that aren't specially reserved for harmonica. The choice of flute sound has a lot going for it, but I can't help feeling that seven rounds of the refrain is overdoing it a bit, despite the lead vocals pressing for more intensity during the last three.

At the five-minute mark the song may feel finished, but a breakdown just after that, with timbales drumming the two-note riff, prepares the listener for another round or two. I have to admit here that I am primarily a jazz listener, in the sense that I like to hear musical interactions, and hear a song change with the input of a soloist – but none of that happens here. It is, after all, a pop song with a flute solo stuck on top.

Concessions are made in the mix to give the flute some deserved space, but it's already a crowded room, with a cluster of people always queuing at the door to come in, including a hard-worked horn section. Consisting of the trusty team from 'Superstition' days, Steve Madaio and Trevor Laurence, on trumpet and tenor saxophone, augmented by Raymond Maldonado and Hank Redd, on trumpet and alto saxophone respectively. These four also contribute to 'I Wish' and 'Sir Duke', and very tight they are too. There's a nifty passage in bars two and four of the refrain here where half the section (or the overdub, it's hard to tell) is written an eighth-note behind the other half, bouncing left and right like a table-tennis match.

Vocally the song has another impressive performance, though the voice sound is thinner than under Cecil and Margouleff's regime. This is probably true of the recorded instruments too – they seem flatter, more two-dimensional. But the voice still manages, as ever, to inject the energy needed to grab the listener's attention. The various ad libs on the out-refrains, as well as the last verse – which because of where it lies in the range provokes a complete tune rewrite – are worth the price of admission alone.

One last comment on 'Another Star': a notable feature that crops up regularly when the track is in danger of needing some glucose is the wild, swirling, you might say flushing, sound of the lower piano strings being excited into abstraction by Stevie's fingers (or even some other body parts). A great noise.

Of these three Latin-flavoured tracks, the first is probably the one that sounds most like its influences, while the other two preserve their distinctive Stevie drumming style, which naturally veers towards the funk side of the spectrum. The extra percussion parts add their own essence too. It does indicate a remarkable breadth to be able to borrow recognisably from several styles and yet preserve an individuality in the material and the performance.

Today we seem to be less tolerant of varied styles next to each other on an album: nowadays they would be collected together into separately themed projects – there would be the *Stevie Wonder Corcovado* album, and the *Stevie 'Salsa' Wonder* album, and so on. It's hard not to admire someone with the aural dexterity and imagination to write and produce so many diverse styles, and do it so convincingly.

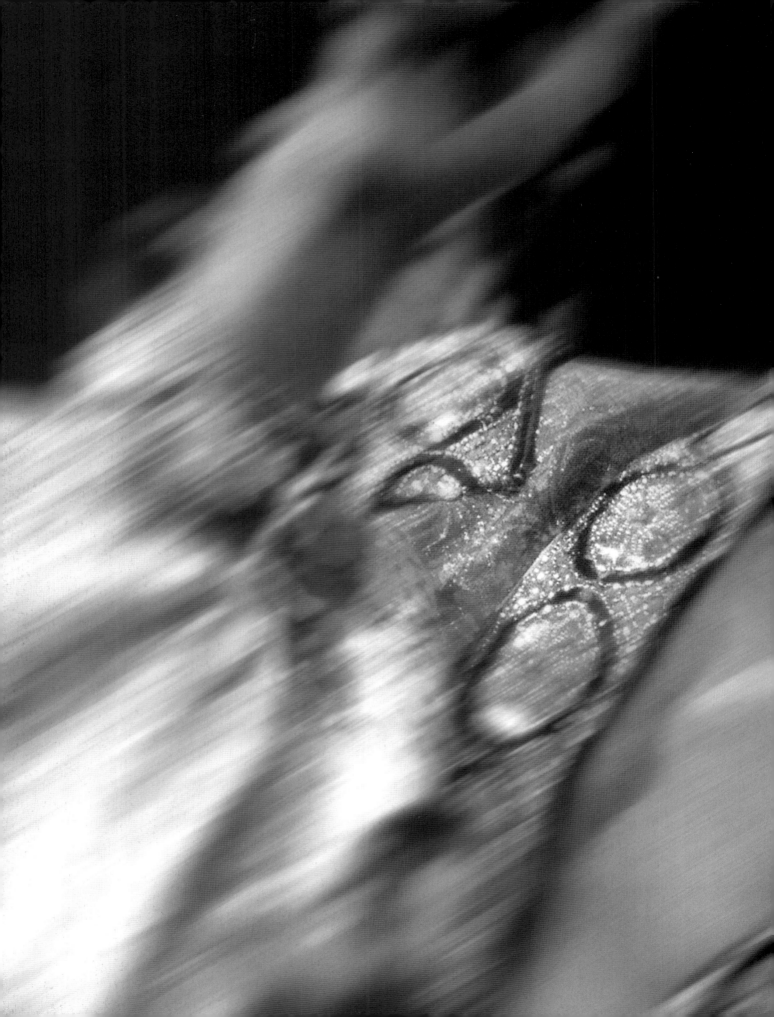

CHAPTER 9
POP SONGS

For someone who always seemed reluctant to write a conventionally structured chorus, Stevie has had an incredible impact on the pop charts. Not that the charts were of much concern to him throughout most of the 1970s – at that time his main focus was the bigger picture, namely the albums, and if the record company could find some singles in there, all well and good. But having started his career in an environment where sales and chorus hooks were vital to the continuing success of the business, maybe it's not surprising that Stevie should eventually have returned to the pop fold.

Two of the tracks included in this chapter come from the album that intentionally marked that return, 1980's *Hotter Than July*. Others manage to be both pop and 'art' simultaneously, a tricky balancing act to pull off, and a talent that very few people have.

'Superwoman'

It does seem strange that 'Superwoman' should have been chosen as a single from *Music Of My Mind* – and it's no great surprise that it didn't exactly crack open the charts, only managing to reach Number 33 on the pop and Number 13 on the R&B chart, and disappearing without trace in the UK. Admittedly it was an edited version of the eight-minute album track, which could hardly have made much sense. The album version is effectively two whole songs linked in lyrical subject matter and in production terms by a Cecil/Margouleff special that gives Tonto its first real outing.

Bearing in mind Stevie's predilection for developmental two-part (or even three-part) compositions, this is another in the grand tradition. It also showcases the type of chord changes seen in 'My Cherie Amour', and which will recur over the next few albums – the major, open, bright, untroubled language suited best to love songs. 'You Are The Sunshine' and 'Knocks Me Off My Feet', are both descendants of the chord colours here, but in 'Superwoman' the subject is the dilemmas of love.

A reflection of his troubles with Syreeta, 'Superwoman' is a meditation on firstly the ambitions of the 'modern' woman, and then, in the second part, a look at how the man still misses his love, even though they couldn't make it work. Stevie's been quoted as saying of the track: "Some people have said they don't see the connection between the two halves – but if you follow the song, it's saying the guy still needs her."[58] To me this smacks of justification after the event, and in truth perhaps the two parts started as unconnected songs. In any case the musical links between them bind the halves together, whether or not the lyrical concept works.

The instrumentation is extremely contained, almost chamber-musical and intimate in its approach. The delicacy of the seven-bar intro is unusual enough – three notes from the Rhodes, echoed by the bass synth (and a fine-sounding bass synth it is). But what's even more unusual is that the three notes, while forming a chord themselves, are suspended over a bass note ringing from the Rhodes that isn't the root of that chord (an F# triad over an E bass). A similar device, though more radical in its chromaticism, reoccurs in 'Too High', over the same bass note. The upper chord is a red herring: after the seven bars (which doesn't feel unnatural, even though you might expect eight), the first chord of 'Superwoman' relates to the bass note rather than the upper colouring.

Having opened with just Rhodes and bass synth, drums and guitar are added at the vocal entry, the first verse. The guitar is played by Buzz Feiten (misspelt Feiton on the album cover) with a light, jazz sound that Stevie always seems to prefer to the big, distorted rock guitar raunch. (Feiten has since worked with, among many others, Aretha Franklin, and is perhaps best known now for his invention of a highly successful guitar tuning system.) Mike Sembello would pick up the baton – or is it pick – where required, using a comparable style. The drums are similarly lightweight, cymbals and sidestick snare hardly disturbing the surface of the pool. With the addition of backing vocals on the second verse, that's all that happens instrumentally.

What's been going on vocally is a description of a woman intent on keeping career and relationship together:

"Mary wants to be a superwoman
But is that really in her head
But I just want to live each day to love her
For what she is."

As it continues, the song becomes more and more tetchy: Mary is trying "to boss the bull around" (another sly reference to Stevie's star sign, perhaps, as well as males in general?), but still the narrator thinks, "I can deal with everything going thru your head". In the end, though, he "just had to say goodbye". The last few choruses are progressively resentful: "I wish I could think of everything going thru your head, your filthy head."

Their daily routine at Electric Lady studios was a 7pm start and a 7am finish

Sounds like a bitter man, and yet the music reflects none of that – we're still in the same controlled but cheerful harmonic place. Despite the acceptant stance of the chorus – "I believe I know you very well ... Wish that you knew me too" – the singer feels his partner has not made the same effort he has.

It was a common enough phenomenon in the late 20th century, the tension between career and domestic bliss, and with no way out of the impasse the relationship had to be sacrificed. But if that was the wrong course of action, would the couple realise their mistake? Cue part two of the track, a simpler song of regret that she's not there, including the seasonal imagery we've seen before (of which Stevie was perhaps over-fond): "When the summer came you were not around." The only complication in the second part is expressed in the lines:

"Our love is at an end
But you say you have changed
But tomorrow will reflect love's past."

The implication is that, despite the fact that's she's now apparently reconsidered their split, he is not keen to have her back, as past history will always impinge upon the future. Of course, on the other hand, these could be *her* wise words in that last line, and in fact he still needs her as much as ever...

The situation is a bit of a conundrum, and if based on fact then it's quite a mature one for a 21-

year-old to have to face. But Stevie did spend a lot of his youth in adult company, which is maybe why his emotional intelligence seems advanced beyond his years. There must have been adult talk in the bus with Martha Reeves, and/or in the car with Clarence Paul and Ted Hull.

Understanding real life problems is one thing – resolving them is something else. It's interesting to compare Stevie's attitudes here with a later track like 'Ordinary Pain' from *Songs In The Key Of Life*. Another two-part song, the first half of 'Ordinary Pain' has Stevie pouring out his heart, wallowing in a bit of self-pity over a broken relationship, and then the second half consists of a female friend lambasting him for being a "masochistic fool". Again, it's clear Stevie was keen to present different perspectives on the same situation, whether or not he was able to act on them, or even necessarily agree with them.

It's hard to imagine that the intensity of Stevie's career would fail to impact on any relationship at the time. According to Margouleff, their daily routine at Electric Lady studios was a 7pm start and a 7am finish – what kind of strain does that put on married life? The work rate must have been punishing for all three on the production team, but they were enthused enough to put in the hours. They knew they were getting into something good.

'Superwoman' was the first track to contain a real 'Tonto section'. It acts as a musical bridge between the two segments of the song, and as a filmic blurring/fast-forward in time, then a refocus once the second part starts. We don't hear any synths before this point; the time slows and a repeated Rhodes note (which we've had before, leading back to a verse/chorus) now leads us somewhere completely different.

A melodic phrase that's echoed on the bass (as in the intro – ah, it all makes sense now) deliberately pulls the wool over our eyes/ears. The notes in that phrase are in groups of three, implying a time signature of 3/4, in a move that anticipates 'Living For The City', and designed to make you lose the pulse of the first part of the tune. It's cleansing the listening palate before the dessert, so to speak – like a musical lemon sorbet, perhaps.

The reason the style sounds so classical is again probably down to the limitations of the technology at the time

Once the three-in-a-bar movement has gone, it's as if time is literally suspended in preparation for the announcement of the new tempo and feel. The tempo of section one was around 112bpm, but the second is 86-92bpm; the listener is taken straight to the slower speed for the transition, which then gradually picks up steam.

The transition consists of an assemblage of lines that forms a modulation from the key of one part (E) to the other (F♯). The reason the style sounds classical is again probably down to the limitations of the technology at the time. You couldn't just stick down a chord: each monophonic voice had to be played separately – which is why Bach's lines were so perfect for Walter/Wendy Carlos, and why Stevie/Cecil/Margouleff synth extravagances sound so cultured (and contrapuntal).

The lines inhabit the area of high and mid strings, but there's not an ounce of string emulation to the sounds. The tone is quite rich, with a touch of the hollowness of a square wave origin, and the sliding portamento effect is engaged, so the effect is relatively sci-fi/futuristic for what is basically a simple pop song.

The arrangement not only gives the track a lift but also sets up part two. The same instrumentation is used, except for the addition of the synths, which carry on – they're inconspicuous during the verses but string-like in their part writing, particularly on the middle-eights.

The glue that binds parts one and two is the type of chordal harmony used: both parts start on the major 7th chord (jazz alert…), both have a rising chord progression, minor for two bars, then major for two (part one is Am, Bm, Cmaj7, D and back to root E).

Stevie was able to draw on the standard song/show tune models of the 1930s and 1940s

Another feature that's by now fully incorporated into Stevie's personal style is the chord at the second half of bars two and four, which is another of the chord-over-a-different-root sounds (in this case it's an A/B, or B11). It re-appears in the second bar of the part two verse (this time as a D/E, or E11).

It's all a long way away from the blues. The harmonic tuition that Clarence Paul (among others) had given Stevie, by showing him the 'standards', allowed him a freedom of chord choice that few other pop writers were using. McCartney's writing, at its best, is imbued with the same sense of historical background – they are both able to draw on the standard song/show tune models of the likes of Cole Porter, Jerome Kern, and other writers of the 1930s and 1940s.

'Isn't She Lovely'
The chord progression of 'Isn't She Lovely' is another one that's reminiscent of a standard from the jazz books. In keeping with the rest of the *SITKOL* album, where there's a general move away from the previous penchant for convoluted chordal and chromatic complexity, this track sticks to the basics of classical and jazz harmony. Its chord sequence particularly brings to mind 'Autumn Leaves' (by Joseph Kosma/Johnny Mercer), but it occurs in a myriad of jazz standards.

Instead of small steps in the bassline, here they are large and bold and solid. This song also has the confidence not to need to go anywhere very special – it knows there's plenty of mileage in the old sequence yet. The middle-four takes one step out of the back door, decides it's too cold and returns to the warmth of the flickering hearth.

'Isn't She Lovely' is a funny old tune – instantly accessible, but not a track in which you keep hearing more detail with repeated listens. What you first perceive is what you get. It's a complete pop song, every hook (and line and sinker and fresh bait) firmly in place.

The way the harmonica insists on re-inforcing the melody, so there's absolutely no way you can forget it (though it eventually does break away for a proper solo), is pure Motown pop sensibility incarnate – whether intentional or not.

All of which makes it hard to see why this song was never issued as a single (by Stevie at least). 'I Wish', 'Sir Duke', 'Another Star' and 'As' were released over the space of a year, from November 1976 to October 1977: the first two scored double Number Ones and the others only appeared around the 30s in the charts. Surely 'Isn't She Lovely' would have made a better single than the last two? (One story is that Stevie didn't want to edit the original down from its 6:30 into a single-friendly length – although oddly an edited version did later surface on his 1996 *Song Review* 'hits' compilation, despite the fact it was never actually a hit...)

Although the song is a celebration of his daughter Aisha's birth, the introductory gurgling sounds you hear are in fact from a baby belonging to a doctor friend of Stevie and Yolanda's. At the same time one of the world's longest drum fills (six bars, lasting about 12 seconds) is happening behind it – it's a complete guide to the land of tom toms, starting at the top, working down to the floor tom and up again. The six bars are a two+four, the two being drums only, then the bass (synth) joins in for the riff.

Even though the chords are (almost) straight ahead (C#m7, F#9, F#m/B, E), Stevie finds a way of chromaticising the movement by inserting passing bass notes (G#, G) stepping down or up to the next root, in a ghost-of-Jamerson way.

More chromatic movement occurs in the bottom line of the chord voicing (B2, A#2, A2, G#2), while the top line again falls, this time through whole steps (G#3, G#3, F#3, E). The reason why I say the chords are only *almost* straight is to do with the presence of the same note on the first two chords: on the second chord it forms a rich colour (9th); on the following chord (which is over a different root) it creates a similar sound to the type seen earlier in 'Superwoman'.

And that's it harmonically, except for how the tune relates to the chords. On the "Isn't she *love-ly*" part in the first bar of the verse, the melody falls to a suspension note (4th, F#), which exactly follows the way the phrase would be spoken by a doting parent – it's almost as if Stevie had analysed the cadence of the spoken phrase and translated it into pitched notes.

Despite his normal working method of groove, music, and tune before words, my guess here would be that the words were written right alongside the tune. The suspension note falls down a step and tension reaches resolution – it's like a musical sighing, this time of contentment. Over the middle section, the tune supplies a top colouring to several of the chords (all 9ths: B3 over the Amaj7, A3 over the G#7) to sweeten the harmony even further.

Despite his normal working method of groove and music first, my guess here would be that the words were written right alongside the tune

The tune itself is such a simple, effective design. Economy is to the fore; the same 'uptake' (the three notes before the bar) is used for the first four lines, with two different endings, then a rising line points out the middle-four, before returning to a version of the original phrase to wind up. Simple, yes? But you try it...

That's the secret of pop music, to make simplicity sound fresh – it doesn't matter if it has a short shelf-life, it's all about immediate impact. There's another theory that says a lot of the best pop tunes are based on nursery rhymes or playground chants, and you can certainly hear 'Isn't She Lovely' that way – with one added hook, which is the unison run at the end.

First a word about the rhythm. Instead of being a straight four beats to the bar, it's in a more bluesy/rock'n'roll 12/8 'shuffle' time signature, where the bar is split into four beats, and each of those split into three (da-da-da, da-da-da and so on). But since there's not a milligram of blues in this track, it's best to call it a pop shuffle here. Anyway, the break at the end is a run of triplet eighth-notes up a pentatonic scale, which signs off with a two-beat stop, before plunging back to the top again, back home.

The instrumental line-up is basic too: drums, synth bass and Rhodes, then voice (no BVs), harmonica and two main synth parts, in which Stevie was assisted by Greg Phillinganes. If you listen at the intro, the part that sounds like Phillinganes to me is the one that comes in the same time as the Rhodes and punches out a chordal punctuation, which disappears later in the track, or at least smooths out into a sustained pad.

The second synth part is an almost identical sound, but even harder to hear; it plays the tune (supported by chordal notes underneath) on the last four bars of the intro, and then becomes stringy/paddy in function, pausing only to take a breath at the ascending run. The part meanders existentially through the song, with no sense of build, no grand design save existence itself. You can't help feeling that if Cecil and Margouleff were still directing proceedings, this part would have been a) audible, and b) more thought-out in terms of adding interest where it was needed.

Perhaps part of the problem by this stage in Stevie's work is the introduction of polyphonic synthesisers. While monophonic keyboards presented their own difficulties, the new ability to busk chordally through a track, playing handfuls of notes at a time, though it's obviously a time-saving short cut, inevitably means less thought goes into each 'handful', so the end result is not quite as considered and crafted.

The production is also generally flatter than we have been used to, in the sense that there seems to be less depth to the mix. It may seem fanciful to talk in terms of another dimension when you just have a left and a right speaker, but compare something like 'Superwoman' (or almost any other C&M production) and you'll be aware of the incredible forward/backward placement.

The harmonica has always been Stevie's first choice for immediate instrumental expression

Nowadays Margouleff has his own company specialising in Dolby 5.1 mixing, and is looking forward to bringing quadraphonic sound into the home. In fact, even while recording the albums with Stevie there was a quad monitoring situation in the studio, run off an API mixing desk. This placed Stevie completely inside the music, and surely had an effect on the way the stereo mix eventually sounded. Stevie's post-C&M engineering/production team gets nowhere near the same holographic effect, and I'm afraid parts like Phillinganes' synth on 'Isn't She Lovely' are wasted.

At least you can't say the same for the harmonica. Although it's not the greatest solo Stevie ever played, it contributes enormously to the innocent/child-like mood. The harmonica has always been Stevie's first choice for instant, immediate instrumental expression, and there are many endearing elements in this performance. The ability to bend notes the way he does is not a skill everyone has.

Famous harmonica players are thin on the ground: even most fellow musicians would only be able

to name Toots Thielemans, Larry Adler, Tommy Reilly, Lee Oskar… then they might be struggling. Of course the instrument is historically never far away from the blues, and it was associated with the 'hobo' sound of the Depression, from Woody Guthrie through to his stylistic successors like Bob Dylan. But Stevie's style is very different to that of a blues player, and that's mostly down to the type of harmonicas he uses.

The first reed instrument that produced notes when you blew and sucked was a Chinese sheng, dating back several thousand years, but the harmonica as we know it goes back to the mid-19th century, and a man called Matthias Hohner (recognise that surname?). He took the earlier designs of the German Buschmann and Bohemian/American Richter, and sent some of his newly fashioned 'mouth organs' to cousins in the States. They were a roaring success, and established the names of both Hohner and the harmonica.

The mechanics were (and are) simple enough: a metal case covers the body, which consists of a row of holes, and inside each of those are two metal reeds, one vibrated by air going in, one by air coming out. In a diatonic harmonica (equivalent to just the white notes on a piano) ten holes are arranged to give a full scale in the middle and enable chord playing at either end. For the blues, that range of notes is fine, provided you have a harmonica in the right key for the tune you want to play (for a G blues you would use a C harmonica, so you can get the 7th note, F.)

For music with a wider harmonic reach, the chromatic harmonica has a clever device that makes the semitones possible. Each hole has four reeds, two as normal, and two a step up, which are normally covered. When you press a lever at the side, it aligns the air hole with the chromatic reeds, blocking off the diatonic ones.

Although most of Stevie's harmonica playing sounds effortless, it's an intricate business, with notes appearing where you don't expect them (talking as a keyboard player, at least). Although you could say 'Fingertips' was more about energy than accuracy, by the time of the mature albums, Stevie

Although most of Stevie's harmonica playing sounds effortless, it's an intricate business, with notes appearing where you don't expect them

had an instantly recognisable sound, as well as musical style. If pushed I would cite 'Boogie On Reggae Woman' as one of the most exciting, expressive harmonica tracks – particularly towards the end, where the technique of bending notes, and notes not quite functioning normally, adds a tension to the track.

On 'Isn't She lovely' the harmonica is more easy-going and melodic. In fact the first solo is so memorable it becomes a tune in itself – which is the aspiration of any soloist. The way every note of the melody is squeezed out, and scooped up to from below, fills it with human vocal inflection. It's often claimed that the instrument able to mimic the human voice most closely is the saxophone – well, not on the evidence here.

The harmonica sticks close to the tune on the first section then splits off on the middle-four, including the short (staccato) skip-like falls from the top note, which are cute but still distinctive.

The same tune happens next time after the third stanza, "life is Aisha…", and then honours are shared between harmonica and the sounds of bathtime for the real Aisha.

That makes seven rounds of the song structure altogether, some sticking close to the tune with embellishments, and some heading off on their own to a bluesier place – for example at the end of round three. Round four (seconds out…) has a great snatch of tune over the middle-four; the repeated notes cry out for words to be set against the melody.

It's at the end of round six that we start wondering how much longer this can be kept up. Probably sensing this, Stevie tries to add spice with some oddly placed blues notes, right up at the dusty end of the harmonica (the bent D over the F♯/B, and the G natural over the Amaj7). It's a perfect illustration of how much he knows about the blues and chromatic tension notes – as well as how to construct a pop song.

His voice, it almost goes without saying, soars over the top of the song, reaching top notes (B3) in the middle-four that make absolutely sure nobody else is going to cover the song in that key.

Enjoyable as it is, the tune (and the intense sweetness) does pall, so eventually I find it has to be limited to something like one playing a year – for the sake of my teeth, if nothing else.

'Master Blaster'

The next pop-infected track, 'Master Blaster (Jammin')', jumps forward to the period of *Hotter Than July*, in 1980. By this stage the Wonderlove band found themselves starting to get more involved in the studio sessions. 'Master Blaster' features Dennis Davis on drums (later with jazz vibes player Roy Ayers), Nathan Watts on bass, guitarists Ben Bridges and Rick Zunigar, Isaiah Sanders on organ, Earl DeRouen on percussion, and the brass team of Hank Redd (sax) and Larry Gittens (trumpet). Shirley Brewer is still there on BVs, with Marva Holcom, Angela Winbush and Alexandra Brown Evans for singing companions. With this level of personnel, you'd expect the result to sound very different to Stevie's one-man multi-tracked approach – and it does.

Stevie had spent more time with Bob Marley in 1979 at a gala for the Black Music Association in Philadelphia. They performed together, and shortly afterwards Stevie wrote the bare bones of 'Master Blaster'. His interest in reggae was long-standing: throughout the Seventies he had jammed and recorded with reggae musicians, and was interested in bringing the music to the mainstream. This time around the musical influence was to manifest itself in a more literal fashion. The song is clearly a tribute to Marley – who was diagnosed with cancer soon after the single was released, and died tragically young in May 1981.

At this point in Stevie's career there must have been a fair amount of pressure to come up with a commercial track, because his most recent album, 1979's double *Journey Through The Secret Life Of Plants* (more of which in Chapter 11), had yielded just the solitary single, 'Send One Your Love'. Although it reached Number Four in the album charts (Number Eight in the UK), the public's disinterest for the project was disappointing for Stevie – and the reality hit home hard when a gig on 'home turf' in Detroit failed to sell out. It was time for drastic action. And if ever there was a pop statement that said, 'Look, I can still write catchy, dancey, pop tunes that will sell, and then sell some more', then 'Master Blaster' was it.

The track received a lot of attention, as it was released well before the host album, whetting the public's appetite for *Hotter Than July*. Chart success was almost inevitable – a Number Five in the

pop chart and an R&B Number One – and the b-side was a six-minute, fully fledged dub version, complete with all the Kingston/Lee Perry studio tricks.

The intro takes us all the way back to 'Superstition', with drums setting up the groove for four bars, and the intriguing break at the front that sounds like a CD player in trouble. But it's OK – the snare and bass drum are just checking oil, water and windshield washer before embarking on their journey.

Far from warning of the troubles of society, the song invokes us to step aside from them

Once they're on the road, the bass drum (which the listener is *very* close to) punches on every beat, the sidestick snare on two and four, and the hi-hat is playing a swung pattern (eighth-notes swing). That's the main groove, but in most bars there's a fill on snare or hi-hat that cuts across the rhythm for a couple of beats, as customary in the reggae style.

Guitars and keys join for a unison riff that introduces the eight-bar verse material, a naturally simple descending line that propels itself with the octave leap of notes three and four of the riff – this was the age of disco, after all. Organ fits surprisingly in the grid next time around – instead of playing on two and four as you might expect (that's left to the guitars), it almost collapses to half the frequency by filling the gap in the riff on beat three.

Brass comes in on the following repetition, and it looks like there's a conscious decision to employ more of the language of reggae in the writing. Arpeggiation, stepping melodically through the chords, is part of that language, and it's being employed in the bass as well as in the brass, which solely plays broken chords for the intro, placed cleverly over the chord changes. That's the introduction, now it's time for the song to start.

It's one of the most optimistic lyrics in the Wonder songbook. Far from warning of the troubles of society, or preaching how to solve them, the song invokes us to step aside from them for a while.

"Though the world's full of problems
They couldn't touch us even if they tried."

The album title appears in the lyric, as does a direct reference to Marley: "Marley's hot on the box". It's party time, and nothing will derail the summer celebrations, despite the fact that: "They want us to join their fighting…" Then Stevie – somewhat unfortunately, given the developments of the ensuing 25 years – moves on to praising the peace in Zimbabwe, and pronounces, "Third World's right on the one".

He manages to create another ideal world, a kind of ecstasy through jammin', while ignoring everyday reality. Personal happiness isn't excluded either:

"'Cause we all just made a pact
We've agreed to get together
Joined as children in Jah."

So the one-man crusade to change the evil ways of the world seems to be curtailed for a while – although bear in mind: "We've only just begun…".

The feelgood factor firmly in place, the song dances its way through three verses and choruses, linked by a passage that's very similar to the instrumental section in 'Sir Duke' – a unison line (based around C this time, minor/pentatonic), four bars in length. This passage actually does very little except break the instrumental groove, so the groove feels fresher when it returns. The next time the link occurs it's twice the length, which gives it more room to explore, before tripping down the scale back to a reprise of the intro (and some ghostly whistling).

Reasons to be cheerful include: the slight awkwardness of the chords in the verse, which turns out to be a plus, and the sheer danceability of the collective groove. And of course there's the backing vocals: the line, "We're in the middle of the makings of the master blaster jammin'" is an 'earworm' in the extreme, and artfully sung. Part of the attraction is the gap between the two BV harmonies (first notes are E♭3 and C3), which gives them a certain fragility and delicacy.

The chords, well they're all major apart from the home chord, and in Stevie's output we're used to hearing a mixture of majors and minors in a descending run like this. Take 'Another Star' (which by the way has an almost identical bassline to this): the chord sequence is very similar up until the

The fact that the major chord sounds rougher, less smooth than its minor counterpart, adds to the earthiness of the track

fourth bar, which is where this tune departs from the rails of normality by keeping to the major (G). That tinge of colour is enough to transform the sequence from just another descending bass sequence into something more characterful. The fact that the major chord sounds rougher, less smooth (in classical terms more ungainly) than its minor counterpart, adds to the earthiness of the track.

The band do sound good together. The drum track is exactly in the pocket, the two guitars share out rhythmic duties sensibly – one with a regular reggae 'skank' over on the right, and the other shaping a similar part to the brass and bass by breaking the chords into single notes. The combination is reminiscent of the clav arrangements from the old days, but it sounds lighter, thanks to the tone colour of the guitars.

As for Stevie himself, instrumentally he's almost absent-without-leave for the whole track, apart from a Rhodes that doubles the intro line, and despite the sleeve credits mentioning a clavinet – if it's in there, I can't spot it. The Rhodes sounds more bell-like than of old: my guess would be that it had been modified with the 'Dyno' system. Around 1978 a company called Dyno-my-piano, run by Chuck Monte, designed an add-on to the Rhodes that allowed the player to change the tone through the use of pedals, beefing up the top end with pre-amps. It's a sound that's familiar from the Michael Jackson ballads of the time – for instance 'She's Out Of My Life', from *Off The Wall* (Greg Phillinganes is also in session on that album).

That particular timbre certainly left its mark. Synthesiser programmers would come to consider it as the norm when designing Rhodes/electric piano patches for synths – something that would have implications for Stevie later in the 1980s.

Stevie is of course present and correct on vocals here, with a suitably Kingston-inflected delay (two delays of dissimilar lengths, one sent left, one right) and a Caribbean delivery, clipped and slightly hard-edged, which again takes the vocal out of the ordinary and into a special area marked 'Wonder reggae/funk'.

Because the voice sounds as if it's adopting a persona, it's not one of Stevie's most heartfelt performances, but it more than fulfils the brief in terms of a catchy, singalong, energetic single. Incidentally the single made Number Two in the UK charts, as had 'Sir Duke' (see Chapter 10), and as would 'Happy Birthday' (see Chapter 11).

'I Love Every Little Thing About You'

This track brings us back to *Music Of My Mind*: having earlier questioned the sense of releasing 'Superwoman' as a single, you can't help wondering why the track that follows it, 'I Love Every Little Thing About You', was never considered potential chart material. How did that slip through the commercial net? The tune's pop potential seems enormous – it's bright, positive, uncomplicated, memorable, everything you'd think a single should be.

Then again, looking at the context… you can imagine why Stevie would want to focus on tracks that underlined his new-found mature/pensive/complex angle of approach. Maybe he felt 'I Love Every Little Thing' was just too bright, too positive, too uncomplicated – too much like you'd think a single should be. With his artistic freedom clutched firmly in hand like a flaming torch, Stevie's disdain for the singles market was plain to see. (Thinking about it, it's just as well he was doing all this in the 1970s – if it was in today's pop market it's unlikely any record company would be so understanding and indulgent.)

One of the first things that strikes you about the sound of 'I Love Every Little Thing About You' is its openness and relative innocence – far removed from the blues/funk influence of a track like 'Love Having You Around', it pitches the song straight into a mainstream pop environment. The tune is just *so* tuneful, the harmonies *so* harmonious, making it perfect crossover material for someone wishing to reach a larger audience. (Ironically, of course, Stevie's true musical potential was eventually realised through his more adventurous album work.)

The tune is just *so* tuneful, the harmonies *so* harmonious, making it perfect crossover material

The origins of this track's sound are filtered through from English pop and American country/rock – in fact it could almost be an identikit match for a Crosby, Stills, Nash & Young number circa 1970's *Déjà Vu* album. (While we're at it, 'Our House' on that album has exactly the kind of baroque descending bassline that Stevie loved so much.)

The musical characteristics that contribute to its marketability are the straight-ahead song construction, the unfussy sound, and the optimism/happiness of the lyrics. The only note of negativity is struck by the first line of each verse, where opinions of friends and outsiders are introduced:

"Though they say you're not my friend", and "Though they say that I am wrong". Despite 'their' views, the singer is convinced he knows better:

"But they don't know what you've done for me
You've made such a happy man out of me."

The next section, which we'll call the pre-chorus, confirms his need to put the doubters right on the subject:

"I'm here to say
I love you more each day
And I just want to tell the world
That I love you so."

At this point you might feel that you've just heard the chorus, as the shape of that segment opens out then resolves, using a similar harmonic technique to the end of the chorus on 'Seems So Long'. The progression is borrowed from church, a chord sitting on a bass note that's not the root note of that chord, but the solidity and re-assurance of that move is perfectly married to the words. (The chords are: A♭/E♭, resolving via E♭9 to the home key A♭.)

Sure enough it's back to a verse, then on to another pre-chorus (which for all you know is really the chorus) until... along comes the genuine chorus, transforming what has seemed an understated love song into a heart-on-sleeve declaration, complete with four "I love" lines in a row. If that's not hooky enough, I can't imagine what is.

Don't let anyone say Stevie is not a great drummer – his choice of timbre at specific points in a song, as well as overall feel, is impeccable

The chorus is built over the first changes of the verse and, quite unusually for Stevie, the chords just oscillate between the home key and four steps away (A♭ and D♭). I say unusually because when Stevie has a chorus its preference is to wander through a few avenues close by, rather than just crossing the street and back again, so to speak. But the effect here is to add to the stability and simplicity of the action.

By the time the chorus strikes up, the drum track finds a new level of energy too with the addition of a ride cymbal, which increases the impact of the chorus. Up until then the drums have been part of a controlled build-up – first leaving room for the bongos, then settling into a rock beat, with space for Stevie's vocalised drum emulations (tschhhhh, aaahh etc), and then finally breaking free. On the end choruses, as the BVs stack up, the drum fills turn exuberant – a finely judged take that excites without overwhelming. Don't let anyone say Stevie is not that great a drummer: his choice of timbre at specific points in a song, as well as the overall feel, is impeccable.

'I Wish'

At least the marketing department had its eye on the ball some of the time around about the release of *Songs In The Key Of Life*. 'I Wish' was the perfect single choice from an album chock-full of releasable delights (including, as we've seen, 'Isn't She Lovely' – one of those that got away). Among the last songs to be completed for *SITKOL*, the music for 'I Wish' was already finished but the lyrical concept at that time was not complementing the rhythmic drive and youthful energy of the song.

'I Wish' was the perfect single choice from an album chock-full of releasable delights

As Stevie tells it: "We were going to write some really crazy words to the song … something about the 'Wheel Of 84'. A lot of cosmic type stuff, spiritual stuff … when you go off to war and all that … but I couldn't do that 'cos the music was too much fun, the words didn't have the fun of the track."[59] (The 'Wheel Of 84', by the way, refers to the cycle of reincarnation.)

A Motown summer picnic, of all things, provided the answer – lots of activities, running around, games of various sorts with everyone joining in, all took Stevie back to his schooldays and lost youth, and that was the key to the song. That evening he went to Crystal studios to record. Full of real/imagined childhood images – such as waking to find no Christmas presents, illicit cigarette smoking, even playing doctors and nurses – the song mourns the passing of those years of (relative) innocence.

As is the case on much of *SITKOL*, some lines trip off the tongue easily, while others have to be pushed every inch of the way (like "Teacher sends you to the principal's office down the hall"). But mostly the thing zips along, as manoeuvrable as a Mini in Rome city centre. Stevie's not-so-little half-sister Renee Hardaway even gets a look-in as a disapproving teacher – "You nasty boy!" – and on the verses Stevie acts the bad boy in the background.

In the *Classic Albums* documentary on the making of *Songs In The Key Of Life*, Stevie is seen overdubbing a drum part – and indeed listening to the album you'd certainly think it was Stevie laying down the rhythm, yet Raymond Pounds (fine name for a drummer) gets a credit on the sleeve for drums. Closer listening reveals there's an extra hi-hat, one each side in fact, as well as an extra drumbeat/handclap doubling the snare on beats two and four, which certainly adds poke to the backbeat. The hi-hat turns into a bit of a naughty schoolboy/rogue element itself by the end.

Watching Stevie lay down that drum track, recording in isolation, you know just by his punctuation exactly where you are in the tune, even before it arrives at the middle breakdown. What's also fascinating to observe is the speed and urgency with which he needs the tape to be rewound to let him drop in on a mistake – a fast worker, that's for sure.

The bassline seems to have been recorded first, then the Rhodes part, which doubles the bass effectively in the left hand, then the synth parts that weave in and out of the Rhodes right-hand part. And all of it 'effortlessly' funky. (Watch out for a flash bit of fingering dead-on three minutes too.) The organisation of the parts reminds us of the old days – it's the equivalent of three clavinets working together. It's also similar to the way the guitars interact in 'Master Blaster'.

Nathan Watts famously plays the bassline. As mentioned before, the keys in which Stevie often writes (with lots of flats) are not ideal for playing on stringed instruments. You can imagine Nathan Watts turning up for a session hoping beyond hope for a nice bright dose of open strings (E, A, D, G etc), and learning the tune is in the very unfriendly key of E♭, as with 'I Wish'. It does make you wonder whether, in order to get a good low root note on a song like 'I Wish' (in the days before five-string basses), a player wouldn't be tempted to tune the bass guitar down a semitone, so that the nice, low, resonating open E-string is now really an E♭. Just a thought…

The *Classic Albums* film is also useful for letting keyboard players of the world examine Stevie's fingering technique. He has no problem playing the right-hand part, mostly black notes, while keeping his thumb pointing down and out in that stabilising position (as described back in Chapter 6). For a classically-trained pianist it looks a little weird, but, as they say, whatever it takes…

The brass foursome are the same team as on 'Another Star', and they get to play a frisky block-chord line on the outro, as well as the 'conversation' (or more of a shouting match) with the vocal on the choruses.

The middle breakdown section in 'I Wish' is the equivalent of the unison line in 'Master Blaster' or 'Sir Duke', in that its function is just to provide a release from the mechanical-grinder bassline, gathering energy for the next burst.

Lyrically and musically, it all adds up to an engrossing vignette: the man, now with his own child, not wanting to let go of his own, less-than-ordinary childhood.

'Lately'

The final track in this chapter could have just as easily been grouped with the ballads, but it always made such an impact on live audiences that it was deemed to have sufficient pop potential to be released as a single. In fact it became a much bigger hit in Britain than the US, reaching UK Number Three on its release in 1981.

The secret of the song's success is partly the over-indulgent sentimentality of the lyric, partly the simplicity and directness of the musical content and arrangement, and partly the phenomenal vocal performance. Some critics have compared Stevie to Elton John, but on the evidence here the piano is a more flexible tool, the voice far more impressive, and the writing more inventive. (See Chapter 4 for Elton's own view on who's best.) 'Candle In The Wind', probably Elton John's most famous ballad, from 1973's *Goodbye Yellow Brick Road*, shares a sentimental approach with 'Lately', but without the same intensity.

Stevie's decision to use just piano and bass synth for accompaniment brings the emotion even closer

Stevie's decision to use just piano and bass synth for accompaniment brings the emotion even closer. There's an intimacy that would be lost if drums were added, as well as a looseness to the flow of events. Stevie assigns the tune over the intro to synth and piano in unison, which forms an attractive hook right from the off. One word about the bass synth – it's not a double bass sample, but

it has nearly all the right characteristics of the acoustic bass, and you can almost hear flesh on string.

In songwriting terms the tune contains building blocks from earlier work, fashioned in a new guise. The first chords hark back to the 'Isn't She Lovely' sequence; the next group, at bar five of the verse, borrow directly from 'Don't You Worry 'Bout A Thing' (including the top voice chromatic descending line); and the beginnings of the refrain use the major/minor move of 'You And I'/'Bird Of Beauty'. The refrain itself uses the rising sequence outlined in 'Superwoman' – the only difference is the chords this time are all dark minor crunches.

The melody is straight from the top drawer, and well shaped for maximum vocal impact

With so much being borrowed, is there anything original in the writing? Absolutely – the melody is straight from the top drawer, completely natural in its lyric setting, and well shaped for maximum vocal impact. The refrain hits the highest note, then comes back down for "cry", all the notes held with perfect vibrato control, and as long as possible.

But the pièce de résistance is the end refrain, where Stevie revives the 'You And I' technique of changing register by extending the rising sequence almost off the page, so the song ends four steps higher than the opening key (it modulates from D♭ to G♭). This means the melody is pushed into its top emoting range, and in one glorious melisma Stevie manages a topmost top-note of D♭3 – which, if it were in an opera, would bring the house down.

From there it's a walk downhill to the finish line, and a surprising final chord out of nowhere (E♭maj7) that says, 'story to be continued'.

If pop sensibility is all about experiencing and then relating in a form that becomes universal in its appeal, then this certainly meets the criteria. But for Stevie Wonder at his best, it's about more than just mass appeal – it's self-expression through quality writing and exceptional performance.

CHAPTER 10
JAZZ/MISCELLANY

Sometimes it's impossible to categorise a Stevie Wonder song. The ingredients may be identifiable, but the personality and individual touch is so strong that it forms its own sub-genre or sub-section. But some songs show a clear interest in, and indeed a love for, music from previous generations of writers/composers in the jazz field, whether white or black. This is acknowledged specifically in the celebratory 'Sir Duke', but jazz can appear anywhere at any time.

If you take jazz to mean improvised solos, then Stevie's harmonica speaks the language of jazz eloquently. If you take jazz to mean a black-inspired rhythmic structure with sophisticated harmonic language and an interest in improvisation in the accompaniment as well as the solos, then virtually all Stevie's songs qualify. As I've mentioned before, the vocal outros – which sound largely improvised – inhabit a parallel world to the great jazz singers.

Even when there's no improvisation in a song, the jazz education Stevie had at the hands of Clarence Paul and various members of the Funk Brothers at Motown manifests itself in the quality of the materials used to build the songs. Mainstream jazz styles per se are left strictly outside the studio door – although there is a later track, 'Sensuous Whisper', on *Conversation Peace*, which employs a jazz feel and features trumpeter Terence Blanchard and saxophonist Branford Marsalis (it still sounds like a pop song though).

Some of the tracks explored in this chapter are included for their use of jazz improvisation, others for the use of jazz materials, and others purely because they create their own sound world.

'You've Got It Bad Girl'

As *Talking Book* starts to become familiar and get under your skin, its less immediate and attention-grabbing tracks start to creep into the subconscious areas of your mind and take root. 'You've Got It Bad Girl' was a prime example for me. There's something about the slitheriness of the eel-like synths, the held-back, understated vocal delivery and the unusual stance of the lyric (by Yvonne Wright) that is strangely captivating. Couple that with some jazz-inspired ad-lib vocals, which I'm not sure completely do what they're supposed to, plus some rare lead synth work from Stevie, and you have an absorbing combination.

The intro certainly sets off with an intriguing compositional device known as 'confuse-the-hell-out-of-the-listener'. Instead of providing, as most intros do, a way in, an easy mode of access, a welcoming explanation, this one starts to play games right from the outset. The slightly squelchy bass synth – sounding more like Tonto on *Zero Time* than the regular SW/C&M bass sound repertoire – plays a three-note riff: root, five steps up and upper root (A0, E1, A1). But it does so in a deliberately misleading way. Instead of repeating the first bar, which is what the ear is half-expecting, or even repeating one-and-a-half bars, which would also make sense, the four bars of intro are a random jigsaw puzzle of a rhythmic game. Because you expect the bottom note to land on the beat, it's a mild shock to find it delayed by an eighth-note (OK, it's hardly going to make your hair stand on end, but it is unexpected). Then it tries to catch up and over-compensates, so it's ahead of itself... and so on.

A run of three half-steps (chromatic upward motion) leads to the entry of the Rhodes, and even there the mystery remains, because the first note is anticipated by an eighth-note push. It's only when the hi-hat starts ticking that you have any idea where the timing is. (Like many a riddle, the answer is obvious once you know it: the intro is just four bars with four beats in each.)

The third/fourth bars are equally unsettling. Instead of the bar being divided into four beats, which by now would be (just about) the expectation, there are six notes in the space of four (quarter-note triplets). And when you think you've had enough of being messed around, here come those gorgeous synth lines – slightly brassy, definitely shiny – slinking in like a troupe of belly dancers, all curvaceous and bendy.

The voicing on the intro is unusual too: starting off three steps apart, the last two notes track each other four steps apart (B2, E3, and E3, A3), giving an open sound to the texture.

Openness and intimacy are the key words throughout the song. Stevie's vocal is smooth and soft-spoken, as are the BVs of Lani Groves and Jim Gilstrap when they arrive on the refrain (again, there's no real chorus as such). The timbre of the BVs is open and attractive, with Jim doubling Stevie, and Lani doubling an octave higher up. The only other outside contribution is conga player Daniel Ben Zebulon, who adds some effects to the intro – you know that thing where they lick their thumb and scrape it along the skin (a similar principle to playing a quica). Elsewhere restraint is the message – even the drums keep a lid on proceedings.

In songwriting terms, 'You've Got It Bad' is almost an exercise in moving chords in a parallel fashion. There are two shapes to be looked at: the first inhabits bars one to five, and is a minor chord (Bm7) that gets shifted up and then down again by whole or half steps – as if you held your left-hand fingers in the same shape on a guitar and slid from fret to fret. The other pattern is at the end of the middle section where the vocal sings the phrase "on a shelf". This time the chord is another of those triads over a different root (D/E or E11), as in 'Superwoman', which steps up a whole, then a half, repeating the cycle before treading back down again.

The gorgeous synth lines – slightly brassy, definitely shiny – slink in like a troupe of belly dancers, all curvaceous and bendy

It feels as if Stevie, rather like a painter, is doing a preliminary study for the full-on version of this kind of activity – the full-on version being the intro and chorus of 'Too High' (which by the way has the same tonal centre as this song). On 'You've Got It Bad' you feel there's an exploratory mind at work (what happens if I do this?), whereas on 'Too High' the freedom of motion is confident (look what I can do). There's a voyage of discovery in progress, that's for sure.

At the other pivotal point in the song – the entry to, and the first eight bars of, the middle section – the chords are based on cycles of 5ths. Four steps up, five down, and so on, much like the verse of 'You Are The Sunshine…', or the moaning souls of 'They Won't Go…'.

One last observation on the chords. The entry to the middle section has a very slick move: having just had the refrain in the home key (Am), the voice holds that note while the harmony lowers by a half-step (G#7♭9), twisting to quite a strange environment for the middle part. The lyrics are also quite odd and elliptical. It's Yvonne Wright's only input on *Talking Book* – she had worked on 'Evil' and 'Girl Blue' from *MOMM*, both good solid songs, but for my taste a mite self-conscious on the poetry-as-lyric front. 'You've Got It Bad Girl' looks at an age-old problem from an unusual angle.

The common interpretation of the expression "got it bad", when it comes to relationships, is that one or more parties has a serious case of the love bug (Duke Ellington employed a similar turn of phrase in 'I Got It Bad (And That Ain't Good)'. In this case – although the lyrics border on the impenetrable in places – things appear more complex. The object of the singer's affection seems instinctively inclined to avoid commitment – or perhaps even physical contact:

"When you believe in a feeling,
That's holding you back from my love,
Then you've got it bad girl, you've got it bad girl."

"When you insist on excluding
The tenderness that's in my kiss,
Then you've got it bad girl…"

…. "Should you depend on an outlet,
Through which an escape can be found,
Then you've got it bad girl."

But the singer isn't giving up easily on his love, insisting there's, "just no way of getting round me". The very last stanza adopts an alternative approach, turning things around by pointing out that, if/when she finds "just a small space" in her mind for his love, "Then you'll have it good girl…"

The particularly good thing in this track is the amount of space the vocals have in which to cut loose. Lani Groves is the first to have the reins removed, over the initial middle section, and her line, which sounds as if it was learned rather than improvised, sits well on top of the complex changes stirring underneath.

What is bizarre, though, is to have another freewheeling element, the lead synth solo, happening simultaneously. They bump at one point, but there's no great damage done, and they whirl off again to their different corners. Maybe that's it – the two soloists are the protagonists in the song: the girl, over on the right, refusing to come into the picture, and the guy in the middle constantly trying to entice her in… No, I didn't think so either, but worth a try.

The synth is full of small grace notes and tiny pitch bends that define a personal playing style

The synth – flutey but not breathy – is full of very small 'grace' notes that lead up to the main note, and tiny pitch bends that define a personal style of synth playing, even at this early stage of development.

By 1972 there was in fact a growing number of players with a personal synth vocabulary: Frank Zappa's record *Waka/Jawaka* features both George Duke (who would almost hijack the Minimoog, but played mostly Rhodes/piano) and Don Preston, the latter navigating a memorable synth solo on the title track. The English 'prog' (progressive) rock movement was on its feet, taking to synths in a big way – and I mean big: Yes released *Fragile* in 1972, showing off the expansive keyboard style of Rick Wakeman, and Tony Banks of Genesis was also incorporating synths into his keyboard set-up. There was Jeff Lynne and the Electric Light Orchestra, Keith Emerson with the amazingly productive Emerson, Lake & Palmer (four albums in two years), Rick Wright of Pink Floyd... the list goes on. And given the variety of results, it proves the synthesiser was an adaptable instrument, capable of being tamed and shaped, given the right ears and fingers. Stevie's controlled synth solo here is a million miles removed from the macho bravado of, say, ELP's *Pictures At An Exhibition*.

Things do hot up on the next middle-16 of 'You've Got It Bad'. More voices are loaded up either side (incorporating more of an improvised feel), while the synth is very busy in the middle of it all. I particularly like the phrase Stevie plays over "things I do" – quite horn-like in its choice of notes (E4, D4, G4, E4 etc). The lead synth is active to the end, in one of the most fluid and note-laden passages Stevie ever delivers. This is emphatically not self-indulgence, though – compared with the saturated prog rock bands, this is a low-fat, low-calorie, light snack.

Personally I would have preferred to hear more synth and fewer vocal lines in this track – fine as they are, the BVs tend to distract from the main vocal business. Having said that, the way the track is mixed does at least allow for co-habitation of so many free-spirited elements.

'Visions'

'Visions' falls into the jazz category here not only because it houses a generous amount of instrumental freedom, but also because the chordal language is as advanced as anything we'd seen before (in 1973), and borrows heavily from, while adding to, jazz harmony.

It's not difficult to see why Stevie himself views this song as one of his best. It's a complete gem, and full of hard-to-open cupboards that contain a variety of treats – not least the up-closeness and shimmering of the guitar tracks.

As explained in Chapter 5, there are three guitar parts, split across the stereo image – electric down the middle and, I would imagine, two takes of acoustic panned left and right. They have separate functions, and interest turns from one to another in different parts of the song, but broadly the acoustic guitars carry the burden of song propulsion (along with the bass, naturally) and the electric guitar is more soloistic in approach.

You'd think three guitars on a track, particularly considering the amount of freedom involved, would be overkill, but not so – all the fills and single lines always avoid each other, as if they were molecules kept apart by an electromagnetic charge. For one thing David Walker's electric is playing mostly above the others' voicings; over the intro Walker plays the motif that is the constant returning point of the song, a jazz colouring (adding a 9th to Bmin and C♯m) in the upper range of the guitar.

The guitar chord voicings lie discreetly in the shadow, while underneath them Malcolm Cecil's double bass contributes a line that also emphasises the jazz-tinged 9th chords (top note of the bubbling-up phrase is C♯). There would be a certain degree of expectation on Cecil to record himself well, and he doesn't disappoint – the bass sound is soft, warm, supportive yet with enough detail to hear fingers on strings. You can't quibble with the intonation either on a line that travels from the bottom of the instrument on a voyage of discovery across the strings/up the neck.

The intro is the kernel of the song here, as it provides a comfortable resting place for the returning traveller. The verse also spends time in the bus depot there (the chords remain static for four bars), before departing on a convoluted journey, with several changes of route along the way.

The bar-per-chord stability of the intro, gently swaying back and forth, lulls the listener into a false sense of security. Soon the ground is shifting beneath our feet, as a passage of descending chords leads to murky depths before landing on the ledge (F♯7aug) that leads back to safety.

The melody is out-of-the-ordinary too, but it matches the mood of the lyric exactly. The structure of the lyric is very controlled – the first and second lines evoke the dream:

"People hand in hand
Have I lived to see the milk and honey land?"

Then the mood changes slightly, and Stevie dips in register, as if he's recoiling at the thought of the word "hate" in the next line:

"Where hate's a dream and love forever stands
Or is this a vision in my mind?"

The pattern of introducing an element of doubt, or reality, persists in the following verses too: "Have we really gone this far through space and time", and "Or do we have to find our wings and fly away" both receive the same musical treatment. The effect is achieved by moving two pairs of chords down a whole step in parallel motion, but it's the nature of the two chord shapes that makes it special. Though both voicings sound sweet and rich on guitar, there is an element of dissonance, as they each contain one of the most jarring intervals (A13 and G13 have a maj7th between 7th and 13th; E7♯9 and D7♯9 have the same interval between 3rd and major 3rd (♯9)).

The augmented chord, the temporary resting place, is also an appropriate choice: it functions like the musical equivalent of a quizzically raised eyebrow. The short pause on the chord elongates that uncertainty, then it's back to the top for another verse.

The middle-eight (or almost eight) brings a steadier rhythm in the panned-left guitar; though muddied by the goings-on elsewhere, it's a clear glimpse of a bossa nova pattern, which comes and goes like waves on Ipanema beach. The inference is clear though – soft guitars, hints of bossa nova, and dense harmonies are all paths back to Jobim/Gilberto. There's even more of a clue in the chord sequence at bar three of the bridge, where the descending semitone line at the top of the accompaniment makes probably its first appearance.

Except it's not as obvious as all that. Stevie modifies the last chord by taking it down a whole rather than half step, which throws the ear somewhat. You get the feeling a lot of thought has gone into both music and lyrics here, in order to tread new ground and push the limits of the personal language forward. The long pause over another augmented/questioning chord reveals more tension in the chords – is it the raised eyebrow or not? The guitarists seem to think it is, but Stevie, in the melody and the chord he's playing on Rhodes, is sure that it's not. Last time around the bridge there's no disagreement, Stevie just ducks out of the way quickly on the vocal melody to leave the guitar and Rhodes hanging for what seems an unfeasible length of time (in fact it's just two bars).

The section with the guitar solos is interesting, as they're not constructed like traditional jazz solos, with a beginning, middle and end. Maybe the producers gave instructions for guitarists Parks

Stevie with jazz legend Miles Davis in 1970 – it was around this time that Davis 'borrowed' young bass protégé Michael Henderson from Stevie's live Wonderlove band

and Walker to be fluttering birds or forest floor animals (don't laugh, I've come across stranger directions), because the solo section is less concerned with notes than the atmosphere induced by the fast finger-picking (tremolando). The attention shifts after eight bars from electric to acoustic, and then it's a wind-down, and sail back to harbour.

There's a tremendous amount of growing up in this song. Whereas a dream of an ideal society might previously have seemed possible, Stevie is coming to terms with the likelihood that Utopia can only exist as a vision and not a reality. In a strong visual image of imagined colour, Stevie insists that he is not living in cloud-cuckooland, but has a grasp on earthly actuality:

"I'm not one who make believes
I know that leaves are green
They only turn to brown when autumn comes around
I know just what I say
Today's not yesterday
And all things have an ending."

There's musical growing up in progress too. For Stevie hardly to play at all on a track is a big step in letting go, and a sign of self-confidence as a writer. The consideration given to all levels of expression, including the understated vocal, is impressive.

This song lies at the core of the *Innervisions* album, with the writer trapped between an idealised spiritual world and the reality of everyday urban life. But Stevie knows exactly where he is in songwriting/production terms – in hindsight it's the height of his most creative period.

'Sir Duke'

The reference in the title of 'Sir Duke' is to one of the most important jazz composers/piano players of the 20th century, Duke Ellington, but the song is a general tribute to musicians past and present. More than that, it's a celebration of music itself – almost a modern hymn to Saint Cecilia, the traditional muse and patron saint of music.

The idea of music as a common language, linking people of different races and creeds, is at the centre of this kind of inclusive, idealistic philosophy. (A good introduction to the communicative power and materials of music is Deryck Cooke's book *The Language Of Music*.) Thing is, it looks great on paper, but doesn't quite hold water. I think it's fair to say that even if it's one language, there are many dialects. A flexible musician intuitively learns the dialects as part of everyday curiosity, as well as intensive study – some musicians can speak in many tongues more easily than others. Stevie perhaps reached his peak in this regard on *Songs In the Key Of Life*, where the breadth of influence is so diverse and the ambition so intense that he'd freely follow the dark synth strings of 'Village Ghetto Land' with the jaunty 'Sir Duke'.

Duke Ellington (born Edward Kennedy Ellington) was there at the beginnings of jazz, having formed his first band in 1917. He moved to New York City in 1923 and found the power of radio propelling him into popularity and recording contracts. The Cotton Club, which also broadcast on the radio, gave Ellington and his band (at that time The Washingtonians) another exposure boost, and from that time to his death in 1974, the Duke was in constant demand worldwide.

As well as writing in the standard song format ('Take The A Train', 'Satin Doll', 'It Don't Mean A Thing (If It Ain't Got That Swing)', 'Sophisticated Lady', etc etc), Ellington was one of the pioneers of jazz composition, taking and developing the style but extending the form, and some of his best music lies in the various suites he wrote in the last 30 years of his life. (Nixon was a huge admirer, saying: "In the royalty of American music, no man swings more or stands higher than the Duke.")

This track was a risk for Stevie. If you write a tribute that doesn't live up to the reputation of the subject, it falls flat on its face. Fortunately the band on 'Sir Duke' are in cracking form, and the playing is so crisp you can feel the starch on the collar. With Pounds on drums, Watts on bass, Sembello and Bridges on guitars (right and left of the stereo image respectively), Stevie on Rhodes, and the resident *SITKOL* horn section, there's no worries about this record being anywhere else but 'in the groove', as the lyrics say.

'Sir Duke' was a risk for Stevie. If you write a tribute that doesn't live up to the reputation of the subject, it falls flat on its face

There's not much more to comment on lyrically — except perhaps to question the inclusion of Glenn Miller. Among the inspirational names mentioned are jazz bandleaders Count Basie and Louis (Satchmo) Armstrong, Ella Fitzgerald, who made her name singing with Duke's band... and then there's Glenn Miller, the white bandleader who, as many people see it, appropriated the Duke's big-band sound, simplified it, commercialised it and sold it in vast bucketloads — exactly the kind of behaviour that Berry Gordy had been trying to subvert. You might understand if it had been Benny Goodman, who at least was a jazz writer. But maybe the point is that Miller was a populariser — he played music for dancing and sheer enjoyment, as a relief and escape from the all-too-harsh reality of WWII. In any case, Miller would be pleased to be in such company.

The chorus is a one-line statement that sums up the mood of the song — "You can feel it all over" — a hugely catchy line that hooked a nation, ensuring a second consecutive Number One in both US singles charts. In fact, much of the world was hooked: it was a Number Two single in the UK, equalling Stevie's highest chart position there up to this point (the previous one was 'Yester-Me...', over seven years earlier). The appeal must have been primarily the groove, then the unexpected melodic and harmonic twist in the chorus, and the immaculate horn section arrangement.

Those horns start as they mean to go on, neat and tidy against just the bass drum and hi-hat. The brass tune is like an early study for 'Master Blaster', running up the notes of the chord, with the occasional chromatic dip down and up again. Destined never to re-appear in the song, like many of Stevie's intros, it sets up the swing feel and jazz ambience a treat. (When the horns stop for a bar, the bass drum suffers from some untidy engineering — you can hear the 'noise gate' opening and closing.)

As we go into the verse, the two guitars work off each other in a sort of banjo-like way, while the bass almost 'sousaphones' its way through the track with a street-band march feel. The middle-four hits half-step world in a big way; the root and chords go three steps down, three up, three down, then five up (all 9th chords, starting on E9, finishing on F♯9), and then they're poised for the chorus.

While the bass and guitars are essentially playing double-time 'oompah' rhythm, the drums stick safely to a pop backbeat snare on beats two and four, ensuring the pop eligibility remains intact. The resultant groove is a street-jazz/swing-funk/hint-of-reggae/pop mix that's probably unique, and establishes its own identity despite the myriad influences.

The chorus starts innocuously enough, but bar two heads off at a tangent, returning to the fold in bar three. Sometimes as a songwriter you'll be looking for a feature to make a particular moment sound distinctive, and I'll wager that Stevie added the 'surprise' chord afterwards. The chorus starts in the home key (B major), and the logical chord move would be down to the relative minor (G#m) – except that's the verse pattern, so he had to find a chord that does the same job and substitute it… Ah, here we are, F minor. With bar three just a half-step down (Emaj7), that provides the perfect point of interest and tension.

Talking of tension, that's also the bit where the vocal line leaps five steps up into top emotive gear, landing on the highest note of the song (B♭3) before settling down a couple of steps. The interval that the high note makes with the chord (a 4th) is unsettling, and is in need of downward resolution (minor 3rd). Interest is maintained by means of some beautifully voiced horn lines (à la big-band) that inhabit bars three and four; you can hear the work that's gone into those two lines, so it's a shame they're discarded after that chorus in favour of repeated-note cattle prods.

The resultant groove is a street-jazz/swing-funk/ hint-of-reggae/pop mix that's probably unique

The eight-bar chorus proceeds without any further disturbing incidents to the instrumental bridge (again a model for 'Master Blaster'), which is a fabulous unison line, tricksy but memorable. It's actually very hard to play on keyboards – as you could hear when Stevie (perhaps a little rusty) tried it once during a BBC radio interview.[60] But Mike Sembello (right-channel guitar) and Nathan Watts on bass don't seem to have any problem with it – they manage to make it sound like falling off a log. The horns deal with it splendidly too, bending and flexing in all the right places. The line itself is all built over the one tonal area (B major/pentatonic with the odd blues 3rd), with some suitable jazz hi-hat to keep things rolling along.

Another verse and many, many choruses make certain that the tune is firmly fixed between our ears – a true celebration of the groove, and of music itself.

'Pastime Paradise'

The second outing for the Yamaha GX-1 synth strings on *SITKOL*, 'Pastime Paradise' falls neatly into the pigeonhole marked 'unclassifiable-but-interesting'. It was given a second lease of life through Coolio's 1995 hit 'Gangsta's Paradise', which used the chorus as a refrain between its rap sections (a new generation weren't aware that the original song was by Stevie, but I'm sure sales of *SITKOL* were revived when they found out).

Pitting a backward-referring/retro Afro-Caribbean percussion track against a forward-looking synth(etic) string track, the song examines the dichotomy between the pervasive negativity of an imperfect past and the positivity of looking forward to an idealised future (not necessarily in this life).

An alternative interpretation might be that 'pastime paradise' refers to the materialistically obsessed 'leisure-culture' of modern times, which Stevie could be contrasting with the ethic of working hard and getting your reward in heaven.

Though the song's ideas are philosophical/spiritual, the non-denominational slant is emphasised by the use not only of a gospel choir – from the West Angeles church of God – but also a Hare Krishna chanting group, who together build a multi-cultural finale.

The other musicians are percussionists Raymond Maldonado and Bobbye Hall, who supply the history-laden percussion track. Starting with cowbell and guiro, congas join in, and something that sounds like wood is hit to provide a backbeat – maybe the side of a drum (even an Eastern mrdanga or dholak). The Hare Krishna musicians also supply a persistent 'chinging' bell pattern.

The synth strings are split and arranged more as a string section with separate parts. It starts with a repeated-note pattern (C5, C4, C4, C4 etc in 16th-notes), coupled with a 'cello' part which I have to say is so note-for-note like 'Eleanor Rigby' that no forgiveness is possible unless it's a conscious tribute. (In fact, in the *Classic Albums* documentary, Stevie does acknowledge a debt by saying that he wanted the track to have the feel of 'Eleanor Rigby'.[61]) The line in question is a scale running up eight steps (A♭2 up a lydian mode), which then repeats a step up.

While we're on things sounding like other things, the key and sound of the chords here is more than a little evocative of Chopin's 'Piano Prelude In C minor', which in turn owes a debt to J.S. Bach's own 'Prelude In C Minor'. There's a fair chance Stevie's classical education would have exposed him to pieces like these, showing just how wide his influences could be.

The groove of 'Pastime Paradise' is given a greater swing by the placement of the bass part: sounding more like the pizzicato (plucking) of an orchestral double-bass section than a synth or electric bass, the rhythmic pattern has a salsa-esque lean to it. The first emphasis falls just a 16th-note before the second beat, and the second note lands on the 'and' of beat two, which means the bass catches the vocal phrasing on "lives" and "past" in the first couple of lines of the verse. This is another reason why a rap artist would be interested in the arrangement of the groove, as it falls straight into a standard hip-hop pattern.

Given the resources used at the end, this song is remarkably restrained in its length – you might think that having assembled those choirs you'd want more out of them, or build an end section that's more structural (Stevie was never averse to stringing out an ending – just look at 'Another Star' and 'As' from the same album). But this time it's all about the colour. As soon as all the elements have made themselves known, the string part announces the coda, and the track abruptly closes with a foreboding crash on a gong.

Coolio called his 'Gangsta's Paradise' a "new negro spiritual", whereas Stevie's version is more inclusive than that; for all the weaknesses of the *SITKOL* album – and it does miss the mark sometimes by cajoling or preaching along the way – there is a genuine effort to include all humanity in its celebrations, aspirations, meditations, mediations, associations, and co-operations.

"Praise to our lives
Living for the future paradise
Shame to anyone's lives
Living in the pastime paradise".

'As'

As an affirmation of eternal adoration between two people, 'As' is just about as convincing as it gets. Not because every line of the lyric makes perfect sense, but because the vocal performance and song structure build to a level of intensity that won't be denied. (I'm referring to the full-length, seven-minute album track here, of course, rather than the truncated single version.)

The listener is transported by repetition to almost a semi-conscious state where time, dreams, reality, all merge into a 'oneness' in love and nature and groove… and if that sounds horrendously pretentious, I'm sorry but that's really what Stevie's after here, and it works.

This is all contained in the music – a constantly rising chorus bassline and harmonic movement reach up and out (but never actually arrive anywhere) for the unattainable state of perfect human love. "Until the day that you are me and I am you"…

A constantly rising chorus bassline and harmonic movement reach up and out for the unattainable state of perfect human love

The first sound you hear is a four-note call from the Fender Rhodes that seems to announce the presence of Herbie Hancock, who was proud to be part of the *SITKOL* experience (Stevie even lent him an Oberheim four-voice polyphonic synth so Herbie could use it on a session of his own). In fact my bet would be that Stevie laid down the first Rhodes track as a basic underlay for the song and then brought Herbie in to be more of a 'free spirit' on top.

In the sound picture the underlying Rhodes track is spread centre and left while Herbie's track (which consists mainly of just right-hand fills) plumbs a path straight down the middle. The overall effect could be created by one player, but it would take some doing to combine both roles, structural and ornamental, in one take. That description of Herbie's role doesn't do his contribution justice of course; it's not merely decorative, because the musical interest and energy he supplies between, and even during, vocal phrases lifts the track immensely.

From the intro (with Stevie singing a 'doo' line that curiously never re-appears) onwards the vocal and Rhodes form a partnership that co-exists to the end of the track. The Rhodes solo even ups the level of funk and prepares for the gritty middle bridge section, "We all know sometimes life's hates and troubles".

Structurally the song is light on verse and bridges – the chorus/refrain is the thing. In fact after the first two minutes – consisting of verse, chorus, middle section, verse – it's that gospel-like chorus pattern all the way to the end. The pattern is only two bars long in itself, but because it's so repeatable and the groove intensity never flags, the next five minutes pass extraordinarily quickly.

Propelled by a samba-esque drum track and Nathan Watts' punchy bass, time takes a back seat as you sink inside the vocal tracks, which are piled high with harmonies and backing vocals courtesy of Stevie and Mary Lee Whitney (also part of the hard-working group on 'Ordinary Pain' from the same album).

The harmonic structure of those two bars is typically black-note based (A♭m to E♭7/B♭ to A♭m7/C♭

to D♭7, each lasting half a bar), and reminiscent of the earlier 'They Won't Go When I Go' movement from *FFF*. Rising basslines generally have an air of optimism, and this one lifts with each move, even though you slip imperceptibly back to where you started every fourth chord. But whereas 'They Won't Go' has a mournful ache at its heart, 'As' is nothing but exuberance and propulsion.

The song starts out in bright major-key fashion, twists through the verse via a series of chord changes that threatens to arrive on the relative minor, but narrowly avoids that minor for another verse and eventually revolves and settles there for the chorus. Far from being a disappointment though, the minor chorus supplies the 'home' for the song to hang its hat.

Greg Brown is credited for drums on the track, but it might as well be Stevie — all the hallmark tom fills and ride cymbal touch are present, with drums high in the energetic mix, even though the basic tempo isn't very fast (102bpm). It's not jazz as such — no hint of a swing to that beat — but the jazz spirit inhabits the track from beginning to end. Herbie's inventive fills and soloing hint at a more chordally complex world, and his sense of playfulness imbues the whole thing with a jazz spirit of adventure.

At the start of his keyboard solo, around 3:00, there's a jewel of a phrase — an ascending line that ends on classic Herbie right-hand tremolo, slightly off-note, dirty but extremely right. Towards the end of the solo Herbie explores the repeated-note Rhodes attack, extracting further levels of grime from the tine.

The jazz/improvising element doesn't belong exclusively to Herbie either — the Dean Parks solo (see 'Visions') also contributes greatly, and of course Stevie's vocal track is pure jazz-by-way-of-gospel invention.

These phrases are in a perfect part of his vocal range – his strong, high area where you think strain might begin to show but it never does

While relying on backing harmonies to keep the song afloat, Stevie is free to wander through the choruses, tied to the "loving you" and the "always", but enjoying the gaps in-between to the full. These phrases are in a perfect part of his vocal range too (based around A♭3) — his strong, high area where you think strain might begin to show but it never does. The only place deliberate strain shows here is on the aforementioned bridge section where, with a sermon-like intensity, Stevie delivers a back-of-the-throat injunction to spread your love wider:

"Change your words into truths and then change that truth into love
And maybe our children's grandchildren
And their great-great grandchildren will tell."

All this is delivered with machine-gun aggression. It's passionate stuff, unfortunately let down by some less inspired images, such as: "Until the dolphin flies and parrots live at sea..." Hmmm. There's some oddly-phrased philosophising too:

"As today I know I'm living but tomorrow
Could make me the past but that I mustn't fear
For I'll know deep in my mind
The love of me I've left behind
Cause I'll be loving you always."

Still, there are plenty of lively lyric images to compensate – an amazing visual storehouse of sun and light, and pretty extraordinary concepts for a sighted let alone a non-sighted person:

"Until the rainbow burns the stars out in the sky…"
"Until the day the earth starts turning right to left…"

The seven minutes and seven seconds is over before you realise it – the repetition/deviation routine is inventive enough to sustain interest. In fact, long after the track has finished, you still can't get it out of your head.

There are plenty of lively lyric images to compensate – an amazing visual storehouse of sun and light

'As' was ambitiously released as a single in October 1977, with 'Contusion', the Wonderlove instrumental, on the b-side. It was the last single to be released from *SITKOL*, and didn't sell particularly well, reaching exactly 36 in both pop and R&B charts, following the Number Ones of 'I Wish' and 'Sir Duke'.

But if Stevie thought that was disappointing, it was nothing compared to the disappointments the next few years would bring in terms of public reaction to his artistic endeavours.

Onstage with Ella Fitzgerald in the late 1970s. Ella recorded a live version of 'You Are The Sunshine Of My Life', and once expressed her (unfulfilled) wish to record an album of Stevie Wonder songs, describing him as like a Gershwin or Porter for the modern generation

CHAPTER 11
LATER WORK,
1979-2005

"As much as we may have feelings about what's happening with music right now, I do believe that in time all that is taken care of."

There was a gap of more than three years between the release of *Songs In The Key Of Life* and Stevie's next album – and when it finally arrived it surprised a lot of people. An expectant public had been waiting patiently (three years was a long wait in those days), but as Stevie would explain on the new album's sleeve notes: "Waiting is not what I meant for you, but to share with me the images of life that god has sent me through, and if this life affords me again the chance to share with you the new and the hidden knowledge, through song, I will move as swiftly as life demands, but never so fast as not to give you my very best." Not much change in the self-imaging department then – but there did turn out to be a fairly drastic transformation in content and musical direction.

Secret Life of Plants

When Stevie issued his double LP *Stevie Wonder's Journey Through The Secret Life Of Plants* in October 1979, the world was split concerning its quality, or even whether it was worthwhile at all. Herbie Hancock has praised its sense of adventure, justifying the experimentation as part of Stevie's musical development. *Rolling Stone* reviewer Ken Tucker had virtually no time for it: "The result is a strange succession of stunted songs, nattering ballads and wandering instrumentals that relies on the tiresome reprises of the most desultory soundtrack albums, the kind you buy for fond memories of the film but then never play".[62]

The idea of a movie soundtrack written by a non-sighted musician might strike you as rather unusual in itself, but it was the subject matter of the movie that raised the most eyebrows. The background runs like this: author Peter Tompkins and biologist Christopher Bird assembled all the information they could from research relating to plant life and any evidence of sensory perception therein, and they published it in the book *The Secret Life Of Plants*. It covers the use of plants as lie detectors, and plants as ecological sentinels, as well as the way they respond to music, and their ability to adapt to and even communicate with humans.

Stevie was reluctant at first – *SITKOL* was still in progress at the time – but Braun later persuaded him and he threw himself into the project

All sorts of evidence is presented to back up the theories – my favourite is the test to see if plants have memory. Two plants are placed in a room, six students are blindfolded, and one of them (without the knowledge of the others) is assigned to completely destroy one of the plants. When the students are then paraded in front of the surviving plant, which has electrodes attached to a polygraph machine, the readings establish (beyond reasonable doubt, apparently) the identity of the killer.

Film producer Michael Braun became interested in developing a screenplay/movie, and already had some music when he asked Stevie to contribute a closing piece for the project. The result, called 'Tree' on the final album, didn't match up with the rest of the score so Braun asked Stevie to write the music for the entire film. Stevie was reluctant at first – *SITKOL* was still in progress at the time – but Braun later persuaded him, and Stevie threw himself into the project.

Concerning Stevie's ability to imagine visual scenes, Braun recalls: "This was a tough picture to score because it deals with things that people have rarely seen on the screen before, so there are no standard ways of composing music for those things, like seeds sprouting or the Venus flytrap catching a bug. I'll bet a lot of veteran composers wouldn't know what to do with some of these sequences – except in the most mundane literalistic way, but Stevie did. He's uncanny."[63]

Stevie was given a tape of the film soundtrack, with Michael explaining what was happening on-screen, and Gary Olazabal counting down time/frame references. Stevie took the tape and chose an appropriate tempo and mood for each section.

It seems like a precarious career move, with hindsight, for Stevie to hitch his wagon to the kind of theories that most of the scientific community would have no time for, and then to make the whole thing his next (double) album. In the press Stevie was cautious, saying that he expected he would score a film about black issues, rather than plants, but he still found the idea intriguing. Maybe he saw the project as a way of expanding his writing capabilities, unfettered by the restrictions of the pop song format. An opportunity to structure the music around an external source, or visual cues, might have seemed like a release from his routine self-generated patterns of working.

Whatever the attraction, Stevie was committed to the album and recording went ahead in a multitude of studios – Crystal, Sigma and Motown's own Hollywood studio among others – using the brand new, hot-off-the-press Sony PCM 1600 digital recorder.

In those days (not so much now, it must be said) you wouldn't expect a soundtrack album to be rich in songs, and sure enough eight out of the 20 tracks on *Secret Life* are instrumentals. The ratio was even higher before Paramount decided to pull the movie, leaving Stevie with an album that would have to stand on its own feet without visuals. He went back to the studio and recorded three more tunes with a vocal, commercial edge. There was another (by now customary) delay due to a final remix, to include more natural ambient sounds, and then after three years planning and working, the album was complete.

An ambitious plan to add flower scent to the record sleeves went awry when it was discovered that the perfume used actually ate into the vinyl. In another pre-publicity ploy, Motown sent copies of the book and a packet of sunflower seeds to the record shops – the explanation was that when the seeds had sprouted, the record would be in the shops. Unfortunately the wait outlasted the flowers.

Let's clear the air straight away. Many people look on this album as a pseudo-classical offering, which allowed Stevie to indulge in near symphonic forms. This couldn't be further from the mark. The instrumental tracks, although they might sound orchestral, offer none of the thematic development of a typical classical symphony. True, there is some thematic linking between various songs (or is it just that the tunes all sound like each other?), but there is little in the way of harmonic or thematic development.

In fact, where harmony/chord structure is concerned, there is an awkwardness in the unexpected here, in contrast to, say, the gratifying surprise of the chorus chord in 'Sir Duke'. And when it's not awkward, it lapses into cliché. There is hardly any evidence of three years labour here – the songs almost have an unfinished air to them.

Part of the problem is the sound. To 21st-century ears, Stevie's Yamaha "dream machine" keyboard strings are plainly not a symphony orchestra. Although Stevie was still keen to use synthesisers to create new sounds, he was in danger of falling into the common synths-as-imitation trap. It's not just the strings – timpani, bass, drums, Indian instrument emulations, all fail to convince on the sonic front.

It could be that the aridity of the musical performances is also related to the presence of so many sequencer operators (six programmers credited in all, including Stevie). The grooves have no swing, and even the non-groove tracks have a rigid feel – exactly opposite to the sensitivity and flexibility of the natural world he's supposed to be portraying.

You get the impression there's a fair amount of new technology on show here, and while that's exciting to use, it can also dull the objective judgement. Why use a sequencer to play a drum part for you, when no one plays drums better on your tracks than you do? The ability to access new sounds would be a partial explanation, and maybe another appeal would be the flexibility of being able to program tracks, then make subsequent changes without having to re-record a drum track each time.

If all that sounds too negative, the news is not entirely bad… Except, having said that, we haven't come to the words yet. The Wright sisters are brought in to contribute lyrically, as is Mike (now Michael if you please) Sembello. Yvonne Wright's song 'Black Orchid' attempts to broaden the canvas with a parallel between the flower and the woman – but the result is wandering and unfocused. Syreeta wrote the words as well as performing on 'Come Back As A Flower', and though she sings with warmth and just the right note of innocence, the concept is as sticky as the stamen of a damp honeysuckle. Which leaves Michael's 'Power Flower', an evocation of Pan, which scores a cringe factor of 119 per cent (I wonder what earned him the credit of "Thank you Michael for being a positive pain"?). Stevie's lyrics range from the naive to the unintelligible, to the incomprehensible and beyond to the unfathomably mawkish.

It's an ironic twist that the first two notes on 'Earth's Creation', the opening track on *Secret Life*, form the interval commonly associated with the devil in classical music language – the tri-tone. (Strangely Prince uses the same interval when he writes 'serious' rock-operatic episodes.) Somewhat self-consciously Stevie uses a 'difficult' time signature, five beats in a bar, to summon up the concept of creation. The notes are similarly difficult, with the synth and string lines clashing in a twisted replay of the triad over a different root.

Soon the so-far contained melodrama slips out of the bag, the theme has arrived, and with an explosion of cymbals, timps and strings (all synthetic), a fanfare figure (eighth-note triplet-based) erupts. It's not unlike the moment of controlled drama in 'Lately' (Chapter 9).

'The First Garden' features a music box/kalimba amid a forest of birds and insects, giving way to an attractive harmonica tune. 'Voyage To India' seems to be going well with a string/piano passage that meanders through several territories, repeating the theme of 'The First Garden'/'Secret Life', but it's ruined at about two minutes by a disastrous modulation (key change), for which the only word can be inept. For the Indian flavour, Ben Bridges brushes the sitar sensitively, but the mood is broken by a crude synth sound/figure, the first four notes of which are borrowed straight from the Beatles'/ Harrison's 'Within You And Without You'. The next four minutes pass by with increased texture but no musical direction.

So that's the first three tracks: all instrumental and, without any visual clues from the movie, all uninvolving. These three would probably make more sense on a soundtrack – you'd certainly be scrutinising the audio less closely. I'm not sure the same excuse can be applied to a vocal track, though, which by its nature attracts more concentration, and would diminish the attention given to

Posing for the camera with a fine early 1980s array of synthesisers

the visual. (The relationship between sound and sight is complex, but one thing is certain: the days of Wagnerian Hollywood soundtracks with whooping French horns and swooping strings set against a sensitive love scene are long gone.)

The first vocal track on the album is 'Same Old Story', a ballad with a South American hue, courtesy of the two acoustic guitars (from Ben Bridges and Sembello). Stevie is on harmonica, piano and bass. There's a slap-happy moment halfway through when the bass appears to go for a note a half-step away from where it should be. Ouch. A little more rehearsal on the slowing down before the chorus wouldn't have gone amiss either.

The tune is OK, but I'm not sure how anyone is supposed to sing with feeling when the lyrics include lines such as: "But with instruments Bose would devise/Would take science by surprise…" (Dr Jagadish Chandra Bose was the early 20th-century scientist who discovered, among other things, that plants can feel a kind of pain.)

'Venus Flytrap' aims to produce some light humour by employing pitch transposers on Stevie's voice to create a character (or even two) against a synthesised jazz-lounge backdrop, and some dodgy 'doo-doo-doo' scatting. The musical build-up to the demise of the fly is heavy-handed, and is

There doesn't seem to have been the usual level of care taken, not just in the composition but also in the performance of many of these songs

followed by an exchange between Stevie and Keita, his son, who asks how the bug was eaten. Stevie's response hardly bolsters the scientific rationale of the project: "by closing its leaves and swallowing it."

You'll be pleased to hear I don't intend to dissect every track on the album (one of my houseplants just flinched at the mere idea), but I felt I had to make the point that there doesn't seem to have been the usual level of care taken, not just in the composition but also in the performance of many of these tunes and songs.

On the subject of composition, it does bring to light the issue of the mechanics of Stevie's writing in general. In the days before computer-aided sequencing, and assuming he didn't type everything out in braille, Stevie would basically have had to create and retain whole arrangements for songs in his head. When you can see notes on paper or on-screen it must make the task of shaping the music that much easier. It's well known that Stevie has a remarkable memory for music and lyrics; when he's on-stage and a problem crops up, he can throw in an impromptu performance of an unrehearsed number at the drop of a hat, just voice and piano. But remembering some of the complex string moves, let alone planning the next one on an album such as this, would be a challenge for anyone.

All of which puts 'Finale', the closing track on *Secret Life Of Plants*, in a different light. An astonishing level of mental and musical organisation must be needed to bring together so many themes in one place. Quoting passages from 'Creation', 'Send One Your Love', 'Secret Life…' etc, the piece assembles ideas and even casts new surroundings for them: for instance 'Come Back As A Flower' is given a fresh coat of samba treatment. (Stevie had been working with Sergio Mendes and Brazil '77, and two of his songs appear on Sergio's album.) There are some cringe moments here too, of course – like the inexplicable clashing cymbals and tasteless time change in the 'Outside My Window' extract, which are a match for any b-list musical.

Highlights/lowlights not mentioned so far include a nine-minute (count 'em) disco track, 'Race Babbling', with a stultifying sequenced drum pattern, mystifying vocals and an emasculated horn section. On the other hand, 'Send One Your Love' is a song with a wider brief: the 'plant' connection here is more symbolic (flowers as a symbol of love) rather than literal – and it sounds more like a Stevie Wonder song. (There's an entertaining 'lounge' instrumental version of this song on the album too, complete with disinterested background chatter and clinking wine glasses – a nice touch that suggests Stevie was well aware of the inevitable fate of some of his more easy-listening numbers.)

The Japanese and African tracks both sound good (the latter, 'Kesse Ye Lolo De Ye', even has a live percussion track, at last); and finally 'A Seed's A Star/Tree' delivers a track where Stevie has some self-belief and the band possess some energy. The top line inner melody uses the by-now overworked half-step routine (5th to ♭6th to 6th), which would serve Michael Jackson well enough on 1982's 'Thriller' single. The 'live' feel engendered by the dubbed announcements and massive applause seems to gee up bass player Nathan Watts in particular.

It's a rare moment of excitement though, and a timely reminder that most of the musical slants on *Secret Life* don't come naturally to the composer. There's little evidence of Stevie's cultural background on display – even the groove numbers sound 'white' somehow, if you'll forgive me for saying so. Preoccupied by the search for sophistication and classical credibility, the album fails to build on past experience of styles (if anything it negates them), without managing to establish worthwhile alternatives. All in all, a disappointing end product, especially bearing in mind how long it took him to produce.

Stevie had used up his 'unsuccessful experiment' voucher that every artist is allowed

Stevie had used up his 'unsuccessful experiment' voucher that every artist is allowed. Expectation again worked wonders with the market place: a Number Four in the charts was more a reflection of loyalty sales than critical acceptance. One reviewer wrote: "After listening very carefully to this new album project from Stevie, I am still not sure just what exactly the purpose of the LP is."[64]

Hotter Than July

Here's another, very different review, this time for an album released less than a year later: "On *Hotter Than July*, the artist's blend of pop hooks and African chants, his synthesized expressions of pipe-and-drum tribal dreams and his powerful vocal mixture of baby talk, galloping gospel singing and flowery melismata all add up to a unique musical style that goes far beyond words in conjuring a natural world one step removed from paradise. Stevie Wonder remains our most gifted pop muralist."[65]

After *Secret Life* Stevie realised he would have to act swiftly with a 'bona fide' Stevie Wonder album. Not that he'd been completely inactive in the commercial pop world – in 1979 he worked with Jermaine Jackson, recording three songs for the singer (the only Jackson brother still signed to

Motown – who was, coincidentally, married to Berry Gordy's daughter). Of the three tracks, 'Let's Get Serious', written with Lee Garrett, was the outstanding one, lending its title to the album, and also featuring Stevie on vocals (Stevie initially had eyes on it for his own purposes too). It was a serious hit: an R&B Number One, Top Ten elsewhere.

Stevie also sessioned on Smokey Robinson's album *Where's The Smoke*, which revitalised Smokey's flagging career. But most of his energies were focused on reversing his current standing with his own audience. He set to work, using various studios, including his own Wonderland studios in LA, and a new, pop-song-filled album was ready for release by the end of September 1980. *Hotter Than July* was to be Stevie's reply to fans disappointed by *The Secret Life Of Plants*.

But the musical world had changed substantially since *Songs In The Key Of Life* – four years is a long time in pop music. Indeed Stevie's track 'Race Babbling' from *Secret Life* reflected the shift towards the disco style that pervaded the singles market in the late 1970s. Discotheques had sprung up in the early 1970s, and gradually the music spread from the clubs into the mainstream. (One of the earliest chart hits with an identifiable 'disco sound' was Gloria Gaynor's 'Never Can Say Goodbye' in 1974.) As the Seventies progressed, tracks became faster and, more crucially, longer.

The 12″ single, the invention of one Tom Moulton, transformed the market for dance music, and became the standard DJ format, which it remains today. In 1977 the *Saturday Night Fever* explosion (largely fuelled by the reborn Bee Gees) launched disco on a massive scale. Other groups/artists were quick to join the rush: Chic ('Dance, Dance, Dance', 'Good times'), Donna Summer ('Love To Love You Baby') and Anita Ward ('Ring My Bell') were among the mainstays of the disco revolution. The engine behind Chic, guitarist Nile Rodgers and bassist Bernard Edwards, had their ears to the ground: Chic tunes appealed not only to black audiences but also the gay club scene, which basically bankrolled the disco market in its early days at least. Rodgers was also in demand as a producer, and in 1980 he revived Diana Ross's career by producing the album *Diana* and single 'Upside Down'. (Nile's impressive 1980s track record would include David Bowie's 'Let's Dance' and Madonna's 'Like A Virgin'.)

It's inconceivable that Stevie's pop style would remain unaffected by such developments. Sure enough, *Hotter Than July* is packed full with dancey, immediate, hooky pop songs that are a universe or so removed from the vagaries of *Secret Life*. Stevie's production (with Gary Olazabal as engineer/mixer) is sharper, cleaner, fuller all round (and shows them getting to grips with new-fangled digital recording), and for sheer outgoing energy it makes the perfect reply to the critics.

Some sounds are modified according to prevalent fashion: the drum kit has a low-tuned snare, and the electric bass is more slappy, played with the thumb hitting the bottom strings and fingers pulling at the top ones. The bass drum is inevitably present on almost every beat (didn't it used to be possible to dance to music without four thuds on the floor every bar... now, where's my walking frame?), the snare is backbeat only, and I mean *only*, and the hi-hat goes 'pea-soup, pea-soup' a lot.

The first obvious track to look at from the album is the one that had the biggest impact. 'Happy Birthday', dedicated to the memory of Martin Luther King, was part of a campaign to declare a US national holiday on King's birthdate, 15th January. Organised with the aid of his widow Coretta King and members of the US Congress, various marches and conventions culminated in a 1982 Washington rally where 50,000 people celebrated what would have been King's 53rd birthday on a freezing January day.

Stevie spoke at the end of the meeting: "These are not easy times, yet they are not hopeless times. We must refresh our souls and uplift our spirits and harmonise with our brothers and sisters."

Race relations had suffered of late: the Klan had resumed activities in the south, and there was talk that new Republican president Ronald Reagan wanted to repeal the Voting Rights Act, potentially removing the vote from many black Americans. Plus the new economic regime, the lifting of the 'burden' of taxes, was inevitably going to widen the poverty gap.

The press noted at the time: "Wonder appeared intuitively to comprehend a bit better than the old civil rights groups ... that the assaults on the sense of pride of blacks have been felt as deeply, maybe even more deeply, as the assaults on their pocketbooks".[66] Stevie's campaigning found fruition when Congress agreed the idea of the holiday in 1983 – the third Monday in January each year would be declared Martin Luther King Jr Day, starting from January 20th 1986.

On the track 'Happy Birthday' Stevie is once again a one-man band (except for the un-credited female BVs). How much of the 'band' is sequenced rather than played is another question. The first thing that strikes you about the sound here is how 'hard' it is in comparison to the rest of the album. It's early days for digital technology, admittedly, but the flatness of the drum sound (plus the Roger Linn thanks on the sleeve) leads you to suspect the presence of a Linn drum machine. Stevie had always managed to get hold of new technology almost before it was known about, but the Linn LM-1 had just been released at the turn of 1979/80. It was the first sampling drum machine, played eight-bit samples of real drums, and heralded the dawn of the programmable rhythm track era.

The synths and bass are programmed here too, chugging away for the duration – but the song is strong enough to take a dull mix and survive (there are people who would wish, purely for musical reasons, that it hadn't...). Stevie seems to sing his heart out, on a song that is musically unremarkable yet solid – annoying yet desperately infectious. You can't help thinking it's odd that a subject Stevie clearly felt passionate about should be matched with such a strangely passionless backing track.

We've already looked at the tracks 'Master Blaster' and 'Lately' (in Chapter 9), but *Hotter Than July* houses a gamut of songs from the socially relevant 'Cash In Your Face', to 'All I Do', an old song from the mid 1960s written with Clarence Paul and Morris Broadnax.

'Cash In Your Face' tells the story of a well-heeled black man and his expectant wife in search of accommodation, coming up against the brick wall of prejudice. The agent makes all sorts of excuses – broken computers, the apartment has already gone to someone else, children not allowed in the block – but the subtext is always a colour issue. "You might have the cash but you can not cash in your face."

It's set to a laidback version of the early Seventies clav numbers, though crucially without the same hookiness of riff. The Linn drumbox is present and very correct (drum machines, after all, don't make mistakes ... and they're never late for a gig either), but the price you pay is a loss of feel – the magical ebbing and flowing of human inaccuracy. There's no discernable anger either, in the backing track or the vocal. There's sincerity, but it doesn't translate into musical energy.

'All I Do' tries to recapture the intensity of first love; originally written when he was 16, the arrangement here is slightly straitjacketed by disco-isms, but still manages to deliver the energy missing elsewhere on the album. The Rhodes/synth bass/drums nucleus provides all the steam necessary for propulsion – and it's a distinctly dirty Rhodes too, just on the edge of distortion (either that or it needs to be repaired).

Stevie, with the Wonderlove band, in concert in the 1980s

And what's the first thing the bass plays? A descending half-step run to the home key. The debt to Jamerson is continually paid – it's also evidenced in the double-time fills Stevie plays before the second chorus, harking back to 'Boogie On Reggae Woman'.

Stevie's vocal is back on form – there's a particularly good bit as he comes out of the first bridge, where you expect the temperature to drop for the verse but he's having none of it. The colour of the backing vocals is interesting too – O'Jays Eddie Levert and Walter Williams, plus Michael Jackson, Jamil Raheem and Betty Wright, all recorded very close up. Motown's snakepit, Studio A, is remembered with the addition of a stock mock glock(enspiel) part.

The economy in the writing serves to emphasise the hook of the chorus, as the verse is built on the same material. The Hank Redd saxophone solo is marred by some fussy flutes behind it, but generally this is vintage Wonder. A similar mixture of Eighties dance influence, jazz-funk, and soul/jazz vocals would serve Al Jarreau well through the decade.

'Rocket Love' hosts the now well-overworked half-step routine (5th to ♭6th to 6th) just one more time, allied to a Brazilian-flavoured chorus groove. The lines: "A female Shakespeare of your time/With looks to blow Picasso's mind" are appealing, as is the string arrangement by Paul Riser (he goes back a long way at Motown) – far from being silky and smooth, it punctuates the vocal with well-placed phrases.

'I Ain't Gonna Stand For It' became the follow-up single to 'Master Blaster' – not quite as successful, but almost Top Ten. With more of a band performance (including extra drums) on top of the drum machine track, the groove is more of a living, breathing animal – proving Stevie could still do it.

It seems as if the technology is dictating the production, sometimes even the composition

'Do Like You' shows the Quincy Jones/Michael Jackson influence at work. Jackson's 'Don't Stop 'Til You Get Enough' from his 1979 *Off The Wall* album (his first 'adult' release) was a recent Number One, and many aspects of 'Do Like You' – from the tempo and feel to the brass parts, gogo bells and wood blocks – point to that song as the inspiration. 'Do Like You' is a cracking track, with the excellent muted harpsichord supplying the guitar funk. The song focuses on Keita's dancing talents – but it could just as easily refer to Jackson, or even Little Stevie Wonder himself, back on the bandstand at Belle Island at the Fourth Of July picnic, showing off his talents to a cheering crowd.

Hotter Than July does signal a return to songwriting form – but it also signals two other, less positive factors. Firstly the dilution of Stevie's idiosyncratic, personal language when it comes to his writing style; and secondly the gradual permeation and increasing dominance of studio technology. It used to be that when Stevie (with Cecil and Margouleff) employed new technology, it was to enhance and add flavour to the overall effect – but the performer was always still in charge. Now it seems as if the technology is dictating the production, sometimes even the composition, pushing aside the quality, the feel and energy of 'real' drum and bass tracks, replacing them with a less vibrant machine-driven 'hologram' substitute.

The presence of simpler songs and catchier hooks was obviously positive in terms of pop audience satisfaction, and for Stevie it must have felt good to be reaching the people again after the *Secret Life* episode. If the price was sacrificing a degree of musical interest, I guess that was one he was willing to pay, and we just have to accept that. It would at least be nice to think the motivation for producing a more commercial record was communicative rather than financial.

We do give our pop artists a hard time, don't we? We don't like it when they experiment too much, and we don't like it when they play too safe. It's a fine line they have to tread in the name of public satisfaction.

We do give our pop artists a hard time, don't we? We don't like it when they experiment too much, and we don't like it when they play too safe

The 1980s

The Stevie Wonder story doesn't stop after *Hotter Than July*, of course – it's just that it tends to become a lot less musically interesting. One thing is plain: Stevie has a gift for melody, and that gift refuses to lie down. But the musical surroundings he chose throughout the 1980s in particular were so often disappointing that a listener could easily be forgiven for jumping ship. No longer a stylistic explorer he became a dedicated follower of fashion, aping the latest sound trends, pushing all the populist buttons, without much evidence of an internal navigation system able to steer a steady course.

One incident is especially revealing. Sometime around 1983, Stevie reportedly suffered a confidence crisis (is it coincidental that this was in-between 'Ebony And Ivory' and 'I Just Called To Say I Love You'?) Guitarist Ray Parker has talked of how Stevie felt crumpled by the weight of expectation every time he worked on new material. The story goes that, while attending the Grammy ceremony that year, Quincy Jones caught up with Stevie on the way to the toilet. It must have been difficult for Stevie to sit by while Michael Jackson collared the awards that had once been his, but such is the stuff of maturity. Anyway, there had been rumours that Jones had been asked to produce Stevie's next album, and although the exact content of their conversation that night is lost to ceramic tiling, it's reported that Quincy gave Stevie a severe talking-to, encouraging him to keep working, and stressing how much he was appreciated.

It would have been fascinating to hear a Wonder/Jones album – you get the feeling Quincy is not a man to mince his words, a trait that could have matched Stevie's need for directional assistance. But it wasn't to be. Instead, Motown must have been wringing their hands when they heard that Stevie's next proposed project (after the hits album *Original Musiquarium*, which had a smattering of new tracks) was to be another soundtrack tie-in.

But the circumstances this time were very different from *Secret Life Of Plants*. Dionne Warwick had put Stevie's name forward to contribute in some way to a soundtrack for the Gene Wilder movie *The Woman In Red*. Stevie wrote some tunes, originally two, then suddenly seven, but when current Motown president Jay Lasker listened, he wasn't over-impressed. He also argued that it was a distraction that would delay the album Stevie had already been working on for the last few years (which would eventually see the light of day as *In Square Circle* in 1985). Perhaps Lasker's main concern was that there was not enough material of commercial interest on the soundtrack to warrant an album release. This propelled Stevie back into the studio, to emerge with almost certainly the most commercial song ever to have passed his lips – 'I Just Called To Say I Love You'. Lasker was pacified, and Berry Gordy was reassured when he learned the film was to be associated with the Motown logo, so the company agreed to the participation.

'I Just Called…' is unquestionably a successful pop song: there's nothing challenging anywhere along the route, the rhythm track is plodding but comfortable, and the songwriting materials are some of the simplest/most accessible Stevie ever laid his fingers on. The paucity of those materials is all too apparent, with not a tiny spark of creative energy on display. Talking of sparks, and how things have changed, Bob Margouleff once described the team that created *Music Of My Mind* as being, "Like three comets streaking through the night with their tails on fire."[67] By contrast, 'I Just Called…' is like a box of soggy fireworks.

The lacklustre chordal arrangement, the annoying synth doubling of the tune, the devoid-of-imagination bassline, the predictability of the harmonic moves, the dire change of key in a desperate attempt to inject some life into a track that's going nowhere… All these characteristics in place at the same time can spell just one thing – massive commercial success. The song duly reached Number One on every available chart – even in the UK, where alarmingly, and somewhat tragically, it remains Stevie's biggest ever hit (and to many people, even more depressingly, the song and the image with which the name Stevie Wonder is now most strongly associated).

Call me an old cynic (yes, I can hear you), but that's not what Stevie's career was to have been about. At one point he had been the voice that expressed a generation's joy and angst, whether black or white, full of sensitivity, anger where necessary, always with musical intelligence and stylistic curiosity. All of which was left at home when he cut 'I Just Called…'. Ultimately disappointing for its casting aside of the very roots he is so proud to proclaim, this song more than any other has become a symbol of Stevie being eaten by pop. In particular it showed him being engulfed by *Eighties* pop, a sound that was inseparable from the emerging technology that produced it.

'I Just Called…', more than any other song, has become a symbol of Stevie being eaten by pop

By the mid 1980s, synth technology had entered the digital realm. So-called 'vintage' analog synthesisers (in synth terms anything from the Seventies is now considered vintage) were replaced by a new generation of keyboards that used digital circuitry to generate more complex timbres. The Yamaha DX7 made the largest impact on the synth market; using a method called Frequency Modulation (FM) to control the characteristics of a sound, it was possible to produce a greater level of detail. Old grit and muddy warmth was replaced, for better or worse, by clarity and definition.

Stevie had a rack of DX7s, plus a Yamaha TX816 – basically eight modules linked together – to produce the range of sounds required for a complete track. The linking together was crucial too: a protocol for communication between synths (and subsequently computers) was agreed between the various musical instrument manufacturers and became known as MIDI (musical instrument digital interface). This made it possible to link together keyboards and modules, and run them from a computer which issued instructions about what notes to play, and when. It was nothing less than a revolution, which utterly transformed the way music has since been created and realised.

There were some drawbacks, though. The new synths tended to sound brittle, hard and thin, lacking in bass and low-mid frequencies (much like the earlier digital recorders). The detail in the top range was welcome, but the sound has since flowed down the glacier of fashion into an icy sea. It was possible to approximate the timbre of a Fender Rhodes piano, but the imitation had none of the warmth and flexibility of touch associated with the real instrument (it was, however, lighter to carry around).

Also, for all its attractions, the drawback of recording your music using computers and MIDI is that it's too tempting to press a button marked 'quantise' – automatic time correction. This moves all the notes by a few milliseconds towards the nearest beat, thus destroying any human feel that, rightly or wrongly, has crept into the track. If you're Stevie Wonder, a musician capable of performing with both a natural groove and superb accuracy, this is a disaster. The instrumental personality is stripped away at one computer command.

What's more, it may be accurate, but it tends to sound just like everyone else's performance. That's probably overstating the case, as it's not just the timing that makes a track but also the choice of notes themselves, but there is an ironing-out of character. And with the layering possibilities of linking keyboards and modules, there's a tendency to go wild, over-the-top, piling on sounds… but somehow ending up with less than the sum of the parts.

Take a track like 'Go Home', from 1985's *In Square Circle*, for an illustration of the soulless nature of the DX7 electric piano, the mechanical bass and drum tracks (don't change that pattern, whatever you do), and tired compositional ideas. 'You Will Know', a ballad from the *Characters* album in 1987, features a similar sound palette, a whole gallery of chime/bell-like electric pianos competing for space on a crowded wall. (Both of these tracks are on *At The Close Of A Century* – no further investment required.)

One more word concerning drum machines. In 1983 Stevie was interviewed by *Songwriter Connection* and stated: "I never thought much of putting drum machines on records. Being a drummer, I thought they were too cheap, and on certain songs you can't get a feel. With a rhythm machine it sounds too mechanical." Which kind of begs the question: so why did he use them? Maybe he just viewed them as a necessary evil at the time, but a passing phase. When asked in an interview for *Keyboard* magazine whether drum machines tended to discourage the idea of a live rhythm feel, Stevie responded: "Well, music is an evolving and revolving spiral. Hopefully it's going up. As much as we may have feelings about what's happening with music right now, I do believe that in time all that is taken care of."

Technology apart, some of Stevie's later musical disappointments might have been averted with the help of a strong, no-nonsense co-producer, which is something that, post Cecil & Margouleff, Stevie seems to have badly lacked. Gary Olazabal gets a co-production credit on *Characters*, but I think a fresh set of more judgemental ears might have been more appropriate.

No apportioning of blame is meant – would you be able to stand up to a man who was once arguably the world's most influential recording artist and still keep your job? You also gets the impression that Stevie's close entourage are reluctant to engage critical faculties, but that's often one of the inevitable trappings of fame/success/royalty.

Conversation Peace

Stevie's visit to Ghana in 1993, although disastrous in organisational terms (equipment went missing, leaving Stevie alone with a piano for the whole gig), triggered a rush of songs, reportedly 40 in six weeks. It makes you curious about Stevie's working methods. If so many songs drop from the trees, like apples in an orchard, would it not make more sense just to pick up the juiciest ones and leave the others for the wasps? Or, then again, maybe there just aren't many juicy ones nowadays...

Whatever the reason, we start to see the same stylistic devices cropping up again and again – and although every writer has their identifying trademarks, overused ingredients lose their emotional potency over time. Again, you can't help wondering how much Margouleff and Cecil were involved with the harvesting/weeding-out process in Stevie's Seventies heyday.

Having said all that, 1995's *Conversation Peace* album does boast a higher ratio of quality songs than anything since 1980's *Hotter Than July*. A 73-minute excursion, with 13 tracks (all well over four minutes long), the album introduces three new "associate producers" in Nathan Watts, Derrick Perkins and Vaughn Halyard. Also new is Van Arden, responsible for engineering and most (but not all) of the mixes. Two tracks, 'My Love Is With You' and 'Sorry', are mixed by none other than Robert Margouleff, along with Brant Biles. (Sad to report there's not much evidence of the old chemistry... but then his involvement was only at the mixing stage.) Guest stars abound: Anita Baker among the jazz stars on 'Sensuous Whisper', plus Ladysmith Black Mambazo, Take 6, and Sounds Of Blackness elsewhere on the album.

The opening track, 'Rain Your Love Down', with its thunder effects (shades of *Secret Life*) and exhortation to the higher being, presents a distinctive angle on changing worldly matters. Stevie seems depressed at the human condition and the inability to deal with "drugs, disease, crime and pain". It's the water as purifier concept, washing sins away in the river, and though you might expect all that to be gospelly and slow, the backing track is chirpy and bright – a strange contrast.

1995's *Conversation Peace* album does boast a higher ratio of quality songs than anything since 1980's *Hotter Than July*

But one thing is clear from the outset – the digital sampler has arrived, and with the sampler come drum loops. Whereas drum machines had to have the rhythm patterns programmed in (or played in via MIDI), samplers catch an audio snapshot of one segment, just a bar or two, of a drummer's actual performance. Loop that around and, lo and behold, you have a drum track. The advantage is that you can capture a live feel and still have the flexibility of programmed control. Because the loops are actual recordings, it often gets impossible to tell what's live and what isn't; but Stevie has said (in the same *Keyboard* magazine interview) that he plays along with samples, adding colour/groove to the basic rhythm track – which is probably the best of both worlds. Certainly this tune starts with a loop, which is replaced/augmented by another loop, which is again augmented by live drums.

One reassuring thing about *Conversation Peace* is that the vocals sound well placed over the backing tracks, as if they are more comfortable with their surroundings than they've been for a while.

Vocally, Stevie is (mostly) in remarkable form, starting this song on a high note (A3), while reaching even higher on the BVs and the bridge (D4). The chorus repeats (ad nauseam, I'm afraid) with no change in the backing save a cutting of the loops, which highlights the quality of the BVs.

Other stand-out tracks include the harp/strings-based 'Taboo To Love' which, although it's almost arranged-to-death (remember the simplicity of 'If It's Magic' on *SITKOL*?), still manages to provide the twists and turns that traditionally single out a Stevie Wonder song.

'My Love Is With You' centres on the problems of handgun control, and the story of Lori Miles and Jeffrey James, both friends and both victims of motiveless gun crime. Again the voice is top of the range, in both senses of the word, quality and pitch. A drama along the lines of 'Living For The City' unfolds in the second verse – where Stevie's voice sounds uncomfortably and worryingly croaky (I did say it was *mostly* in remarkable form).

'Tomorrow Robins Will Sing' revisits Jamaica, featuring some "intro reggage chatting" (sic) by Edley Shine. As usual the stylistic referencing is loose, and indeed the heavy backbeat works completely counter to any true regga(g)e feel. It's unfortunate that the jazz of 'Sensuous Whisper' should bring to mind 'Venus Fly Trap'... but the piano-playing takes me unfairly straight there. In fact the song explores new territory – a Nineties jazz-funk loop-intensive piece, with a walking bass that insists on doing an Olympic marathon, but should stop for a drink once in a while.

'For Your Love' was the album's mid-tempo ballad, released as a single, but causing few ripples. By the time the listener arrives at the title track, 'Conversation Peace', two things happen: firstly you realise that the sound of the drum loops is now very wearing; but secondly you realise that Stevie can still sing and arrange great vocal tracks. The shape of the line on the chorus and the way it interacts with the splendid punchy, scoopy, BVs is masterful. The highest note is reserved for last – a melisma that pushes the chorus line beyond the beyond (E4). The rideout of what is undoubtedly a powerful song features a large cast intoning the words of the title, including Yolanda, Aisha and Keita, Milton and Calvin Hardaway, and their mother Lula.

Possible reasons for the delay of the new album might be the the deaths of two inspirational figures

A double live album, *Natural Wonder*, followed in November of 1995. Recorded in Japan and Israel, featuring Stevie's band and the Tokyo Philharmonic orchestra, the choice of songs ranges from 1960s to 1990s material, with more than a slight leaning towards the 1970s repertoire. The retrospective box set, *At The Close Of A Century*, neatly rounds off the discography – at least at the time of writing. But not for long...

A Time 2 Love

If the latest record company schedule can be relied upon (Stevie's still nominally with Motown, though they've now been subsumed into Universal), a new Stevie Wonder album – his first in nine years, and roughly his 27th in total, not counting compilations – is due to be released in May 2005. Of course it's already been postponed several times over the space of a year, so you never know.

Entitled *A Time 2 Love*, there were no pre-release copies available as this book went to the printers, but there are a few details already known about the album, and a single 'So What The Fuss' to listen to. Stevie performed 'What The Fuss' as far back as June 2004, when he appeared on the *Oprah Winfrey Show* to plug the supposedly imminent album – he also sang a duet with his daughter Aisha called 'How Will I Know', another song from the new collection. More prospective titles include 'If The Creek Don't Rise' and 'If Your Love Cannot Be Moved'. Other than his children, album guests will include a female Nigerian talking-drummer, classical orchestral musicians, the West Los Angeles choir, recorded in church, Doug E. Fresh, "doing a little beat-box thing", India.Arie, Alicia Keys, and a few more surprise guests.

'So What The Fuss', on which he's backed by guitar playing from Prince and BVs from En Vogue, is a relatively punchy affair, with a live-band rather than programmed feel, phat and squelchy analog synth, and the funk firmly to the fore – albeit in a slightly over-slick format (and Prince's guitar work unfortunately lends a rather dated Eighties feel to proceedings). Lyrically Stevie is in aggressive, take-no-prisoners mode, with the chiding "shame on us" refrain – though some of the verse lyrics are less than world-shattering (but it was always thus). It's gratifying to hear the vocal skills are still intact – physical changes notwithstanding, the voice is as trim and agile as ever.

Here's what Stevie himself has said about his work on the new album: "In these nine years I've done more than just the songs that will be on the album. And it's going good. In these nine years I've found the songs that feel most comfortable for me."

Possible reasons for the album's postponement in 2004 might have included the loss of two inspirational figures in Stevie's life during that year. 'Uncle' Ray Charles died on June 10th, and less than a month later, on July 6th 2004, Stevie's ex-wife, muse, writing partner and long-time friend Syreeta Wright succumbed after a two-year struggle with cancer.

In the months that followed, despite the continued lack of activity on the record front, Stevie's profile was as high as it's been for several years: he won the 2004 Johnny Mercer award as the "Songwriters' Songwriter", as well as *Billboard's* 'Century Award', their highest honour for creative achievement; he paid respects by performing 'I Got A Woman' at the Ray Charles tribute concert; he organised and starred in his ninth annual *House Full Of Toys* benefit concert for underprivileged children; and he joined an all-star cast at the 47th *Grammy Awards* ceremony in February 2005 to perform a version of The Beatles' 'Across The Universe' in aid of the Asian tsunami appeal.

Whatever the 2005 album might bring, there is still a vast, expectant audience counting the days to its release. It's a new Stevie Wonder album, after all. *Conversation Peace* did seem to reveal a more relaxed, assured writer, confident of his musical place in the grand scheme of things. Ten years on, assuming that confidence has remained, or even grown as a new generation of artists discover the debt they owe to the man, we live in hope that Stevie can fully exploit or revisit the heights of his talent, as explored in the 1970s.

Maybe the strangulating desire to keep up in the musical fashion stakes will have been assuaged by now. And although Stevie's need to keep abreast of technological developments has probably not diminished, at least the rate of change in that fast-moving world has slowed enough to enable musicians to establish their own working methods, freeing up space in the head for creating music rather than worrying about technical details.

Albert Einstein was right when he said, "Perfection of means and confusion of ends seems to characterise our age". Stevie has certainly stumbled along the way, but his ability to keep an end in range has been remarkable. His songs of social commentary have changed the everyday lives of many people, and if some of the lyrics appear naive in a cruel world, well, we can put that down to his generous spirit.

The flexibility of his voice, its emotional range and imagination, helped establish a new freedom of phrasing and improvisation which still reverberates – sometimes in a mannered way, but mainly as a liberating model for a generation of younger singers. Bob Margouleff jokingly referred to it as "black yodeling – I call it the Swiss influence in R&B, those appoggiaturas, those gymnastic lines… Stevie is an acrobat with his voice, there's no two ways about it."[69]

Stevie's other crucial legacy resulted from his adoption of the synthesiser as an exciting, versatile and, yes, musical instrument – aided again of course by the seers Margouleff and Cecil. The names of Margouleff and Cecil have to be reiterated in the context of the four classic albums from the early-to-mid 1970s. The pair may have been the medium, rather than the message, but both elements

Stevie has the ability to process experience and express it in a readily available form

worked inextricably together for a while. As they modestly put it themselves: "We sort of helped [Stevie] squeeze the paint onto the palette, but he used the brush to paint the picture."[70] And those sonically unique 'pictures' happened to be some of the most affirmative, questioning, probing, internally examining, joyous, touching, all-embracing music of the 20th century.

As a writer Stevie has so far never equalled the intensity of personal expression associated with his work of the 1970s. It was a time when all the right circumstances coalesced – his cultural background, business environment, personal situation, all contributed to an inner life in need of working-out and expression. When Berry Gordy says that Stevie has the ability to process experience and express it in a readily accessible form, that's probably the highest compliment a record company boss could pay an artist.

Put simply, Stevie Wonder is just an extraordinary musician. I'll leave the final words to Herbie Hancock, who summed up the man's life and work very neatly, and offered the ultimate compliment when he said: "I can't imagine the world being the same if we had not been exposed to the great songs of Stevie Wonder."

Stevie performing live at the Ray Charles tribute concert in September 2004

REFERENCES/QUOTE SOURCES

1 *The Wonder Years: Life And Times With Stevie Wonder*, Ted Hull with Paula L. Stahel
2 as 1
3 Marvin Gaye in conversation with David Ritz, quoted in *Rhythms Of Wonder*, Sharon Davies
4 *Keyboard* magazine interview, July 1995
5 *Rhythms Of Wonder*, Sharon Davies
6 *Color* magazine, 1949
7 *To Be Loved*, Berry Gordy
8 *Standing In The Shadows Of Motown* (movie), 2002
9 *as 8*
10 *Blind Faith*, Dennis Love & Stacy Brown
11 as 10
12 *Stevie Wonder*, John Swenson
13 *Dancing In The Street*, Suzanne E. Smith
14 *Where Did Our Love Go?*, Nelson George

15 as 5
16 as 1
17 *Innervisions*, Martin E. Horn
18 as 12
19 as 1
20 Interview with author, 2005
21 as 5
22 Jack Saylor, sportswriter, quoted in *Where Did Our Love Go?*, Nelson George
23 as 14
24 as 12
25 as 12
26 Interview with journalist Mark Plummer
27 Bob Moog quoted in *Vintage Synthesisers*, Mark Vail
28 *Stevie Wonder*, Constanze Elsner
29 *Mix* magazine, November 2003
30 John Diliberto, *Keyboard* magazine, January 1984
31 as 14
32 as 5
33 as 30

34 as 12
35 *Classic Albums (Songs In The Key Of Life)*
36 *Hotwired*, 1996
37 as 29
38 as 5
39 as 12
40 Lenny Kaye, *Rolling Stone*, issue 144 – 27/9/73
41 as 35
42 as 12
43 as 35
44 as 10
45 as 17
46 as 4
47 Vince Aletti, *Rolling Stone*, issue 228 – 16/12/76
48 as 8
49 'The Father Of Gospel Music', *Score* magazine, 1994
50 *Gospel Women Of The Night*, Wilfred Mellers
51 Jon Landau, *Rolling Stone*, issue 162 – 6/6/74
52 as 8
53 From *Crawdaddy,* quoted in

Innervisions, Martin E. Horn
54 as 12
55 as 5
56 as 47
57 as 47
58 as 5
59 *Musician* magazine (details unknown)
60 *40 Years Of Wonder*, BBC Radio 2
61 as 35
62 Ken Tucker, *Rolling Stone*, issue 309 – 24/1/80
63 as 5
64 Bob Killbourn, *Blues & Soul* magazine
65 Stephen Holden, *Rolling Stone*, issue 336 – 5/2/81
66 Herbert Denton, *Washington Post*
67 as 60
68 *www.stevie-wonder.com*
69 as 60
70 as 60
71 as 60

GLOSSARY OF MUSICAL TERMS

chromatic – a passage or movement from one note to another that uses semitones (half-steps).

counterpoint – two or more simultaneous lines with separate directions and timings.

grace note – short note played just before the main note and normally adjacent to the main note, a step or half-step away. The Italian term for this (as used in classical music) is either 'acciaccatura', for a fast-moving grace note, or 'appoggiatura', for a gentler rise or fall.

monophonic – (in a keyboard/synth context) capable of playing only one note at a time.

note/pitch positions – described as on a MIDI keyboard: C3 = middle C, C4 an octave above, etc.

octave – an interval of 12 semitones, eight rungs of a major scale (eg C to the next C above or below).

oscillator – see 'synthesis terms'.

pentatonic – a five-note scale, most easily illustrated by playing the black notes of a piano or other keyboard, and containing

rungs 1, 2, 3, 5, and 6 of a major scale.

pitch bend – normally a wheel or a joystick at the front left of the keyboard, assigned to raise or lower the pitch by a given amount.

polyphonic – capable of playing more than one note at a time. Early synths were four or eight-voice polyphonic.

portamento – literally 'carrying', describes smooth glide from one note to another: the amount of this applied to a sound affects the speed at which the oscillator moves to the next note played on the keyboard. Turned off it goes straight there, and with a reasonable amount it glides within a second or so.

quarter-notes etc – in a bar of four beats there are four quarter-notes (crotchets), eight eighth-notes (quavers) and 16 16th-notes (semiquavers).

scale – a series of notes going up or down; notes within a scale are referred to by their position in the sequence (eg 5th, 7th etc)

semitone – the smallest distance from one note to the next in western music, referred to in the text as a half-step (see also

chromatic). A tone is two semitones and is referred to as a step, or whole step.

sidestick – hitting the rim of the snare rather than the skin of the drum (also rimshot).

synthesis terms – an oscillator is the raw material, the source of the sound; the filter controls the timbre, or the number of upper/lower frequencies in that sound, by cutting or boosting certain frequencies; the envelope shapes the sound over time, varying attack, decay, sustain and release; a modular synth is assembled from custom modules that require linking or patching together to configure the sound; a patch cord links different areas or modules of a modular synth, or bypasses hard-wired connections in a portable synth.

tremolo/vibrato – tremolo is a slight, rapid variation in volume (tremolando is a very fast, stuttering effect). Vibrato is a slight, rapid variation (wobble) in pitch.

triad – the simplest three-note chord made up from the root, 3rd and 5th step of a major or minor scale.

INDEX

AUTHOR'S ACKNOWLEDGEMENTS

I have worked on this book in many rooms of a dusty, noisy, shell of a house, listening to a new-born baby screaming in the next room, confident in the knowledge that he was well looked after, thanks to the extraordinary efforts of his mother, Heather Lodder. When I was ignoring circumstances around me, she was dealing directly with them, and for that she is owed a mountain of thanks. Thanks are also owed to Tony and Nigel at Backbeat for having the confidence, and above all Paul Quinn for his overwhelmingly patient and necessary guidance through the editing stages of the writing process.

"Today's not yesterday, and all things have an ending."
Stevie Wonder, 'Visions'